Patrick Fraser Tytler

The history of Scotland from the accession of Alexander III. to the union

Vol 3

Patrick Fraser Tytler

The history of Scotland from the accession of Alexander III. to the union
Vol 3

ISBN/EAN: 9783743345300

Manufactured in Europe, USA, Canada, Australia, Japa

Cover: Foto ©ninafisch / pixelio.de

Manufactured and distributed by brebook publishing software (www.brebook.com)

Patrick Fraser Tytler

The history of Scotland from the accession of Alexander III. to the union

THE HISTORY OF SCOTLAND,

FROM THE

ACCESSION OF ALEXANDER III. TO THE UNION.

BY

PATRICK FRASER TYTLER,
F.R.S.E. AND F.A.S.

NEW EDITION.

IN TEN VOLUMES.
VOL. III.

EDINBURGH:
WILLIAM P. NIMMO.
1866.

CONTENTS OF THE THIRD VOLUME.

CHAP. I.

ROBERT THE SECOND.

1370–1390.

	Page
Accession of Robert the Second,	1
Unexpected opposition by the Earl of Douglas,	ib.
Obscurity of the motives which guided him,	2
Spirited conduct of Sir Robert Erskine, and the Earls of March and Moray,	ib.
Douglas renounces his opposition,	ib.
Coronation of the king,	3
Indolent character of the new monarch,	4
Situation of the country,	5
Condition of England,	6
Same subject continued,	7
Scotland enters into a new treaty with France,	8
Symptoms of hostility on the part of England,	9
Parliament held at Scone, March 2, 1371,	10
Death of the Black Prince,	11
And of Edward Third,	ib.
Causes of animosity between the two countries,	12
The Earl of March sacks and burns the town of Roxburgh,	13
The Borderers fly to arms,	ib.
Warden raid by Hotspur,	14
Singular dispersion of the English army,	ib.
Mercer, a Scottish naval adventurer, infests the English shipping,	15
The fleet consists of Scottish, French, and Spanish privateers,	ib.
Mercer is taken by Philpot, a London merchant,	16
Observations on the mutual situation of the two countries,	ib

CONTENTS

	Page
Perpetual infringements of the truce,	17
Berwick taken by Sir Alexander Ramsay,	ib.
Retaken by the Earl of Northumberland,	18
Conflict between Sir Archibald Douglas and Sir Thomas Musgrave,	ib.
Invasion of Scotland by John of Gaunt,	19
Cessation of hostilities,	ib.
Insurrection of Tyler, during which the Earl of Lancaster finds a retreat in Scotland,	20
New treaty with France,	ib.
Truce with England expires, and war recommences,	21
John of Gaunt again invades Scotland,	ib.
He advances to Edinburgh,	ib.
Truce between France and England notified in Scotland,	22
A party of French knights arrive in Scotland, and Lancaster retreats to England,	ib.
The king desirous for peace, but the nobles determine to continue the war,	23
They break the truce and invade England,	ib.
Parliament meets at Edinburgh,	24
Its various provisions,	25
Same subject continued,	26
Expedition of John de Vienne, admiral of France, into Scotland,	27
The French determine to attack England at the same time by sea,	28
Vienne's fleet arrives in Scotland,	29
Difficulty of finding them quarters—discontent of the Scots,	ib.
Scottish peasantry rise against them,	30
Scottish king arrives at Edinburgh,	ib.
He is anxious for peace, but is overruled,	31
An army of thirty thousand horse assembled near Edinburgh,	ib.
Council of war, and regulations for the conduct of the army,	ib.
Commencement of the campaign,	32
King of England assembles a great army,	33
Tactics of the Scots and French,	34
Disadvantages under which the English made war in Scotland,	ib.
Discontent of the French, in not being allowed to fight,	35
Anecdote of Vienne and Douglas,	ib.
Richard the Second pushes on to the capital,	ib.
Devastations committed by the English,	ib.
Edinburgh burnt,	ib.
Dreadful distress of the army,	36
Richard compelled to retreat,	ib.
Scots and French break into England by the western marches,	ib.

CONTENTS.

	Page
Ravage Cumberland,	36
Return to Scotland,	37
Discontent of the Scots, who refuse to furnish transports for the French,	ib.
Miserable condition of the army of Vienne,	38
The French admiral at length obliges himself to pay all damages, and his knights are allowed to return,	ib.
Reflections upon the expedition,	39
Continuation of the war, and invasion of England,	40
Scottish descent upon Ireland,	41
Character of Sir William Douglas,	ib.
He assaults and plunders Carlingford, and ravages the Isle of Man,	42
Lands at Lochryan, and joins his father and the Earl of Fife in the west of England,	ib.
Great invasion of England determined on in a parliament held at Edinburgh,	43
Description of the army,	ib.
Plan of the campaign,	ib.
Army separates into two divisions,	44
Second division, under the Earl of Douglas, pushes on to Durham,	ib.
Hotspur and the barons of Northumberland assemble their power, and occupy Newcastle,	45
The Scots present themselves before the town,	ib.
Skirmish between the knights, in which Douglas wins the pennon of Hotspur,	46
Defiance of Hotspur,	ib.
The Scots are suffered to continue their retreat,	ib.
Encamp in Redesdale, near Otterburn,	47
Douglas prevails on the Scottish barons to interrupt their retreat, and assault the castle of Otterburn,	ib.
His motives for this,	ib.
His judicious choice of the ground,	ib.
Hotspur pursues Douglas at the head of eight thousand foot and six hundred lances,	48
Battle of Otterburn, and death of Douglas,	49
English totally defeated—captivity of Hotspur,	50
Reflections upon the battle,	51
Causes of the defeat of the English,	ib.
Distinguished prisoners,	52
No important consequences result from this defeat,	53
State of Scotland—age and infirmities of the king,	54
The Earl of Fife chosen regent—his character,	ib.

	Page
His injudicious administration,	55
Three years' truce,	56
Death of Robert the Second,	ib.
His character,	ib.
Commerce of Scotland,	57

CHAP. II.

ROBERT THE THIRD.

1390–1424.

	Page
Coronation of John earl of Carrick,	59
He assumes the name of Robert the Third,	ib.
Character of the new king,	60
State of the country,	ib.
Earls of Fife and Buchan, their great power,	61
Anecdote illustrative of the times,	62
Indolence of the king—intrusts the Earl of Fife with the management of the government,	63
Mutual situation of the two countries,	ib.
Truce of eight years,	64
Atrocious conduct of the Earl of Buchan,	ib.
His natural son, Duncan Stewart, ravages Aberdeenshire,	ib.
Combat at Gasklune—the ketherans defeat the lowland barons,	65
Disorganized state of the country,	66
Combat on the North Inch of Perth between the clan Kay and the clan Quhete,	67
Its results,	68
Government of the northern parts of the kingdom committed to the king's eldest son, David earl of Carrick,	ib.
State of the two countries,	ib.
Prevalence of chivalry and knight-errantry,	69
Anecdotes connected with this,	70
Parliament at Perth, April 28, 1398,	71
David earl of Carrick, created Duke of Rothesay,	ib.
His character,	72
Bands entered into between the king and his nobles,	ib.
Same subject,	73
Observations on the state of the country,	74

CONTENTS. ix

	Page
Albany resigns the office of governor,	75
Parliament held at Perth, January 27, 1398,	ib.
Its proceedings,	76
Duke of Rothesay made king's lieutenant, and a council appointed to advise him,	ib.
Further proceedings of the parliament,	77
Same subject continued,	78
Accession of Henry the Fourth, and reported murder of King Richard,	80
Revolution in England, and deposition of Richard the Second,	79
Reports arise that Richard is still alive,	81
A real or pretended Richard appears in Scotland,	82
Situation of that country,	ib.
Contentions between the Earls of March and Douglas, regarding the marriage of the Duke of Rothesay,	83
Rothesay is married to Elizabeth Douglas,	84
The Earl of March enters into a correspondence with England,	ib.
Flies to the English court,	ib.
Borderers recommence their ravages,	ib.
March, along with Hotspur, invades Scotland,	86
Expedition of Henry the Fourth into Scotland,	ib.
Details of this invasion,	87
Henry's moderation,	ib.
Same subject continued,	88
Meeting of the Scottish parliament, February 21, 1401,	89
Its proceedings,	90
Same subject continued,	91
Wild and reckless character of the Duke of Rothesay,	101
Contrast between his character and that of his uncle Albany,	102
Death of the queen and the Earl of Douglas,	103
Intrigues of Sir John de Ramorgny,	104
Character of this intimate of the prince,	ib.
Albany and Ramorgny form a plot for the destruction of the prince,	105
He is murdered by their contrivance,	106
Conduct of the Scottish parliament,	108
Albany resumes his situation as governor,	ib.
Conflict at Nesbit Moor—Scots defeated,	109
Scots invade England,	110
Battle of Homildon Hill,	112
Scots entirely defeated,	114
Causes of this,	115

	Page
Events which followed the defeat,	116
Cruelty of Hotspur,	117
Conspiracy of the Percies,	118
Its connexion with Scotland,	119
Battle of Shrewsbury,	120
Able conduct of the Earl of March,	121
Death of Hotspur,	122
The Duke of Albany retreats,	ib.
Murder of Sir Malcolm Drummond,	123
Alexander Stewart seizes Kildrummie, and marries the Countess of Mar,	ib.
Extraordinary proceedings at the castle of Kildrummie,	124
State of Scotland,	125
The heir of the throne is committed to the charge of the Bishop of St Andrews,	126
Effects of the captivity of the nobles on the state of the country,	ib.
Reports that Richard the Second is kept in Scotland,	127
Conspiracy of the Countess of Oxford,	128
Conspiracy of Scrope and Northumberland,	129
Scrope and Mowbray seized and beheaded,	130
Percy and Lord Bardolf fly into Scotland,	ib.
Albany's administration becomes unpopular with some of the nobles,	131
They determine to send the heir of the throne to France,	132
The prince on his passage is treacherously captured by the English,	133
And confined in the Tower,	ib.
Albany's satisfaction at this event,	ib.
Skirmish at Lang-Hermandston, and death of Sir David Fleming,	134
Death of Robert the Third,	135
Character of this monarch,	ib.
Meeting of the parliament at Perth,	137
Declaration that James the First is king, and nomination of the Duke of Albany as regent,	ib.
Political condition of the country in its relations with France and England,	ib.
Piracies of the English cruisers,	138
Scots retaliate under Logan, but are defeated,	139
Stewart earl of Mar becomes a naval adventurer,	ib.
The Earls of Douglas and March return to Scotland,	140
Doctrines of Wickliff appear in Scotland,	141

CONTENTS.

	Page
History and fate of John Resby,	141
He is burnt for heresy,	142
Consequences of this persecution,	ib.
Expiration of the truce,	143
Teviotdale Borderers recommence hostilities,	ib.
Henry the Fourth complains of the Earl of Douglas neglecting to return to his captivity,	144
Douglas is finally ransomed,	ib.
Fast castle taken, and Roxburgh burnt by the Scots,	145
Sir Robert Umfraville, admiral of England, seizes fourteen Scottish ships, and ravages the country,	ib.
Rebellion of the Lord of the Isles,	146
Causes of his discontent,	ib.
Assembles his army at Inverness, and ravages Moray,	148
The Earl of Mar advances against him,	149
Great battle at Harlaw,	150
Particulars of the battle,	ib.
Severe loss of the lowlanders,	151
Lord of the Isles retires,	ib.
Statute in favour of the heirs of those slain at Harlaw,	152
Albany's northern expedition,	153
His negotiations for the return of his son from captivity,	154
Death of Henry the Fourth,	ib.
Policy of England to maintain pacific relations with Scotland,	ib.
Foundation of the University of St Andrews,	155
Same subject,	156
Policy of Henry the Fifth with regard to Scotland,	157
Albany's profligate administration,	158
He procures the return of his son Murdoch,	159
And succeeds in detaining James the First in captivity,	ib.
Resolves to assist France, and to invade England,	160
Parallel between the policy of Edward the Third and Henry the Fifth, as to Scotland,	161
Albany sacrifices the national happiness to his own ambition,	162
His expedition into England, called the "Foul Raid,"	163
Exploits of Sir Robert Umfraville,	ib.
Embassy of the Duke of Vendome to Scotland,	164
Seven thousand Scots sent to France under the Earls of Buchan and Wigtown,	ib.
Albany the governor dies at Stirling,	ib.
His character,	165

	Page
His son Murdoch succeeds to his power, and assumes the office of governor,	165
His weak administration,	ib.
Henry the Fifth carries James the First with him to France,	166
James refuses to command the Scots auxiliaries to cease fighting against the English,	ib.
Intrigues of James the First for his return, and his communications with Scotland,	ib.
Death of Henry the Fifth,	167
Regency of Bedford and Gloucester,	ib.
Negotiations for the return of James the First,	168
Marriage of James the First to the daughter of the Earl of Somerset,	169
Seven years' truce,	ib.
James returns to his dominions,	170

CHAP. III.

JAMES THE FIRST.

1424–1437.

	Page
Character of James the First,	171
Advantages of his education in England,	172
His coronation at Scone,	173
His caution in his first proceedings,	174
Assembles his parliament,	ib.
Lords of the Articles,	175
Proceedings of the parliament,	ib.
Proclamation against private wars and feuds,	ib.
Against riding with too numerous an attendance,	ib.
Appointment of officers or ministers of Justice,	176
Laws against sturdy mendicants,	ib.
Statutes regarding the "Great Customs," and the dilapidations of the crown lands,	177
Tax upon the whole lands of the kingdom,	178
Mode of its collection,	179
Same subject continued,	180
Taxation of ecclesiastical lands,	ib.
State of the fisheries,	181

CONTENTS.

	Page
Mines of gold and silver,	182
Impolitic restrictions upon commerce,	183
Enactment against the purchase of pensions and ecclesiastical benefices,	184
Against rookeries,	ib.
Statute for the encouragement of archery,	185
Reflections upon James's first parliament,	186
His measures for the destruction of the house of Albany,	187
Difficulty of tracing his project,	ib.
Mode in which he proceeds against Murdoch and the principal nobles,	188
Parliament summoned to meet at Perth, March 12, 1424,	189
James imprisons Duke Murdoch, along with twenty-six of the principal nobility,	190
Possesses himself of the strongest castles in the country,	ib.
Trial and condemnation of Walter Stewart, eldest son of Albany,	191
He is executed,	192
Trials of the Duke of Albany, Alexander his second son, and the Earl of Lennox,	ib.
They are condemned and executed,	193
Their fate excites pity,	ib.
James's unnecessary cruelty,	194
Forfeiture of the estates of Albany and Lennox,	195
The imprisoned nobles are liberated,	ib.
Deliberations of the parliament proceed,	ib.
Symptoms of the decay of the forest timber,	196
Regulations concerning commerce,	ib.
Administration of justice,	197
Striking statute as to the dispensing justice "to the poor,"	ib.
State of the highlands,	198
Statutes against the growth of heresy,	ib.
Reflections upon this subject,	199
Reflections upon the destruction of the house of Albany,	200
The queen is delivered of a daughter,	201
Projected marriage between the Dauphin of France and the infant princess,	202
State of France,	ib.
Embassy of the Archbishop of Rheims and the Lord Aubigny to Scotland,	ib.
Embassy from the court of Scotland to France,	203
Embassy from the States of Flanders to Scotland,	204

CONTENTS.

	Page
James procures ample privileges for the Scottish merchants who trade to Flanders,	204
The king and nobles of Scotland engage in commercial adventure,	ib.
Tax of twelve pennies upon every pound,	205
Rude estimate of the annual income of the people of Scotland,	ib.
Meeting of the parliament at Perth, March 11, 1425,	206
Picture of the condition of the country, conveyed by its regulations,	ib.
Institution of the "Session,"	207
Register for all charters and infeftments,	ib.
Committee appointed to examine the books of the law,	208
Directions for the transcription and promulgation of the acts of the legislature,	209
Defence of the country,	ib.
Commerce of the country,	210
Singular statute as to hostillars, or innkeepers,	211
Regulations of weights and measures,	212
James concludes a treaty with Denmark,	213
He determines in person to bring his northern dominions under legitimate rule,	ib.
Summons his parliament to meet at Inverness,	214
Condition of the highlands,	ib.
Same subject continued,	215
James repairs in person to Inverness,	ib.
His seizure of the northern chiefs,	216
Some are instantly executed,	217
James's clemency to the Lord of the Isles,	ib.
Rebellion of this prince,	218
James's active measures against him,	ib.
Alexander's penance,	219
James imprisons the Lord of the Isles in Tantallon castle,	ib.
The Countess of Ross, his mother, confined in the monastery of Inchcolm,	ib.
Anecdote illustrative of the disordered state of the highlands,	220
Same subject continued,	221
The king again assembles his parliament,	222
Provisions against the barons sending procurators to attend in their place,	ib.
Indications of James's government becoming unpopular,	223
Statutes regarding the prices of work,	ib.
And the encouragement of agriculture,	ib.

CONTENTS.

XV

	Page
Rebuilding of the castles beyond the "Mounth,"	224
Against carrying the gold out of the country,	ib.
Regarding judges and the administration of justice,	225
Important change as to the attendance of the smaller barons in parliament,	226
Principle of representation introduced,	ib.
Speaker of the commissaries,	ib.
Reflections on this change, and the causes of its introduction,	227
Statutes regarding the destruction of wolves,	228
Regarding the fisheries,	ib.
Foreign commerce,	ib.
Lepers,	ib.
Against simony, or "Barratrie,"	229
Prices of labour,	ib.
This meeting of the three Estates denominated a General Council,	230
Difficult to understand the distinction between a Parliament and a General Council,	ib.
Embassy of the Archbishop of Rheims to Scotland,	231
Conditions of the marriage between the Princess Margaret and the Dauphin finally agreed on,	ib.
Cardinal Beaufort requests a meeting with James, which is declined,	232
Benevolent law as to the labourers of the soil,	ib.
Sumptuary laws as to dress,	233
Laws as to the arming of the lieges,	234
Arms of gentlemen,	ib.
Of yeomen,	ib.
Of burgesses,	ib.
State of the navy,	235
Tax of providing vessels laid on barons possessing lands within six miles of the sea,	ib.
The queen is delivered of twin sons,	236
Truce between the kingdoms renewed for five years,	ib.
State of the highlands,	237
Rebellion of Donald Balloch,	ib.
He defeats the Earl of Mar at Inverlochy,	ib.
Desperate combat between Angus Dow Mackay and Angus Murray, at Strathnaver,	238
The king assembles an army, and undertakes an expedition into the highlands,	239
Three hundred robbers hanged,	ib.

	Page
Donald Balloch betrayed, and his head sent to James,	239
Pestilence breaks out,	240
Its symptoms—and effects on the popular mind,	ib.
Total eclipse of the sun, called the " Black Hour,"	241
Advantageous offers of the English government for the establishment of peace,	ib.
The Estates of the realm meet in a General Council,	ib.
The treaty, to which the temporal barons had consented, unfortunately is broken off by disputes amongst the clergy,	242
Trial and condemnation of Paul Crawar for heresy,	ib.
His doctrines,	243
Conduct of the king,	244
James pursues his plan for weakening the aristocracy,	245
His designs against the Earl of Dunbar,	ib.
He determines to resume the immense estates of March,	246
Parliament assembled at Perth, January 10, 1434,	247
The cause between the king and the Earl of March solemnly pleaded,	248
March is deprived of his estates,	ib.
He is created Earl of Buchan,	249
And retires in resentment to England,	ib.
Before separating, James requires the barons to give their bonds of adherence and fidelity to the queen,	250
The king acquires the large estates of Alexander earl of Mar, on the death of this baron,	ib.
Sir Robert Ogle invades the Scottish marches,	251
He is defeated at Piperden by the Earl of Angus,	ib.
The Princess Margaret sent to France with a splendid suite,	ib.
The English attempt to interrupt her, but are unsuccessful,	252
The king deeply resents this,	ib.
The marriage is celebrated at Tours,	253
King James renews the war, and lays siege to Roxburgh,	ib.
He abruptly dismisses his forces,	254
Assembles a General Council at Edinburgh,	ib.
Its provisions,	255
Conspiracy formed against the king by Sir Robert Graham and the Earl of Athole,	ib.
Character of Graham,	ib.
Probable causes of the conspiracy,	256
The nobles readily enter into Graham's designs,	257
Their object merely to abridge the royal prerogative,	ib.
They select Graham to present their remonstrances to the king,	258

	Page
He exceeds his commission, and is imprisoned,	258
He is afterwards banished, and his estates confiscated,	ib.
Retires to the highlands, and sends to James a letter of defiance,	259
James fixes a price upon his head,	ib.
Graham communicates with the discontented nobles,	ib.
Induces the Earl of Athole and Sir Robert Stewart to conspire against the king,	260
James determines to keep his Christmas at Perth,	261
Facilities which this affords to the conspirators,	ib.
Stopt on his journey by a highland woman,	ib.
Neglects her warning,	ib.
Conspirators determine to murder the king on the night of 20th February,	262
Sir Robert Stewart, the chamberlain, removes the bolts of the king's bed-chamber,	ib.
James unusually cheerful,	ib.
Heroic conduct of Catherine Douglas,	264
The murder,	265
James makes a desperate resistance,	266
He is overpowered and slain,	267
The murderers escape to the highlands,	ib.
But are soon taken,	268
They are tortured and executed,	ib.
Audacious defence of Sir Robert Graham,	269
Character of James the First,	270
Prominent features in his reign,	271
Causes which produced his inexorable firmness and occasional cruelty,	272
His conduct towards the house of Albany,	ib.
His encouragement of his clergy,	273
His personal accomplishments,	274
And excellence in all knightly exercises,	ib.
His children,	275

END OF THE REIGN OF JAMES THE FIRST.

HISTORICAL REMARKS

ON THE

DEATH OF RICHARD THE SECOND.

	Page
OBSCURITY which hangs over the accounts of Richard's death,	279
Reports of his having escaped to Scotland,	ib.
Statement of the author's views on this point,	280
Proofs of his escape to Scotland,	ib.
Evidence of Bower,	ib.
Same subject,	281
Evidence of Winton,	283
Same subject continued,	284
Opinion as to Winton's testimony,	285
His caution accounted for,	ib.
Corroborations of his evidence as to Swinburn and Waterton,	286
Proofs from a MS. in Advocates' Library,	288
Conclusions from the above evidence,	289
Passages from the Chamberlain Accounts,	ib.
Same subject,	290
Their unquestionable authenticity,	ib.
Inferences to be deduced from them,	291
Proofs from contemporary English writers,	ib.
From Walsingham,	292
From Otterburn,	ib.
From a contemporary French MS.,	293
Chronicle of Kenilworth,	ib.
Of Peter de Ickham,	ib.
Assertions of the king's escape by contemporary writers,	294
Conspiracy of the Earls of Kent, Surrey, and Salisbury,	ib.
Passage as to Maudelain personating the king,	295
Observations on this,	296
Richard's reported death at Pontefract,	298
Exposition of the body, and funeral service at St Paul's,	299
Passage descriptive of the ceremony, from a contemporary French MS.,	ib.
Observations upon this,	300
Assertions in a contemporary French MS. that it was not the body of the king,	ib.

CONTENTS.

	Page
But of Maudelain the priest,	301
Arguments to show it was not the body of the king which was exposed,	302
Burial at Langley,	303
Froissart's account of Richard's deposition extremely inaccurate,	304
Reports of Richard's escape, which arose soon after this exposition,	ib.
Frequent conspiracies against Henry, always accompanied with the assertion that Richard is alive,	ib.
Eight Franciscan friars hanged in London for asserting this,	305
Prior of Launde executed for the same offence,	ib.
And Sir Roger de Clarendon,	ib.
Proofs of this from Henry's proclamations in the Fœdera Angliæ,	ib.
Reports in 1402,	306
Rebellion of the Percies in 1403,	307
Evidence in their letter of defiance in 1403, contradicted by their manifesto in 1405,	308
Conspiracy of Serle and the Countess of Oxford in 1404,	309
Opinion as to Serle having procured Warde to personate the king,	ib.
Henry's assertion not to be credited—contradicted by the silence of Walsingham and Otterburn,	310
Proofs from the conduct of Henry after this conspiracy,	311
King believed to be alive by the French,	ib.
Epistle by Creton, addressed to Richard in 1405,	312
Conspiracy of Scrope and Northumberland in 1405,	313
Proofs from this conspiracy,	ib.
Letter of Northumberland to the Duke of Orleans,	314
State of parties in Scotland at this time,	315
Same subject continued,	316
Prince James taken prisoner by the English,	ib.
Consequences of Henry becoming possessed of James the First, at the same time that Albany gets possession of Richard,	317
Conspiracy by Northumberland and Lord Bardolf in 1407,	318
Suppression of this conspiracy,	ib.
Conspiracy of the Earl of Cambridge and Lord Scroop, in 1415,	319
Proofs arising out of this conspiracy that Richard is alive,	320
Evident contradiction and falsehood of the account given in the Parliamentary Rolls,	321
Same subject,	322
Explanation of the real object of the conspirators,	323
Same subject,	324

	Page
Conspiracy of 1417,	325
Alleged plot of the Duke of Orleans to bring in the "Mamuet" of Scotland,	ib.
Evidence of Lord Cobham that Richard is alive in 1417,	326
Observations on this evidence,	327
Conclusion,	328
NOTES AND ILLUSTRATIONS,	333

HISTORY
OF
SCOTLAND.

CHAP. I.

ROBERT THE SECOND.

1370—1390.

CONTEMPORARY PRINCES.

Kings of England.	Kings of France.	Rome.	(Popes.)	Avignon.
Edward III.	Charles V.	Gregory XI.		
Richard II.	Charles VI.	Urban VI.		Clement VII.

DAVID THE SECOND, the only son of Robert the First, dying without children, the succession to the throne opened to Robert the High Steward of Scotland, in consequence of a solemn act of the parliament, which had passed during the reign of his grandfather, Robert the First, in the year 1318.* The High Steward was the only child of the Lady Marjory Bruce, the eldest daughter of Robert the First, and of Walter the High Steward of Scotland; and his talents in discharging the difficult duties of regent, had already shown him to be worthy of the crown, to which his title was unquestionable. Previous, however, to his coronation, opposition arose from an unexpected quarter. William earl of Douglas, one of the most powerful of the

* Fordun & Goodal, vol. ii. p. 290.

Scottish nobles, being at Linlithgow at the time of the king's death, publicly proclaimed his intention of questioning the title of the Steward to the throne; but the motives which induced him to adopt so precipitate a resolution are exceedingly obscure. It is certain that Douglas could not himself lay claim to the throne upon any title preferable to that of Robert; but that the common story of his uniting in his person the claims of Comyn and of Baliol is entirely erroneous, seems not so apparent.* Some affront, real or imaginary, by which offence was given to the pride of this potent baron, was probably the cause of this hasty resolution, which, in whatever feeling it originated, was abandoned as precipitately as it was adopted. Sir Robert Erskine, who, in the former reign, had risen into great power, and then commanded the castles of Edinburgh, Stirling, and Dumbarton. instantly advanced to Linlithgow at the head of a large force. He was there joined by the Earls of March and Moray; and a conference having taken place with Douglas, he deemed it prudent to declare himself satisfied with their arguments, and ready to acknowledge a title which he discovered he had not strength to dispute.† It was judged expedient, however, to conciliate so warlike and influential a person as Douglas, and to secure his services for the support of the new government. For this purpose the king's daughter, Isabella, was promised in marriage to his eldest son, upon whom an annual pension was settled; and the earl himself was promoted to the high offices

---

* The story is to be found in Bower, the continuator of Fordun, vol. ii. p. 382; and in the MS. work, entitled, Extracta ex Chronicis Scotiæ, fol. 225. It was repeated by Buchanan, attempted to be proved to be erroneous by the learned Ruddiman, and again revived by Pinkerton, in his History of Scotland, vol. i. p. 10. See Illustrations, letter A.

† Winton, vol. ii. pp. 304 and 514.

of King's Justiciar on the south of the Forth, and Warden of the East Marches.* To the rest of the barons and nobles who supported him, the High Steward was equally generous. The promptitude of Sir Robert Erskine was rewarded by the gift of three hundred and thirty-three pounds, an immense present for that time; whilst the services of March and Moray, and of Sir Thomas Erskine, were proportionably acknowledged and requited.†

This threatened storm having passed, the High Steward, accompanied by a splendid concourse of his nobility, proceeded to the Abbey of Scone, and was there crowned and anointed king, on the 26th of March, 1371, by the Bishop of St Andrews, under the title of Robert the Second.‡ To confer greater solemnity on this transaction, which gave a new race of monarchs to the throne, the act of settlement by Robert the First was publicly read; after which, the assembled prelates and nobles, rising in their places, separately took their oaths of homage. The king himself then stood up, and declaring that he judged it right to imitate the example of his illustrious grandfather, pronounced his eldest son, the Earl of Carrick and Steward of Scotland, to be heir to the crown, in the event of his own death. This nomination was

* Chamberlain Accounts, vol. ii. p. 26. Ibid. pp. 9, 10.
† Ibid. vol. ii. pp. 26, 27.
" Et in solucione facta Domino Willelmo Comiti de Douglas, circa contractum matrimoniale inter filium ipsius Comitis, et Isabellam filiam regis, ut patet per literas regis de predicto, et ipsius Comitis de rc. ons^s. super computum, V^o. li:
" Et in soluc: facto dno. Robto. de Erskine et de dono regis concess: sibi per literam ons. et cancellat. sr. compotum et ipsius Dni. Roberti de rc. ons. super computum III^c, xxxiii li. vi s. viii d."
‡ Robertson's Records of the Parliament of Scotland, p. 119, sub anno 1371. It is there stated, that all the barons and prelates took the oaths of homage, except the Bishop of Dumblane and Lord Archibald de Douglas, who only took the oath of fidelity. Yet this seems contradicted by the "Act of Settlement."

immediately and unanimously ratified by consent of the clergy, nobility, and barons, who came forward and took the same oaths of homage to the Earl of Carrick, as their future king, which they had just offered to his father; and upon proclamation of the same being made before the assembled body of the people, who crowded into the abbey to witness the coronation, the resolution of the king was received by continued shouts of loyalty, and the waving of thousands of hands, which ratified the sentence. An instrument, reciting these proceedings, was then drawn up, to which the principal nobles and clergy appended their seals, and which is still preserved amongst our national muniments: a venerable record, not seriously impaired by the attrition of four centuries and a half, and constituting the charter by which the house of Stewart long held their title to the crown.*

Robert the High Steward, who now succeeded to the throne, had reached his fifty-fifth year, a period of life when the approaches of age produce in most men a love of repose, and a desire to escape from the care and annoyance of public life. This effect was to be seen in the character of the king. The military and ambitious spirit, and the promptitude, resolution, and activity which we observe in the High Steward during his regency, had softened down into a more pacific and quiet nature. He possessed strong good sense, and a judgment in state affairs matured by experience; but united to this was a love of indolence and retirement, little suited to the part which he had to act, as head of a fierce and lawless feudal nobility, and the

---

* Robertson's Index to the Charters, Appendix, p. 11. "Clamore consono ac manu levata in signum fidei dationis." A fac-simile of this deed has been engraved, and will be found in the first volume of the Acts of the Parliament of Scotland, sub anno 1371.

guardian of the liberty of the country, against the unremitting attacks of England. Yet, to balance this inactivity of mind, Robert enjoyed some advantages. He was surrounded by a family of sons grown to manhood. The Earl of Carrick, Robert earl of Fife afterwards Duke of Albany, and Alexander lord of Badenoch, were born to him of his first marriage with Elizabeth More, daughter to Sir Adam More of Rowallan;* David earl of Strathern, and Walter lord of Brechin, blest his second alliance with Euphemia Ross, the widow of Randolph earl of Moray; whilst seven daughters connected him by marriage with the noble families of the Earl of March, the Lord of the Isles, Hay of Errol, Lindsay of Glenesk, Lyon, and Douglas. To these legitimate supports of the throne must be added, the strength which he derived from a phalanx of eight natural sons, also grown to man's estate, and who, undepressed by a stain then little regarded, held their place among the nobles of the land.† Although, after his accession to the throne, the king was little affected with the passion for military renown, and thus lost somewhat of his popularity amongst his subjects, he possessed other qualities which endeared him to the people. He was easy of access to the meanest suitor; affable and pleasant in his address; and while possessing a person of a commanding stature and dignity, his manners were yet so tempered by a graceful and unaffected humility, that what the royal name lost in pomp and terror, it gained in confidence and affection.‡

In the political situation of the country at this

---

* Records of the Parliament of Scotland, p. 119, sub anno 1371.
† Duncan Stewart's History of the Royal Family of Scotland, pp. 56, 57, 58.
‡ Fordun a Goodal, vol. ii. p. 383.

period, there were some difficulties of a formidable nature. A large portion of the ransom of David the Second, amounting to fifty-two thousand marks, was still unpaid;* and if the nation had been reduced to the brink of bankruptcy, by its efforts to raise the sum already collected, the attempt to levy additional instalments, or to impose new taxes, could not be contemplated without alarm. The English were in possession of a large portion of Annandale, in which Edward continued to exercise all the rights of a feudal sovereign; they held, besides, the castles of Roxburgh and Lochmaben, with the town and castle of Berwick;† so that the seeds of war and commotion, and the materials of national jealousy, were not removed; and however anxious the English and Scottish wardens might show themselves to preserve the truce, it was scarcely to be expected that the fierce borderers of both nations would be long controlled from breaking out into their accustomed disorders. In addition to these adverse circumstances, the kingdom, during the years immediately following the accession of Robert the Second, was visited by a grievous scarcity. The whole nobility of Scotland appear to have been supported by grain imported from England and Ireland; and a famine which fell so severely upon the higher classes, must have been still more intensely experienced by the great body of the people.‡

But Scotland, although, as far as her political circumstances are considered, undoubtedly not in a prosperous condition, enjoyed a kind of negative security, from the weakness of England. Edward the Third

---

* Records of the Parliament of Scotland, sub anno 1371, p. 120.
† Rotuli Scotiæ, vol. i. pp. 944, 947, 951, 958, 963, 965.
‡ Ibid. vol. i. pp. 963, 965, 966, 967, 968. The evidence of the Rotuli Scotiæ contradicts the assertions of Bower, vol. ii. Fordun a Goodal, p. 383.

was no longer the victorious monarch of Cressy and Poictiers. His celebrated son, the Black Prince, a few years before this, had concluded his idle though chivalrous expedition against Spain; and after having been deceived by the monarch whom his valour had restored to the throne, again returned to France, drowned in debt, and broken in constitution. Prince Lionel, whom Edward had hoped to make King of Scotland, was lately dead in Italy, and still severer calamities were behind. Charles the Fifth of France, a sovereign of much wisdom and prudence, had committed the conduct of the war against England to the Constable de Guesclin, a captain of the greatest skill and courage; and Edward, embarrassed at the same time with hostilities in Flanders and Spain, saw, with deep mortification, the fairest provinces, which were the fruits of his victories, either wrested from him by force of arms, or silently lost, from inactivity and neglect. In his attempts to defend those which remained, and to regain what was lost, the necessity of fitting out new armies called for immense sums of money, which, though at first willingly granted by parliament, weakened and impoverished the country; and the loss of his greatest captains, his own feeble health, and the mortal illness of the Black Prince, rendered these armies unavailable, from the want of experienced generals.

From this picture of the mutual situation of the two countries, it may be imagined that both were well aware of the benefits of remaining at peace. On the part of Scotland, accordingly, it was determined to respect the truce, which in 1369 had been prolonged for a period of fourteen years, and to fulfil the obligations as to the punctual payment of the ransom; whilst

England continued to encourage the commercial and friendly intercourse which had subsisted under the former monarch.* Yet, notwithstanding all this, two events soon occurred, which must have convinced the most superficial observer that the calm was fallacious, and would be of short duration. The first of these was a new treaty of amity with France, the determined enemy of England, which was concluded by the Scottish ambassadors, Wardlaw bishop of Glasgow, Sir Archibald Douglas, and Tynninghame dean of Aberdeen, at the castle of Vincennes, on the 30th June, 1371; in which, after an allusion to the ancient alliances between France and Scotland, it was stipulated that, in consideration of the frequent wrongs and injuries which had been sustained by both these realms from England, they should be mutually bound, as faithful allies, to assist each other against any aggression made by that country. After some provisions calculated to prevent any subjects of the allied kingdoms from serving in the English armies, it was declared that no truce was henceforth to be concluded, nor any treaty of peace agreed on, by either kingdom, in which the other was not included; and that in the event of a competition at any time taking place for the crown, the King of France should maintain the right of that person who was approved by a majority of the Scottish Estates, and defend his title if attacked by England. Such was the treaty, as it appears ratified by the Scottish king at Edinburgh, on the 28th October, 1371;† but at the same time certain secret articles were proposed, upon the part of France, of a still more decisive and hostile character. By these the French

---

* Rotuli Scotiæ, vol. i. sub. annis 1372, 1373.
† Records of the Parliament of Scotland, sub anno 1371, pp. 122, 124.

monarch engaged to persuade the pope to annul the existing truce between England and Scotland; to pay and supply with arms a large body of Scottish knights; and to send to Scotland an auxiliary force of a thousand men-at-arms, to co-operate in a proposed invasion of England. These articles, however, which would again have plunged the kingdoms into all the horrors of war, do not appear to have been ratified by Robert.*

The other event to which I allude, afforded an equally conclusive evidence of the concealed hostility of England. When Biggar, High Chamberlain of Scotland, repaired to Berwick to pay into the hands of the English commissioners a portion of the ransom which was still due, it was found that the English king, in his letters of discharge, had omitted to bestow his royal title on Robert. The chamberlain, and the Scottish lords who accompanied him, remonstrated in vain against this unexpected circumstance. They declared that they paid the ransom in the name and by the orders of their master the King of Scotland; and unless the discharge ran in the same style, it was null, and could not be received. Edward, however, continued obstinate: he replied, that if David Bruce had been content to accept the discharge without the addition of the kingly title, there was no good reason why his successor should quarrel with it for this omission; and he drew up a deed declaring that the letter complained of was, in every respect, as full and unchallengeable as if Robert had been therein designed the King of Scotland.† With this the Scottish commissioners were obliged for the present to be satisfied; and having paid the sum under protest, they returned

* Records of the Parliament of Scotland, sub anno 1371, p. 122.
† Rotuli Scotiæ, vol. i. p. 953.

home, aware from what had passed, that however enfeebled by his continental disasters, Edward still clung to the idea that, in consequence of the resignation of Baliol, he himself possessed the title to the kingdom of Scotland, and might yet live to make it good.*

Notwithstanding these threatening appearances, the country continued for some years to enjoy the blessings of peace; and the interval was wisely occupied by the sovereign in providing for the security of the succession to the crown; in regulating the expenses of the royal household, by the advice of his privy council; in the enactment of wise and useful laws for the administration of justice, and the punishment of oppression. For these purposes, a parliament was held at Scone, on the 2d of March, 1371, and another meeting of the Estates took place in April, 1373, in which many improvements were introduced, and some abuses corrected.† It seems at this period to have been customary for the lords of the king's council to avail themselves of the advice of private persons, who sat along with them in deliberation, although not elected to that office. This practice was now abolished. Sheriffs and other judges were prohibited from asking or receiving presents from litigants of any part of the sum or matter in dispute; several acts were passed relative to the punishment of murder, in its various degrees of criminality; ketherans, or masterful beggars, were declared not only liable to arrest, but, in case of resistance, to be slain on the spot; and all malversation by judges was pronounced cognizable by a jury, and

---

* Records of the Parliament of Scotland, pp. 126, 127, sub anno 1372. Chamberlain Accounts, vol. ii. p. 3.
† Records of the Parliament of Scotland, p. 124. The parliament consisted of the dignified clergy, the earls, barons, and free tenants *in capite*, with certain burgesses summoned from each burgh.

punishable at the king's pleasure. These enactments point to a state of things in which it was evidently far easier to make laws than to carry them into execution.*

In the meantime, England was visited with two great calamities. Edward prince of Wales, commonly called the Black Prince, to the universal regret of the nation, and even of his enemies, died at Westminster; and his illustrious father, broken by the severity of the stroke, and worn out with the fatigues of war, survived him scarcely a year. Anxious for the tranquillity of his kingdom, it had been his earnest wish to conclude a peace with France; but even this was denied him; and he died on the 1st of June, 1377, leaving the reins of government to fall into the hands of a boy of eleven years of age, the eldest son of the Black Prince, who was crowned at Westminster, on the 11th July, 1377, by the title of Richard the Second. Edward the Third was a monarch deservedly beloved by his people, and distinguished for the wisdom and the happy union of firmness and lenity which marked his domestic administration; but his passion for conquest and military renown, which he gratified at an immense expense of money and of human life, whilst it served to throw that dangerous and fictitious splendour over his reign which is yet scarcely dissipated, was undoubtedly destructive of the best and highest interests of his kingdom. Nothing, indeed, could afford a more striking lesson on the vanity of foreign conquest, and the emptiness of human grandeur, than the circumstances in which he died: stript of the fairest provinces which had been the fruit of his

* Records of the Parliament of Scotland, pp. 124, 125, sub anno 1371. A parliament was held by Robert the Second at Scone, on the 3d of April, 1373, of which an important document has been preserved, touching the succession to the crown. Ibid. sub anno 1373.

victories, the survivor of his brave son and his best captains, and at last pillaged and deserted in his last moments by his faithless mistress and ungrateful domestics. His death delivered Scotland for the time from apprehension, and weakened in a great measure those causes of suspicion and distrust which have already been described.

But, although the action of these was suspended, there were other subjects of mutual irritation, which could not be so easily removed. The feudal system, which then existed in full vigour in Scotland, contained within itself materials the very reverse of pacific. The power of the barons had been decidedly increasing since the days of Robert the First; the right of private war was exercised by them in its full extent; and, on the slightest insult or injury offered to one of their vassals by the English Wardens of the Border, they were ready to take the law into their own hands, and, at the head of a force, which for the time defied all resistance, to invade the country, and inflict a dreadful vengeance. In this manner, the king was frequently drawn in to support, or at least to connive at, the atrocities of a subject too powerful for him to control or resist; and a spark of individual malice or private revenge would kindle those materials, which were ever ready to be inflamed, into the wide conflagration of a general war.

The truth of these remarks was soon shown. At the fair of Roxburgh, a gentleman, belonging to the bedchamber of the Earl of March, was slain in a brawl by the English, who then held the castle in their hands. March, a grandson of the great Randolph, was one of the most powerful of the Scottish nobles. He instantly demanded redress, adding, that, if it was not given, he would not continue to respect the truce; but his representation was treated with scorn, and, as the earl did not reply, it was imagined he had forgotten the affront. Time passed on, and the feast of St Laurence arrived, which was the season for the next fair to be held, when the town was again filled with the English, who, in unsuspicious security, had taken up their residence for the purposes of traffic or pleasure. Early in the morning, March, at the head of an armed force, surprised and stormed the town, set it on fire, and commenced a pitiless slaughter of the English, sparing neither age nor infancy. Many who barricaded themselves in the booths and houses, were dragged into the streets and murdered, or met a more dreadful death in the flames; and the earl, at his leisure, drew off his followers, enriched with plunder, and glutted with revenge.*

This atrocious attack proved the commencement of a series of hostilities, which, although unauthorized by either government, were carried on with obstinate and systematic cruelty. The English borderers flew to arms, and broke in upon the lands of Sir John Gordon, one of March's principal assistants in the recent attack upon Roxburgh. Gordon, in return, having collected his vassals, invaded England, and carried away a large booty in cattle and prisoners; but, before he could cross the Border, was attacked in a mountain-pass by Sir John Lilburn, at the head of a body of knights and men-at-arms, double the number of the Scots. The skirmish was one of great obstinacy, and constituted what Froissart delights in describing as a fair point of arms, in which there were many empty saddles, and many torn and trampled banners; but, although

* Fordun a Goodal, vol. ii. p. 384. Winton, vol. ii. p. 306. Walsingham, p. 198.

grievously wounded, Gordon made good his retreat, took Lilburn prisoner, and secured his plunder.* This last insult called down the wrath of the English warden, Henry Percy earl of Northumberland, who, loudly accusing the Scots of despising the truce, at the head of an army of seven thousand men, broke across the Border, and encamped near Dunse, with the design of laying waste the extensive possessions of the Earl of March, which were situated in that quarter. But this "Warden Raid," which involved such great preparations, ended in a very ridiculous manner. The great proportion of the English consisted of knights and men-at-arms, whose horses were picketed on the outside of the encampment, under the charge of the sutlers and camp-boys, whilst their masters slept on their arms in the centre. It was one of the injunctions of the good King Robert's testament, to alarm the encampments of the English

> "By wiles and wakening in the nycht,
> And meikil noise made on hycht ;†

and in this instance Percy suffered under its success. At the dead of night, his position was surrounded, not by an army, but by a multitude of the common serfs and varlets, who were armed only with the rattles which they used in driving away the wild beasts from their flocks; and such was the consternation produced amongst the horses and their keepers, by the sounding of the rattles, and the yells and shouting of the assailants, whose numbers were magnified by the darkness, that all was thrown into disorder. Hundreds of horses broke from the stakes to which they were picketed, and fled masterless over the country; num-

* Winton, vol. ii. p. 309. † Fordun a Goodal, vol. ii. p. 232.

hers galloped into the encampment, and carried a panic amongst the knights, who stood to their arms, and every moment expected an attack: but no enemy appeared; and when morning broke, the Earl of Northumberland had the mortification to discover at once the ridiculous cause of the alarm, and to find that a great proportion of his best soldiers were unhorsed, and compelled, in their heavy armour, to find their way back to England. A retreat was ordered; and, after pillaging the lands of the Earl of March, the warden recrossed the border.*

It was unfortunate, that these infractions of the truce, which were decidedly injurious to the best interests of both countries, were not confined to the eastern marches. The Baron of Johnston, and his retainers and vassals, harassed the English on the western border;† while at sea, a Scottish naval adventurer, of great spirit and enterprise, named Mercer, infested the English shipping, and, at the head of a squadron of armed vessels, consisting of Scottish, French, and Spanish privateers, scoured the channel, and took many rich prizes. The father of this bold depredator is said by Walsingham to have been a merchant of opulence, who resided in France, and was in high favour at the French court. During one of his voyages, he had been taken by a Northumbrian cruiser, and carried into Scarborough;‡ in revenge of which insult, the son attacked this sea-port, and plundered its shipping. Such was the inefficiency of the government of Richard, that no measures were taken against him; till at last Philpot, a wealthy London

---

* Fordun a Goodal, vol. i. p. 385. Winton, vol. ii. p. 309.
† Winton, vol. ii. p. 311.
‡ Rotuli Scotiæ, vol. ii. p. 16, 20th June, 2 Rich. II.

merchant, at his own expense fitted out an armament of several large ships of war, and attacking Mercer, entirely defeated him, took him prisoner, and captured his whole squadron, among which were fifteen Spanish vessels, and many rich prizes.*

It would be tedious and uninstructive to enter into any minute details of the insulated and unimportant hostilities which, without any precise object, continued for some years to agitate the two countries: committed during the continuance of a truce, which was publicly declared to be respected by both governments, they are to be regarded as the outbreakings of the spirit of national rivalry engendered by a long war, and the effects of that love of chivalrous adventure which was then at its height in Europe. The deep-laid plans of Edward the Third, for the entire subjugation of Scotland, were now at an end; the character of the government of Richard the Second, or rather of his uncles, into whose hands the management of the state had fallen, was, with regard to Scotland, decidedly just and pacific; and the wisest policy for that country would have been, to have devoted her whole attention to the regulation of her internal government, to the recruiting of her finances, and the cultivation of those arts which form the true sources of the prosperity and greatness of a kingdom. Had the king been permitted to follow the bent of his own disposition, there is reason to think that these principles would have been adopted; but the nobility was still too powerful and independent for the individual character of the sovereign to have much influence; and the desire of plunder, and the passion for military adven-

* Walsingham, p. 211.

ture, rendered it impossible for such men to remain at peace.

Another cause increased these hostile feelings. Although the alliance with France was no longer essentially advantageous to Scotland, yet the continuance of the Scottish war was of importance to France, in the circumstances in which that country was then placed; and no means were left unemployed to secure it. The consequence of all this was the perpetual infringement of the truce by hostile invasions, and the reiterated appointment of English and Scottish commissioners, who were empowered to hold courts on the Borders for the redress of grievances. These repeated Border raids, which drew after them no important results, are of little interest. They had the worst effect, as they tended greatly to increase the exasperation between the two countries, and to render more distant and hopeless the prospect of peace; and they become tedious when we are obliged to regard them as no longer the simultaneous efforts of a nation in defence of their independence, but the selfish and disjointed expeditions of an aristocracy, whose principal objects were plunder and military adventure. It was in one of these that the castle of Berwick was stormed and taken by a small body of adventurers, led by Alexander Ramsay, who, when summoned by the Scottish and English wardens, proudly replied, " that he would give up his prize neither to the monarch of England nor of Scotland, but would keep it while he lived for the King of France." Some idea may be formed of the ignorance of the mode of attacking fortified towns in those days, from the circumstance that the handful of Scottish borderers, who were led by this intrepid soldier, defended the castle for some time against the Earl of

Northumberland, at the head of ten thousand men, assisted by miners, mangonels, and all the machinery for carrying on a siege.*

It was in this siege that Henry Percy, afterwards so famous under the name of Hotspur, first became acquainted with arms; and a quarrel, which had begun in a private plundering adventure, ended in a more serious manner. After making himself master of Berwick, the Earl of Northumberland, along with the Earl of Nottingham, and Sir Thomas Musgrave, the governor of Berwick, invaded the southern parts of Scotland; and Sir Archibald Douglas, having under him a considerable force, had advanced against him; but being unable to cope with the army of Percy, he retired, and awaited the result. As he had probably expected, Musgrave, who enjoyed a high reputation for military enterprise, pushed on to Melrose, at the head of an advanced division; and suddenly on the march found himself in the presence of Douglas and the Scottish army: a conflict became unavoidable, and it was conducted with much preparatory pomp and formality. Douglas called to him two sons of King Robert, who were then under his command, and knighted them on the field; Musgrave conferred the same honour on his son; and although he was greatly outnumbered by the Scots, trusting to the courage of his little band, who were mostly of high rank, and to the skill of the English archers, began the fight with high hopes. But after a short and desperate conflict, accompanied with a grievous slaughter, the English were defeated. It was the custom of Sir Archibald Douglas, as we learn from Froissart, when he found the fight becoming hot, to dismount, and attack the

* Walsingham, p. 219. Froissart, par Buchon, vol. vii. pp. 44, 48.

enemy with a large two-handed sword; and on this occasion, such was the fury of his assault, that nothing could resist it.* Musgrave and his son, with many other knights and esquires, were taken prisoners; and Douglas, who felt himself unequal to oppose the main army of Percy and the Earl of Nottingham, fell back upon Edinburgh. The succeeding years were occupied in the same course of Border hostilities; whilst in England, to the miseries of invasion and plunder, was added the calamity of a pestilence, which swept away multitudes of her inhabitants, and by weakening the power of resistance, increased the cruelty of her enemy.†

At length, John of Gaunt, the Duke of Lancaster, who at this time directed the counsels of his nephew Richard the Second, approached Scotland at the head of a powerful army, although he declared his object to be solely the renewal of the truce, and the establishment of peace and good order between the two countries. Sir Archibald Douglas, Lord of Galloway, along with the Bishops of Dunkeld and Glasgow, and the Earls of Douglas and March, were immediately appointed commissioners to open a negotiation; and having consented to a cessation of hostilities, Lancaster disbanded his army, and agreed to meet the Scottish envoys in the following summer in a more pacific guise, at the head of his usual suite. The conference accordingly took place, and the Earl of Carrick, the heir of the throne, managed the negotiations on the part of Scotland; which concluded in an agreement to renew the truce for the space of three years, during which

---

* Froissart, par Buchon, vol. vii. p. 57.
† Rotuli Scotiæ, June 7, 2 Rich. II., and March 5, 5 Rich. II., vol. ii. pp. 16, 42.

time the English monarch consented to delay the exaction of the remaining penalty of the ransom of David the Second, of which twenty-five thousand marks were still due.*

It was at this time that the famous popular insurrection, which was headed by Wat Tyler, had arrived at its height in England; and Lancaster, who was suspected of having given countenance to the insurgents, and who dreaded the violence of a party which had been formed against him, found himself in an awkward and perilous dilemma. He begged permission of the Earl of Carrick to be permitted to retreat for a short season into Scotland; and the request was not only granted, but accompanied with circumstances which marked the courtesy of the age. The Earl of Douglas, along with Sir Archibald Douglas lord of Galloway, conducted him with a brilliant retinue to Haddington; from which they proceeded to Edinburgh, where the Abbey of Holyrood was fitted up for his reception. Gifts and presents were made to him by the Scottish nobles; and here he remained till the fury of the storm was abated, and he could return in safety, escorted by a convoy of eight hundred Scottish spears, to the court of his nephew.† This friendly conduct, and the desire of remaining at peace, which was felt by both monarchs, might have been expected to have averted hostilities for some time; yet such was the influence of a restless aristocracy, that previous to the expiry of this truce, Scotland again consented to be involved in a negotiation with the French king, which eventually entailed upon the nation the calamities of a war, undertaken with no precise object, and carried on at an immense expense of blood and treasure.

* Rymer, vol. vii. p. 312.   † Winton, vol. ii. pp. 315, 316.

The foundation of this new treaty appears to have been those secret articles regarding an invasion of England, which have been already mentioned. A prospect of the large sum of forty thousand franks of gold, to be distributed amongst the Scottish nobles, and an engagement to send into Scotland a body of a thousand men-at-arms, with a supply of a thousand suits of armour, formed a temptation which could not easily be resisted; and although no definite agreement was concluded, it became evident to England, that her enemy had abandoned all pacific intentions.*

When the truce expired, the war was renewed with increased rancour. Lochmaben, a strong castle, which had been long in the hands of the English, was taken by Sir Archibald Douglas;† and the Duke of Lancaster invaded Scotland at the head of a numerous army, and accompanied by a fleet of victualling ships, which anchored in the Forth near Queensferry. But the expedition was singularly unfortunate. Although it was now the month of March, the Scottish winter had not concluded, and the cold was intense. Lancaster, after exhausting the English northern counties in the support of his host, pushed on to Edinburgh, which his knights and captains were eager to sack and destroy. In this, however, they were disappointed; for the English commander, mindful of the generous hospitality which he had lately experienced, commanded the army to encamp at a distance from the town, and issued the strictest orders that none should leave the ranks. For three days, parties of the Scots could be seen carrying off everything that was valuable, and transporting their goods and chattels beyond the Forth.

* Records of the Parliament of Scotland, sub anno 1383, p. 131.
† Winton, vol. ii. p. 317.

Numbers of the English soldiers, in the meantime, began to be seized with sickness, occasioned by exhalations from the marches; and within a short time, five hundred horses died of cold. When at length permitted to advance to Edinburgh, the soldiers, as was to be expected, found nothing to supply their urgent wants: the Scots had even carried off the straw roofs of their wooden houses; and having retreated into the woods and strongholds, quietly awaited the retreat of the English; and began their usual mode of warfare, by cutting off the foraging parties which, disregarding the orders of Lancaster, were compelled, by the calls of hunger, to leave the encampment.* In the meantime, Sir Alexander Lindsay had attacked and put to the sword the crew of one of the English ships, which had made good a landing on the ground above Queensferry; and the King of Scotland had issued orders to assemble an army, for the purpose of intercepting Lancaster in his retreat to England.

At this crisis, ambassadors arrived from France, to notify the truce lately concluded between that country and England; whilst, at the same time, in the spirit of military adventure, then so prevalent, a party of French knights and esquires, tired of being idle at home, took shipping for Scotland; and, on their arrival at Edinburgh, found the Scottish parliament deliberating on the propriety of prosecuting the war. The king and the nobles were divided in their opinion. Robert, with true wisdom, and a desire to promote the best interests of his people, desired peace; and whilst he received the French knights with kindness and courtesy, commanded them and his nobles to lay aside all thoughts of hostilities. Meanwhile Lancaster had pro-

* Walsingham, pp. 308, 309.

fited by the interval allowed him, and made good his retreat; which was accompanied, as usual in these expeditions, with the total devastation of the country through which he passed, and the plunder of the immense estates of the Border earls. To them, and to the rest of the nobility, the king's proposal was particularly unsatisfactory; nor are we to wonder, that when their fields and woods, their manors and villages, were still blackened with the fires of the English, and their foot had been in the stirrup to pursue them, the counter order of the king, and the message of the French envoys regarding the truce, came rather unseasonably.

These, however, were not the days when Scottish barons, having resolved upon war, stood upon much ceremony, either as to the existence of a truce, or the commands of a sovereign. It was, accordingly, privately determined by the Earls of Mar and Douglas, along with Sir Archibald the lord of Galloway, that the foreign knights who had travelled so far to prove their chivalry, should not be disappointed; and after a short stay at Edinburgh, they were surprised by receiving a secret message from Douglas, requiring them to repair to his castle at Dalkeith, where they were warmly welcomed; and, again taking horse, found themselves, in three days' riding, in the presence of an army of fifteen thousand men, mounted on active hackneys, and lightly armed, after the fashion of their country.* With this force they instantly broke into the northern counties of England; wasted the towns and villages with fire and sword; wreaked their vengeance upon

* Froissart, vol. ix. p. 27. Walsingham, p. 309. About this time, the remaining part of Teviotdale, which, since the battle of Durham, had been in the hands of the English, was recovered by the exertions of the Earl of Douglas. Winton, vol. ii. p. 322.

the estates of the Earls of Northumberland and Nottingham; and returned with a large booty in prisoners and cattle. We learn from Froissart, that the King of Scotland was ignorant of this infraction of the truce; and in much concern immediately despatched a herald to explain the circumstances to the English court.* But it is more probable, that, knowing of the intended expedition, he was unable to prevent it. However this might be, its consequences were calamitous; for, as usual, it brought an instantaneous retaliation upon the part of the Earl of Northumberland; and the French knights, on their return to their own country, spoke so highly in favour of the pleasures of a Scottish "raid," and the facilities offered to an attack upon England in this quarter, that the King of France began to think seriously of carrying the projected treaty, to which we have already alluded, into immediate execution, and of sending an army into Scotland.

An interval, which cannot be said to belong either to peace or to war, succeeded these events, and offers little of general interest: the Border inroads being continued with equal and unvaried cruelty; but in a meeting of the parliament, which took place at Edinburgh, a few provisions were passed regarding the state of the country, which are not unworthy of notice.† It was determined that those greater and lesser barons to whom the sovereign, in the event of war, had committed certain divisions of the kingdom should have their array of men-at-arms and archers in such readiness, that, as soon as required, they should be ready to pass to the Borders in warlike apparel, with horse, arms,

---

* Froissart, par Buchon, vol. ix. p. 28. Rotuli Scotiæ, vol. ii. 1385, p. 63.
† Records of the Parliament of Scotland, sub anno 1385, p. 133.

and provisions; so that the lands through which the host marched should not be wasted by their exactions.

It appears that grievous injury had been suffered, owing to the total want of all law and justice in the northern districts of the kingdom. Troops of feudal robbers, chiefs who lived by plunder, and owned no allegiance either to king or earl, traversed the Highland districts, and enlisted into their service malefactors and *ketherans*, who, without respect to rank or authority, burnt, slew, and plundered, wherever their master chose to lead. This dreadful state of things called for immediate attention; and to the Earl of Carrick, the heir to the throne, was the arduous affair intrusted. He was commanded to repair instantly to the disordered districts, at the head of a force which might ensure obedience; to call a meeting of the wisest landholders of these northern parts; and, having taken their advice, to adopt such speedy measures as should strike terror into the guilty, and restore order and good government throughout the land.*

The large district of Teviotdale, which had long been in the possession of the English, having been now cleared of these intruders, and restored to the kingdom by the arms of the Earl of Douglas, it became necessary to adopt measures for the restoration of their lands to those proprietors who had been expelled from them during the occupation of the country by the enemy. It was ordered, that all persons in Teviotdale who had lately transferred their allegiance from the King of England to the King of Scotland, should, within eight days, exhibit to the Chancellor their charters, containing the names of the lands and possessions which they claimed as their hereditary right,

* Cartulary of Aberdeen, Advoc. Library, pp. 104, 105.

wherever they happened to be situated; along with the names of those persons who now possessed them, and of the sheriffdoms within whose jurisdiction they were situated. The object of this was to enable all those persons, who, on the part of the claimants in Teviotdale, were about to receive letters of summons from the Chancellor, to present their letters with such diligence to the sheriffs, as to enable these officers within eight days to expedite the proper citations. It was besides ordained, that the Chancellor should direct the king's letters to the various sheriffs, commanding them to summon all persons who then held, or asserted their right to hold, any lands, to appear before the king and council, bringing with them their charters and titledeeds, that they might hear the final decision on the subject.*

The next provision of the parliament introduces us to a case of feudal oppression, strikingly characteristic of the times; and evinces how feeble and impotent was the arm of the law against the power of the aristocracy. William de Fentoun complained, that he had been unjustly expelled from his manor of Fentoun, by a judgment pronounced in the court of the baron of Dirleton. He immediately appealed to the Sheriff of Edinburgh, and was restored. Again was he violently thrust out: upon which he carried his cause before the king's privy council; and by their solemn award his lands were once more restored. In the face of this last decision by the sovereign and his council, this unfortunate person continued to be excluded from his property by the Baron of Dirleton, who, against all law, violently kept him down; so that he was compelled, in extreme distress, to appeal to the parliament.

* Records of the Parliament of Scotland, sub anno 1385, p. 133.

This case of reiterated tyranny and oppression having been proved by the evidence of the sheriff, it was resolved that Fentoun, without delay, should be reinstated by the royal power; and that the rents due since the period of his expulsion should be instantly restored to him. Whether this final judgment by the court of last resort was more successful than the former sentences against this feudal tyrant, cannot now be discovered; but it is very possible that Fentoun never recovered his property. The remaining provisions of the parliament are of little moment, and relate chiefly to the amicable arrangement of some disputes which had arisen between the Earls of Buchan and of Strathern, both of them sons of the king.

An event of great interest and importance now claims our attention, in the expedition of John de Vienne, the Admiral of France, into Scotland. It is one of the miserable consequences of war, and the passion for conquest, that they almost indefinitely perpetuate the evils which they originally produce. A nation once unjustly attacked, and for a time treated as a conquered people, is not satisfied with the mere defence of its rights, or the simple expulsion of its invaders: wounded pride, hatred, the desire of revenge, the love of plunder, or of glory, all provoke retaliation; and man delights to inflict upon his enemy the extremity of misery from which he has just escaped himself. France accordingly began to ponder upon the best mode of carrying the war into England; and the representations of the knights who had served in the late expedition of Douglas, had a strong effect in recommending an invasion through Scotland. They remarked, that the English did not fight so well in their own country as on the continent;* and without adverting to the true cause of Douglas's success in the skill with which he seized the moment when Lancaster's army had dispersed, and his rapid retreat before the English wardens could assemble their forces, they contrasted the obstinacy with which the English disputed every inch of ground in France, with the facility with which they themselves had been permitted to march and plunder in England.

It was accordingly determined to fulfil the stipulations of the last treaty, and to attack the English king upon his own ground, by sending a large body of auxiliaries into Scotland, and co-operating with that nation in an invasion. For this purpose, they selected John de Vienne, Admiral of France, and one of the most experienced captains of the age; who embarked at Sluys, in Flanders, with a thousand knights, esquires, and men-at-arms, forming the flower of the French army, besides a body of cross-bowmen and common soldiers, composing altogether a force of two thousand men. He carried along with him fourteen hundred suits of armour for the Scottish knights, and fifty thousand franks of gold,† to be paid, on his arrival, to the king and his barons. It was determined to attack England at the same time by sea; and a naval armament for this purpose had been prepared at a great expense by the French: but this part of the project was unsuccessful, and the fleet never sailed.

Meanwhile all seemed to favour the expedition of Vienne. The wind was fair, the weather favourable,

---

* Froissart, par Buchon, vol. ix. p. 162.
† Winton, vol. ii. p. 324. He says there were eight hundred knights, of which number a hundred and four were knights-bannerets; and besides this, four hundred arblasts, or crossbows.

for it was in the month of May; and the transports, gleaming with their splendid freight of chivalry, and gay with innumerable banners, were soon wafted to the Scottish coast, and cast anchor in the ports of Leith and Dunbar. They were warmly welcomed by the Scottish barons; and the sight of the suits of foreign armour, then highly prized, with the promise of a liberal distribution of the French gold, could not fail to make a favourable impression.* On the arrival of the admiral at Edinburgh, he found that the king was then residing in the district which Froissart denominates the wild of Scotland; meaning, perhaps, his palace of Stirling, which is on the borders of a mountainous country. His speedy arrival, however, was looked for; and till then the Earls of Moray and Douglas took charge of the strangers. To provide lodgings for them all in Edinburgh was impossible; and in the efforts made to house their fastidious allies, who had been accustomed to the hôtels of Paris, we are presented with a striking picture of the poverty of this capital, when contrasted with the wealth and magnitude of the French towns. It became necessary to furnish quarters for the knights in the adjacent villages; and the necessity of billeting such splendid guests upon the burgesses, farmers, and yeomen, occasioned loud and grievous murmurs. Dunfermline, Queensferry, Kelso, Dunbar, Dalkeith, and many other towns and villages not mentioned by Froissart, were filled with strangers, speaking a foreign language, appropriating to themselves, without ceremony, the best of everything they saw, and assuming an air of

* The proportion in which the French money was distributed amongst the Scottish nobles, gives us a pretty correct idea of the comparative consequence and power of the various members of the Scottish aristocracy. See Rymer, vol. vii. pp. 484, 485.

superiority which the Scots could not easily tolerate. Mutual dissatisfaction and hatred naturally arose; and although the Earls of Douglas and Moray, who were well contented with an expedition which promised them the money of France, as well as the plunder of England, continued to treat the French with kindness and courtesy, the people and the lesser barons began to quarrel with the intruders, and to adopt every method for their distress and annoyance. All this is feelingly described by the delightful and garrulous historian of the period: " What evil spirit hath brought you here? was," he tells us, " the common expression employed by the Scots to their allies. Who sent for you? Cannot we maintain our war with England well enough without your help? Pack up your goods and begone; for no good will be done as long as ye are here! We neither understand you, nor you us. We cannot communicate together; and in a short time we shall be completely rifled and eaten up by such troops of locusts. What signifies a war with England? the English never occasioned such mischief as ye do. They burned our houses, it is true: but that was all; and with four or five stakes, and plenty green boughs to cover them, they were rebuilt almost as soon as they were destroyed." It was not, however, in words only that the French were thus ill-treated. The Scottish peasants rose against the foraging parties, and cut them off. In a month, more than a hundred men were slain in this manner; and, at last, none ventured to leave their quarters.*

At length the king arrived at Edinburgh, and a council was held by the knights and barons of both nations, on the subject of an immediate invasion of

* Froissart, par Buchon, vol. ix. pp. 155, 157.

England. And here new disputes and heartburnings arose. It was soon discovered that Robert was averse to war. " He was," says Froissart, whose information regarding this expedition is in a high degree minute and curious, " a comely tall man, but with eyes so bloodshot, that they looked as if they were lined with scarlet; and it soon became evident that he himself preferred a quiet life to war; yet he had nine sons who loved arms." The arguments of his barons, joined to the remonstrances of Vienne, and the distribution of the French gold, in the end overcame the repugnance of the king; and the admiral had soon the satisfaction of seeing an army of thirty thousand horse assembled in the fields near Edinburgh.

Unaccustomed, however, to the Scottish mode of carrying on war, and already disposed to quarrel on account of the injuries they had met with, the French were far from cordially co-operating with their allies; so that it was found necessary to hold a council of officers, and to draw up certain regulations, for the maintenance of order during the expedition, which were to be equally binding upon the soldiers of both nations. Some of these articles are curious and characteristic: No pillage was permitted in Scotland under pain of death; the merchants and victuallers who followed or might resort to the camp, were to be protected, and have prompt payment; any soldier who killed another was to be hanged; if any varlet defied a gentleman, he was to lose his ears; and if any gentleman challenged another, he was to be put under arrest, and justice done according to the advice of the officers. In the case of any riot arising between the French and the Scots, no appeal to arms was to be permitted; but care was to be taken to arrest the ringleaders, who were to be punished by the council of the officers. When riding against the enemy, if a French or a Scottish man-at-arms should bear an Englishman to the earth, he was to have half his ransom; no burning of churches, ravishing or slaughter of women or infants, was to be suffered; and every French and Scottish soldier was to wear a white St Andrew's cross on his back and breast; which, if his surcoat or jacket was white, was to be broidered on a division of black cloth.*

It being now time to commence the campaign, the army broke at once across the marches, and after a destructive progress, appeared before the castle of Roxburgh. The king's sons, along with De Vienne the admiral, and the Earls of Douglas, Mar, Moray, and Sutherland, were the Scottish leaders; but Robert himself, unwieldy from his age, remained at Edinburgh. Roxburgh castle, strong in its fortifications, and excellently situated for defence, offered little temptation to a siege. For many months it might have been able to defy the most obstinate attacks of the united powers of France and Scotland; and all idea of making themselves masters of it being abandoned, the army pushed on towards Berwick, and with difficulty carried by assault the two smaller fortalices of Ford and Cornal, which were bravely defended by an English knight and his son.† Wark, one of the strongest Border castles, commanded by Sir John Lusborn, was next assaulted; and, after a severe loss, stormed and taken, chiefly, if we may believe Froissart, by the bravery of the French; whilst the country was miserably wasted by fire and sword, and the plunder and the prisoners slowly driven after the host, which ad-

* Records of the Parliament of Scotland, sub anno 1385, pp. 135, 136.
† Winton, vol. ii. p. 324.

vanced by Alnwick, and carried their ravages to the gates of Newcastle. Word was now brought that the Duke of Lancaster, and the barons of the bishoprics of York and Durham, with the Earls of Northumberland and Nottingham, had collected a powerful force, and were advancing by forced marches to meet the enemy; and here it became necessary for the captains of the different divisions to deliberate whether they should await them where they were, and hazard a battle, or fall back upon their own country. This last measure the Scots naturally preferred. It was their usual mode of proceeding to avoid all great battles; and the result of the war of liberty had shown the wisdom of the practice. Indeed, outnumbered as they always were by the English, and far inferior to them in cavalry, in archers, in the strength of their horses, and the temper of their arms, it would have been folly to have attempted it. But Vienne, one of the best and proudest soldiers in Europe, could not enter into this reasoning. He and his splendid column of knights, esquires, and archers, were anxious for battle; and it was with infinite reluctance that he suffered himself to be overpersuaded by the veteran experience of Douglas and Moray, and consented to fall back upon Berwick.

In the meantime, the King of England assembled an army more potent in numbers and equipment than any which had visited Scotland for a long period. It was the first field of the young monarch; and his barons, eager to demonstrate their loyalty, attended with so full a muster, that, according to a contemporary English historian, three hundred thousand horses were employed.* The unequal terms upon

* Walsingham, pp. 316, 537. Otterburn, p. 161.

which a richer and a poorer country make war on each other, were never more strikingly evinced than in the result of these English and Scottish expeditions. The Scots, breaking in upon the rich fields of England, mounted on their hardy little hackneys, which lived on so little in their own country, that any change was for the better; carrying nothing with them but their arms; inured to all weathers, and fearlessly familiar with danger, found war a pastime, rather than an inconvenience; enriched themselves with plunder, which they transported with wonderful expedition from place to place, and at last safely landed it at home. Intimately acquainted with the seat of war, on the approach of the English, they could accept or decline battle, as they thought best: if outnumbered, as was generally the case, they retired, and contented themselves with cutting off the convoys or foraging parties, and securing their booty; if the English, from want of provisions, or discontent and disunion amongst the leaders, commenced their retreat, it was infested by their unwearied enemy, who instantly pushed forward, and, hovering round their line of march, never failed to do them serious mischief. On the other hand, the very strength, and warlike and complicated equipment of the English army, proved its ruin, or at least totally defeated its object; and this was soon seen in the result of Richard's invasion. The immense mass of his host slowly proceeded through the border counties by Liddesdale and Teviotdale,* devouring all as they passed on, and leaving behind them a black desert. In no place did they meet an enemy; the Scots had stript the country of everything but the green crops on the

* In the Archæologia, vol. xxii., Part i., p. 13, will be found an interesting paper, describing the army of Richard and its leaders, printed from a MS. in the British Museum, and communicated by Sir Harris Nicolas.

ground; and empty villages, which were given to the
flames, and churches and monasteries, razed and plundered, formed the only triumphs of the campaign.

One event, however, is too characteristic to be omitted. When the news of this great expedition reached
the camp of Douglas and Vienne, who had fallen back
towards Berwick, the Scots, although aware of the
folly of attempting to give battle, yet deemed it prudent to approach nearer, and watch the progress of
their enemy. Here, again, the impatient temper of
the French commander broke out, and he insisted that
their united strength was equal to meet the English;
on which the Earl of Douglas requested him to ride
with him to a neighbouring eminence, and reason the
matter as they went. The admiral consented, and was
surprised when they arrived there to hear the tramp
of horse, and the sound of martial music. Douglas
had, in truth, brought him to a height which hung
over a winding mountain-pass, through which the
English army were at that moment defiling, and from
whence, without the fear of discovery, they could count
the banners, and perceive its strength. The argument
thus presented was not to be questioned; and Vienne,
with his knights, permitted themselves to be directed
by the superior knowledge and military skill of the
Scottish leaders.*

Meanwhile, King Richard pushed on to the capital.
The beautiful Abbeys of Melrose and Dryburgh were
given to the flames; Edinburgh was burned and plundered, and nothing spared but the Monastery of Holyrood. It had lately, as we have seen, afforded a retreat
to John of Gaunt, the king's uncle, who now accompanied him, and, at his earnest entreaty, was excepted

* Froissart, par Buchon, vol. ix. p. 144.

from the general ruin. But the formidable expedition of the king was here concluded, and that unwise and selfish spirit of revenge and destruction, which had wasted the country, began to recoil upon the heads of its authors.* Multitudes perished from want, and provisions became daily more scarce in the camp. In such circumstances, the Duke of Lancaster advised that they should pass the Forth, and, imitating the example of Edward the First, attack and overwhelm the northern counties. But Richard, who scrupled not to accuse his uncle of treasonable motives, in proposing so desperate a project, which was, in truth, likely to increase the difficulties of their situation, resolved to retreat instantly by the same route which he had already travelled.

Before this, however, could be effected, the Scottish army, with their French auxiliaries, broke into England by the western marches; and, uniting their forces with those of Sir Archibald Douglas lord of Galloway, ravaged Cumberland with a severity which was increased by the accounts of the havoc committed by the English. Towns, villages, manors, and hamlets, were indiscriminately plundered and razed to the ground; crowds of prisoners, herds of cattle, wagons and sumpter-horses, laden with the wealth of burghers and yeomen, were driven along; and the parks and pleasure grounds of the Earls of Nottingham and Stafford, of the Mowbrays, the Musgraves, and other Border barons, swept of their wealth, and plundered with a merciless cruelty, which increased to the highest pitch the animosity between the two nations, and ren-

* Froissart, vol. ix. p. 147, asserts, that the English burnt St Johnston, Dundee, and pushed on as far as Aberdeen; but I have followed Walsingham and Fordun, who give the account of their ravages as it is found in the text.

dered the prospect of peace remote and almost hopeless. After this destruction, the united armies made an unsuccessful assault upon the city of Carlisle,* the fortifications of which withstood their utmost efforts; and upon this repulse, which seems to have renewed the heartburning between the French and Scots, they again crossed the Border, the French boasting that they had burnt, destroyed, and plundered more in the bishoprics of Durham and Carlisle than was to be found in all the towns of Scotland put together.†

When the army reached their former quarters, and proceeded to encamp in Edinburgh and the adjacent country, an extraordinary scene presented itself. The land, so late a solitary desert, was in a few hours alive with multitudes of the Scots, who emerged from the woods and mountain passes, driving their flocks and cattle before them, accompanied by their wives and children, and returning with their chattels and furniture to the burnt and blackened houses which they had abandoned to the enemy. The cheerfulness with which they bore these calamities, and set themselves to repair the havoc which had been committed, appears to have astonished their refined allies; but the presence of two thousand Frenchmen, and the difficulty of finding them provisions, was an additional evil which they were not prepared to bear so easily; and when the Admiral of France, to lighten the burden, abandoned his design of a second invasion of England, and permitted as many as chose to embark for France, the Scots refused to furnish transports, or to allow a single vessel to leave their ports, until the French knights had paid them for the injuries they had inflicted by

* Winton, vol. ii. p. 325, affirms they would not assault Carlisle, for "thai dred tynsale of men."
† Fordun a Goodal, vol. ii. p. 401. Froissart, par Buchon, vol. ix. p. 155.

riding through their country, trampling and destroying their crops, cutting down their woods to build lodgings, and plundering their markets. To these conditions Vienne was compelled to listen; indeed, such was the miserable condition in which the campaign had left his knights and men-at-arms, who were now for the most part unhorsed, and dispirited by sickness and privation, that, to have provoked the Scots, might have led to serious consequences. He agreed, therefore, to discharge the claims of damage and reparation which were made against his soldiers; and for himself came under an obligation not to leave the country till they were fully satisfied, his knights being permitted to return home.

These stipulations were strictly fulfilled. Ships were furnished by the Scots, and, to use the expressive language of Froissart, "divers knights and squires had passage, and returned into Flanders, as wind and weather drove them, with neither horse nor harness, right poor and feeble, cursing the day that ever they came upon such an adventure; and fervently desiring that the Kings of France and England would conclude a peace for a year or two, were it only to have the satisfaction of uniting their armies, and utterly destroying the realm of Scotland." Some knights who were fond of adventure, and little anxious to return to France in so miserable a condition, passed on to Denmark, Norway, and Sweden; others took shipping for Ireland, desirous of visiting the famous cavern known by the name of the purgatory of St Patrick;[*] and Vienne himself, after having corresponded with his government, and discharged the claims which were brought against him, took leave of the king and nobles of Scotland, and returned to Paris.

[*] See Rymer, Fœdera, vol. viii. p. 14.

Such was the issue of an expedition, fitted out by France at an immense expense, and which, from being hastily undertaken, and only partially executed, concluded in vexation and disappointment. Had the naval armament which was to have attacked England on the south been able to effect a descent, and had the Constable of France, according to the original intention, co-operated with Vienne, at the head of a large body of Genoese cross-bowmen and men-at-arms,* the result might perhaps have been different; but the great causes of failure are to be traced to the impossibility of reconciling two systems of military operations so perfectly distinct as those of the Scots and the French, and of supporting, for any length of time, in so poor a country as Scotland, such a force as was able to offer battle to the English with any fair prospect of success. One good effect resulted from the experience gained in this campaign. It convinced the Scots of the superior excellence of their own tactics, which consisted in employing their light cavalry solely in plunder, or in attacks upon the archers when they were forced to fight, and in opposing to the heavy-armed cavalry of the English their infantry alone, with their firm squares and long spears. It also taught them, that any foreign auxiliary force of the heavy-armed cavalry of the continent was of infinitely greater encumbrance than assistance in their wars with England, as they must either be too small to produce any effect against the overwhelming armies of that country, or too numerous to be supported, without occasioning severe distress.

Upon the departure of the French, the war continued with great spirit; and from the imbecility of the government of Richard the Second, a feeble opposition

* Froissart, par Buchon, vol. ix. p. 162.

was made against the successes of the Scots. The systematic manner in which their invasions were conducted, is apparent from the plan and details of that which immediately succeeded the expedition of Vienne. It was remembered by the Scottish leaders, that in the general devastation which had been lately inflicted upon the English Border counties, that portion of Cumberland, including the rich and fertile district of Cockermouth and the adjacent country, had not been visited since the days of Robert Bruce; and it was judged proper to put an end to this exemption. Robert earl of Fife, the king's second son, James earl of Douglas, and Sir Archibald Douglas lord of Galloway, at the head of thirty thousand light troops, passed the Solway, and for three days* plundered and laid waste the whole of this beautiful district; so that, to use the expression of Fordun, the feeblest in the Scottish host had his hands full: nor do they appear to have met with the slightest opposition. A singular and characteristic anecdote of this expedition is preserved by this historian. Amid the plunder, an ancient Saxon charter of King Athelstane, with a waxen seal appended to it, was picked up by some of the soldiers, and carried to the Earl of Fife, afterwards the celebrated Regent Albany. Its lucid brevity astonished the feudal baron: "I, King Adelstane, giffys here to Paulan, Oddam and Roddam, als gude and als fair, as ever thai myn war; and thairto witnes Mald my wyf." Often, says the historian, after the earl became Duke of Albany and Governor of Scotland, when the tedious and wordy charters of our modern days were recited in the causes

---

* Fordun a Goodal, vol. ii. p. 403. "Exercitum caute et quasi imperceptibiliter ducebat usque ad Cokirmouth, * * per terram a diebus Domin Roberti de Bruce regis a Scotis non invasam."

which came before him, he would recall to memory this little letter of King Athelstane, and declare there was more truth and good faith in those old times than now, when the new race of lawyers had brought in such frivolous exceptions and studied prolixity of forms.* It is singular to meet with a protestation against the unnecessary multiplication of words and clauses in legal deeds at so remote a period.

At the time of this invasion, another enterprise took place, which nearly proved fatal to its authors: a descent upon Ireland by Sir William Douglas, the natural son of Sir Archibald of Galloway, commonly called the Black Douglas. This young knight appears to have been the Scottish Paladin of those days of chivalry. His form and strength were almost gigantic; and what gave a peculiar charm to his warlike prowess, was the extreme gentleness of his manners: sweet, brave, and generous, he was as faithful to his friends as he was terrible to his enemies. These qualities had gained him the hand of the king's daughter Egidia: a lady of such beauty, that the King of France is said to have fallen in love with her from the description of some of his courtiers, and to have privately despatched a painter into Scotland to bring him her picture; when he found, to his disappointment, that the princess had disposed of her heart in her own country.†

At this time the piracies of the Irish on the coast of Galloway provoked the resentment of Douglas, who, at the head of five hundred lances, made a descent upon the Irish coast at Carlingford, and immediately assaulted the town with only a part of his force, finding it difficult to procure small boats to land the whole. Before, however, he had made himself master of the

* Fordun a Goodal, vol. ii. p. 403.   † Ibid.

outworks, the citizens, by the promise of a large sum of money, procured an armistice; after which, under cover of night, they despatched a messenger to Dundalk for assistance, who represented the small number of the Scots, and the facility of overpowering them. Douglas, in the meantime, of an honest and unsuspicious temper, had retired to the shore, and was busied in superintending the lading of his vessels, when he discerned the approach of the English, and had scarce time to form his little phalanx, before he was attacked not only by them but by a sally from the town. Yet this treacherous conduct was entirely unsuccessful: although greatly outnumbered, such was the superior discipline and skill of the Scots, that every effort failed to pierce their columns, and they at length succeeded in totally dispersing the enemy; after which the town was burnt to the ground, the castle and its works demolished, and fifteen merchant ships, which lay at anchor, laden with goods, seized by the victors.* They then set sail for Scotland, ravaged the Isle of Man as they returned, and landed safely at Lochryan in Galloway; from which Douglas took horse and joined his father, who, with the Earl of Fife, had broken across the Border, and was then engaged in an expedition against the western districts of England.

The origin of this invasion requires particular notice, as it led to important results, and terminated in the celebrated battle of Otterburn. The Scots had not forgotten the miserable havoc which was inflicted upon the country by the late expedition of the King of England; and as this country was now torn by disputes between the weak monarch and his nobility, it was deemed a proper juncture to retaliate. To decide upon

* Fordun a Hearne, pp. 1073, 1074. Winton, vol. ii. p. 335, 336.

this a council was held at Edinburgh.? The king was now infirm from age, and wisely anxious for peace; but his wishes were overruled, and the management of the campaign intrusted by the nobles to his second son, the Earl of Fife, upon whom the hopes of the warlike part of the nation chiefly rested, his elder brother, the Earl of Carrick, who was next heir to the crown, being of a feeble constitution, and little able to endure the fatigues of the field. It was resolved that there should be a general muster of the whole military force of the kingdom at Jedburgh, preparatory to an invasion, upon a scale likely to ensure an ample retribution for their losses.*

The rumour of this great summons of the vassals of the crown soon reached England; and the barons, to whom the care of the Borders was committed, began to muster their feudal services, and to prepare for resistance. On the day appointed, the Scots assembled at Yetholm, a small town not far from Jedburgh, and situated at the foot of the Cheviot Hills. A more powerful army had not been seen for a long period. There were twelve hundred men-at-arms and forty thousand infantry, including a small body of archers, a species of military force in which the Scots were still little skilled, when compared with the formidable power of the English bowmen. It was now necessary to determine in what manner the war should begin, and upon what part of the country its fury should first be let loose; and, when the leaders were deliberating upon this, a prisoner was taken and carried to head-quarters, who proved to be an English gentleman, despatched by the Border lords for the purpose of collecting information. From him they understood that the wardens

* Froissart, par Buchon, vol. xi. p. 363.

of the marches did not deem themselves strong enough at that time to offer battle, but that, having collected their power, they had determined to remain quiet till it was seen in what direction the Scottish invasion was to take place, and then to make a counter expedition into Scotland; thus avoiding all chance of being attacked, and retaliating upon the Scots by a system of simultaneous havoc and plunder.

Upon receiving this information, which proved to be correct, the Earl of Fife determined to separate his force into two divisions, and for the purpose of frustrating the designs of the English, to invade the country both by the western and eastern marches. He himself, accordingly, with Archibald lord of Galloway, and the Earls of Sutherland, Menteith, Mar, and Strathern, at the head of a large force, being nearly two-thirds of the whole army, began their march through Liddesdale, and passing the borders of Galloway, advanced towards Carlisle. The second division was chiefly intended to divert the attention of the English from opposing the main body of the Scots; it consisted of three hundred knights and men-at-arms, and two thousand foot, besides some light-armed prickers and camp-followers,* and was placed under the command of the Earl of Douglas, a young soldier, who, from his boyhood, had been trained to war by his father, and who possessed the hereditary valour and military talent of the family. Along with him went the Earls of March and Moray; Sir James Lindsay, Sir Alexander Ramsay, and Sir John St Clair, three soldiers of great experience; Sir Patrick Hepburn

---

* Winton, vol. ii. p. 337, gives a much higher number; but we may here trust rather to Froissart, who affirms that he had no more than "three hundred men-at-arms, and two thousand infantry."

with his two sons, Sir John Haliburton, Sir John Maxwell, Sir Alexander Fraser, Sir Adam Glendinning, Sir David Fleming, Sir Thomas Erskine, and many other knights and squires.

With this small army, the Earl of Douglas pushed rapidly on through Northumberland, having given strict orders that not a house should be burnt or plundered till they reached the Bishopric of Durham. Such was the silence and celerity of the march, that he crossed the Tyne near Branspeth, and was not discovered by the English garrisons to be in the heart of this rich and populous district, until the smoke of the flaming villages, and the terror of the people, carried the first news of his arrival to the city of Durham. Nor did the English dare at present to oppose him, imagining his force to be the advanced guard of the main army of the Scots: a natural supposition, for the capture of their spy had left them in ignorance of the real designs of the enemy. Douglas, therefore, plundered without meeting an enemy; whilst Sir Henry Percy, better known by his name of Hotspur, and his brother Ralph, the two sons of the Earl of Northumberland, along with the Seneschal of York, the Captain of Berwick, Sir Mathew Redman, Sir Ralph Mowbray, Sir John Felton, Sir Thomas Grey, and numerous other Border barons, kept themselves, with their whole power, within the barriers of Newcastle,* and the Earl of Northumberland collected his strength at Alnwick.

Meanwhile, having wasted the country as far as the gates of Durham, the Scottish leaders returned to Newcastle with a rapidity equal to their advance, and in the spirit of the times, determined to tarry there

* Winton, vol. ii. p. 338. Froissart, par Buchon, vol. xi. p. 377.

two days, and try the courage of the English knights. The names of Percy and of Douglas were at this time famous: Hotspur having the reputation of one of the bravest soldiers in England, and the Earl of Douglas, although his younger in years, being little inferior in the estimation in which his military prowess was held amongst his countrymen. In the skirmishes which took place at the barriers of the town, it happened that these celebrated soldiers came to be personally opposed to each other; and after an obstinate contest, Douglas won the pennon of the English leader, and boasted aloud, before the knights who were present, that he would carry it to Scotland, and plant it, as a proof of his prowess, on his castle of Dalkeith. "That, so help me God!" cried Hotspur, "no Douglas shall ever do; and ere you leave Northumberland you shall have small cause to boast."—"Well, Henry," answered Douglas, "your pennon shall this night be placed before my tent; come and win it if you can!"*

Such was the nature of this defiance; and Douglas knew enough of Percy to be assured that, if possible, he would keep his word. He commanded, therefore, a strict watch to be maintained; struck the pennon into the ground in front of his tent, and awaited the assault of the English. There were occasions, however, in which the bravadoes of chivalry gave way to the stricter rules of war; and as the English leaders still entertained the idea that Douglas only led the van of the main army, and that his object was to draw them from their entrenchments, they insisted that Percy should not hazard an attack which might bring them into jeopardy. The Scots, accordingly, after in vain expecting an attack, left their encampment, and pro-

* Froissart, par Buchon, vol. xi. pp. 377.

ceeded on their way. Passing by the tower of Ponteland, they carried it by storm, razed it to the ground, and still continuing their retreat, came, on the second day, to the village and castle of Otterburn, situated in Redesdale,* and about twelve miles from Newcastle. This castle was strongly fortified, and the first day resisted every attack; upon which most of their leaders, anxious not to lose time, but to carry their booty across the Borders, proposed to proceed into Scotland.

Douglas alone opposed this, and entreated them to remain a few days and make themselves masters of the castle, so that in the interval they might give Henry Percy full time, if he thought fit, to reach their encampment, and fulfil his promise. This they at length agreed to; and having skilfully chosen their encampment, they fortified it in such a way as should give them great advantage in the event of an attack. In its front, and extending also a little to one side, was a marshy level, at the narrow entrance of which were placed their carriages and wagons laden with plunder and behind them the horses, sheep, and cattle which they had driven away with them. These were committed to the charge of the sutlers and camp-followers, who, although poorly armed, were able to make some resistance with their staves and knives. Behind these, on firm ground, which was on one side defended by the marsh, and on the other flanked by a small wooded hill, were placed the tents and temporary huts of the leaders and the men-at-arms; and having thus taken every precaution against a surprise, they occupied themselves during the day in assaulting the castle, and at night retired within their encampment.† But this

---

* Winton, vol. ii. pp. 339, 340.
† Froissart, par Buchon, vol. xi. p. 385.

did not long continue. By this time it became generally known that Douglas and his little army were wholly unsupported; and the moment that Percy ascertained the fact, and discovered that the Scottish earl lay encamped at Otterburn, he put himself at the head of six hundred lances, and eight thousand foot, and, without waiting for the Bishop of Durham, who was advancing with his power to Newcastle, marched straight to Otterburn, at as rapid a rate as his infantry could bear.*

Hotspur had left Newcastle after dinner, and the sun was set before he came in sight of the Scots encampment. It was a placid evening in the month of August, which had succeeded to a day of extreme heat, and the greater part of the Scots, worn out with an unsuccessful attack upon the castle, had taken their supper and fallen asleep. In a moment they were awakened by a cry of "Percy, Percy!" and the English, trusting that they could soon carry the encampment from the superiority of their numbers, attacked it with the greatest fury. They were checked, however, by the barrier of wagons, and the brave defence made by the servants and camp-followers, which gave the knights time to arm, and enabled Douglas and the leaders to form the men-at-arms before Hotspur could reach their tents. The excellence of the position chosen by the Scottish earl was now apparent; for, taking advantage of the ground, he silently and rapidly defiled round the wooded eminence already mentioned, which completely concealed his march, and when the greater part of the English were engaged in the marsh, suddenly raised his banner, and set upon them in flank. It was now night; but the moon shone brightly, and—

* Froissart, par Buchon, vol. xi. p. 284.

the air was so clear and calm, that the light was almost equal to the day. Her quiet rays, however, fell on a dreadful scene; for Percy became soon convinced that he had mistaken the lodgings of the servants for those of their masters; and, chafed at the disappointment, drew back his men on firm ground, and encountered the Scots with the utmost spirit. He was not, indeed, so well supported as he might have been, as a large division of the English under Sir Mathew Redman and Sir Robert Ogle,* having made themselves masters of the encampment, had begun to plunder, and his own men were fatigued with their march; whilst the Scots, under Douglas, Moray, and March, were fresh and well-breathed. Yet. with all these disadvantages, the English greatly outnumbered the enemy; and in the temper of their armour and their weapons were far their superior.†

For many hours the battle raged with undiminished fury; banners rose and fell; the voices of the knights shouting their war-cries, were mingled with the shrieks and groans of the dying, whilst the ground, covered with dead bodies and shreds of armour, and slippery with blood, scarce afforded room for the combatants, so closely were they engaged, and so obstinately was every foot of earth contested. It was at this time that Douglas, wielding a battle-axe in both hands, and followed only by a few of his household, cut his way into the press of English knights, and throwing himself too rashly upon the spears, was borne to the earth, and soon mortally wounded in the head and neck. Yet at this time none knew who had fallen, for the English pressed on; and a considerable interval elapsed

---

* Winton, vol. ii. p. 340.
† Froissart, par Buchon, vol. xi. p. 389.

before the Earls of March and Moray again forced them to give back, and cleared the spot where Douglas lay bleeding. Sir James Lindsay was the first to discover his kinsman; and, running up hastily, eagerly inquired how it fared with him. "But poorly," said Douglas. "I am dying in my armour, as my fathers have done, thanks be to God, and not in my bed; but if you love me, raise my banner and press forward, for he who should bear it lies slain beside me." Lindsay instantly obeyed; and the banner of the crowned heart again rose amid the cries of "Douglas!" so that the Scots believed their leader was still in the field, and pressed on the English ranks with a courage which at last compelled them to give way.* Hotspur, and his brother Sir Ralph Percy, surrendered after a stout resistance; and along with them nearly the whole chivalry of Northumberland and Durham were either slain or taken. Amongst the prisoners were the Seneschal of York, the Captain of Berwick, Sir Mathew Redman, Sir Ralph Langley, Sir Robert Ogle, Sir John Lilburn, Sir Thomas Walsingham, Sir John Felton, Sir John Copland, Sir Thomas Abingdon, and many other knights and gentlemen,† whose ransom was a source of great and immediate wealth to the Scots. There were slain on the English side about eighteen hundred and sixty men-at-arms, and a thousand were grievously wounded.‡ We are informed by Froissart, that he received his account of this expedition from English and Scottish knights who were engaged in it; and "of all the battles," says he, "which I have made mention of heretofore in this history, this

---

* Froissart, par Buchon, vol. xi. pp. 393, 394, 395. Winton, vol. ii. pp. 340, 341, 342.
† Froissart, par Buchon, vol. xi. p. 398.　　‡ Ibid. vol. xi. p. 420.

of Otterburn was the bravest and the best contested; for there was neither knight nor squire but acquitted himself nobly, doing well his duty, and fighting hand to hand, without either stay or faintheartedness." And as the English greatly outnumbered the Scots, so signal a victory was much talked of, not only in both countries, but on the continent.*

The joy which was naturally felt upon such an occasion, was greatly overclouded by the death of Douglas. His conduct became the theme of universal praise; and his loss was the more lamented, as he had fallen in this heroic manner in the prime of manhood. All the soldiers mourned for him as their dearest friend; and the march to Scotland resembled more a funeral procession than a triumphant progress, for in the midst of it moved the car in which was placed the body of this brave man. In this manner was it conveyed by the army to the Abbey of Melrose, where they buried him in the sepulchre of his fathers, and hung his banner, torn and soiled with blood, over his grave.†

The causes of this defeat of Hotspur, by a force greatly his inferior, are not difficult to be discovered. They are to be found in the excellent natural position chosen by Douglas for his encampment; in the judicious manner in which it had been fortified; and in the circumstance of Percy attempting to carry it at first by a coup-de-main; thus rendering his archers, that portion of the English force which had ever been most decisive and destructive in its effects, totally useless.‡ The difficulties thrown in the way of the English by the intrenchment of wagons, and the defence of the

---

* Froissart, par Buchon, vol. xi. p. 401.   † Ibid. vol. xi. p. 422.
‡ Ibid. vol. xi. p. 389. " Et etoient si joints l'un à l'autre et si attachés, que trait d'archers de nul coté n'y avoit point de lieu."

camp followers, were of the utmost consequence in gaining time; and the subsequent victory forms a striking contrast to the dreadful defeat sustained by the Scots at Dupplin, in consequence of the want of any such precaution.* Even at Otterburn, the leaders, who were sitting in their gowns and doublets at supper when the first alarm reached them, had to arm in extreme haste; so that Douglas's harness was in many places unclapsed, and the Earl of Moray fought all night without his helmet;† but minutes, in such circumstances, were infinitely valuable, and these were gained by the strength of the camp. One circumstance connected with the death of Douglas is too characteristic of the times to be omitted. His chaplain, a priest of the name of Lundie, had followed him to the war, and fought during the whole battle at his side. When his body was discovered, this warrior clerk was found bestriding his dying master, wielding his battle-axe, and defending him from injury. He became afterwards Archdeacon of North Berwick.‡

On hearing of the defeat at Otterburn, the Bishop of Durham, who, soon after Percy's departure, had entered Newcastle with ten thousand men, attempted, at the head of this force, to cut off the retreat of the Scots; but, on coming up with their little army, he found they had again intrenched themselves in the same strong position, in which they could not be attacked without manifest risk; and he judged it prudent to retreat,§ so that they reached their own country without further molestation. So many noble prisoners had not been carried into Scotland since the days of Bruce;‖ for although Hotspur's force did not

* History, supra. vol. ii. p. 12. † Winton, vol. ii. p. 339.
‡ Froissart, par Buchon, vol. xi. p. 393. § Ibid. vol. xi. p. 419.
‖ Winton, vol. ii. p. 343.

amount to nine thousand men, it included the flower of the English Border baronage. The remaining division of the Scots, under the Earl of Fife, amounting, as we have seen, to more than a third part of the whole army, broke into England by the west marches, according to the plan already agreed on; and after an inroad, attended by the usual circumstances of devastation and plunder, being informed of the successful conclusion of the operations on the eastern border, returned without a check to Scotland.

It is impossible not to agree with Froissart, that there never was a more chivalrous battle than this of Otterburn: the singular circumstances under which it was fought, in a sweet moonlight night;* the heroic death of Douglas; the very name of Hotspur; all contribute to invest it with that character of romance, so seldom coincident with the cold realities of history; and we experience, in its recital, something of the sentiment of Sir Philip Sidney, "who never could hear the song of the Douglas and Percy without having his heart stirred as with the sound of a trumpet." But it ought not to be forgotten, that it was solely a chivalrous battle: it had nothing great in its motive, and nothing great in its results. It differs as widely, in this respect, from the battles of Stirling and Bannockburn, and from the many contests which distinguish the war of liberty, as the holy spirit of freedom from the petty ebullitions of national rivalry, or the desire of plunder and revenge. It was fought at a time when England had abandoned all serious designs against the independence of the neighbouring country; when the king, and the great body of the Scottish people, earnestly desired peace;

* It was fought on Wednesday, 5th August. Macpherson's Notes on Winton, vol. ii. p. 516.

and when the accomplishment of this desire would have been a real blessing to the nation: but this blessing the Scottish nobles, who, like their feudal brethren of England and France, could not exist without public or private war, did not appreciate, and had no ambition to see realized. The war originated in the character of this class, and the principles which they adopted; and the power of the crown, and the influence of the commons, were yet infinitely too feeble to check their authority: on the contrary, this domineering power of the great feudal families was evidently on the increase in Scotland, and led, as we shall see in the sequel, to dreadful results.

But to return from this digression. The age and indolence of the king, and his aversion to business, appear to have now increased to a height which rendered it necessary for the parliament to interfere; and the bodily weakness of the Earl of Carrick, the heir-apparent, who had been injured by the kick of a horse. made it impossible that much active management should be intrusted to him. From necessity, more than choice or affection, the nation next looked to Robert's second son, the Earl of Fife; and in a meeting of the three Estates, held at Edinburgh in 1389, the king willingly retired from all interference with public affairs, and committed the office of governor of the kingdom to this ambitious and intriguing man, who, at the mature age of fifty, succeeded to the complete management of the kingdom.* A deep selfishness, which, if it secured its own aggrandizement, little regarded the means employed, was the prominent feature in the character of the new regent. His faults, too, were redeemed by few great qualities, for he possessed

* Fordun & Goodal, vol. ii. p. 414. He died in 1419, aged eighty.

little military talent; and although his genius for civil government has been extolled by our ancient historians, his first public act was one of great weakness.

Since the defeat at Otterburn, and the capture of Hotspur, the Earl Marshal, to whom the English king had committed the custody of the marches, had been accustomed to taunt and provoke the Scottish Borderers to renew the quarrel, and had boasted, that he would be ready to give them battle, if they would meet him in a fair field, though their numbers should double his. These were the natural and foolish ebullitions that will ever accompany any great defeat, and ought to have been overlooked by the governor; but, instead of this, he affected to consider his knightly character involved; and prepared to sacrifice the true interests of the country, which loudly called for peace, to his own notions of honour. An army was assembled, which Fife conducted in person, having along with him Archibald Douglas, and the rest of the Scottish nobles. With this force they passed the marches, and sent word to the Earl Marshal, that they had accepted his challenge, and would expect his arrival; but, with superior wisdom, he declined the defiance; and, having intrenched himself in a strong position, refused to abandon his advantage, and proposed to wait their attack. This, however, formed no part of the project of the Scots, and they returned into their own country.* In such absurd bravadoes, resembling more the quarrels of children than any grave or serious contest, did two great nations employ themselves, misled by those ridiculous ideas which had arisen out of the system of chivalry, whose influence was now paramount throughout Europe.

* Fordun a Goodal, vol. ii. p. 414. Winton, vol. ii. p. 346.

Not long after this, a three-years' truce having been concluded at Boulogne between England and France, a mutual embassy of French and English knights arrived in Scotland, and, having repaired to the court, which was then held at Dunfermline, prevailed upon the Scots to become parties to this cessation of hostilities; so that the king, who, since his accession to the throne, had not ceased to desire peace, enjoyed the comfort of at last seeing it, if not permanently settled, at least in the course of being established.* He retired, soon after, to one of his northern castles at Dundonald, in Ayrshire, where, on the thirteenth May, 1390, he died at the age of seventy-four, in the twentieth year of his reign.† The most prominent features in the character of this monarch have been already described. That he was indolent, and fond of enjoying himself in the seclusion of his northern manors, whilst he injudiciously conferred too independent a power upon his turbulent and ambitious sons, cannot be denied; but it ought not to be forgotten, that, at a time when the liberties of the country were threatened with a total overthrow, the Steward stood forward in their defence, with a zeal and energy which were eminently successful, and that he was the main instrument in defeating the designs of David the Second and Edward the Third, when an English prince was attempted to be imposed upon the nation. The policy he pursued, after his accession, so far as the character of the king was then allowed to influence the government, were essentially pacific; but the circumstances in which the nation was placed were totally changed; and to

---

* Rotuli Scotiæ, vol. ii. pp. 89, 99.
† Winton, vol. ii. pp. 350, 351. Some fine remains of this ancient castle still exist. Stat. Account, vol. vii. p. 619.

maintain peace between the two countries became then as much the object of a wise governor, as it formerly had been his duty to continue the war. Unfortunately, the judgment of the king was not permitted to have that influence to which it was entitled: and many years were yet to run before the two nations had their eyes opened, to discern the principles best calculated to promote their mutual prosperity.

During the whole course of this reign, the agriculture of Scotland appears to have been in a lamentable condition; a circumstance to be traced, no doubt, to the constant interruption of the regular seasons of rural labour; the ravages committed by foreign invasion, and the havoc which necessarily attended the passage even of a Scottish army from one part of the country to another. The proof of this is to be found in the frequent licenses which were granted by the English king, allowing the nobles and the merchants of Scotland to import grain into that country, and in the fact that the grain for the victualling of the Scottish castles, then in the hands of the English, was not unfrequently brought from Ireland.* But the commercial spirit of the country during this reign was undoubtedly on the increase; and the trade which it carried on with Flanders appears to have been conducted with much enterprise and activity. Mercer, a Scottish merchant, during his residence in France, was, from his great wealth, admitted to the favour and confidence of Charles the Sixth; and, on one occasion, the cargo of a Scottish merchantman, which had been captured by the English, was valued as high as seven thousand marks, an immense sum for those remote times.† The staple source of export

* Rotuli Scotiæ, vol. i. pp. 963, 965, 966, 968, 975.
† Walsingham, p. 239.

wealth continued to consist in wool, hides, skins, and wool-fells. We have the evidence of Froissart, who had himself travelled in the country, that its home manufactures were in a very low condition.

CHAP. II.

ROBERT THE THIRD.

1390—1424.

CONTEMPORARY PRINCES.

Kings of England.	Kings of France.	Rome.	(Popes.) Avignon.
Richard II.	Charles VI.	Boniface IX.	Clement VII.
Henry IV.	Charles VII.	Innocent VII.	Benedict XIII.
Henry V.		Gregory XII.	
		Alexander V.	
		John XXIII.	
		Martin V.	

The remains of Robert the Second were committed to the sepulchre in the Abbey of Scone; and on the 14th August, 1390, being the morning succeeding the funeral, the coronation of his successor, John earl of Carrick, took place, with circumstances of great pomp and solemnity.* Next day, which was the Assumption of the Virgin, his wife, Annabella Drummond countess of Carrick, a daughter of the noble house of Drummond, was crowned queen; and on the following morning, the assembled prelates and nobles, amidst a great concourse of the people, took their oaths of allegiance, when it was agreed that the king should change his name to that of Robert the Third; the appellative

* Winton, vol. ii. pp. 361, 362. Fordun a Goodal, vol. ii. p. 418. Chamberlain Accounts, vol. ii. p. 196. The funeral expenses amounted to £253, 19s. 9d.

John, from its associations with Baliol, being considered ominous and unpopular.

The character of the monarch was not essentially different from that of his predecessor. It was amiable, and far from wanting in sound sense and discretion; but the accident which had occasioned his lameness, unfitted him for excelling in those martial exercises which were then necessary to secure the respect of his nobility, and compelled him to seek his happiness in pacific pursuits, and domestic endearments, more likely to draw upon him the contempt of his nobles, than any more kindly feelings. The name of king, too, did not bring with it, in this instance, that high hereditary honour which, had Robert been the representative of a long line of princes, must necessarily have attached to it. He was only the second king of a new race; the proud barons who surrounded his throne had but lately seen his father and himself in their own rank; had associated with them as their equals, and were little prepared to surrender, to a dignity of such recent creation, the homage or the awe which the person on whom it had fallen did not command by his own virtues. Yet the king appears to have been distinguished by many admirable qualities. He possessed an inflexible love of justice, and an affection for his people, which were evinced by every measure where he was suffered to follow the dictates of his own heart; he was aware of the miseries which the country had suffered by the long continuance of war, and he saw clearly that peace was the first and best blessing which his government could bestow, and for the establishment and continuance of which almost every sacrifice should be made. The soundness of these views could not be doubted. They were the dictates of a clear and correct thinking mind, which, confined by circumstances to thoughtfulness and retirement, had discovered the most judicious line of policy, when all around it was turbulence and error, and a few centuries later they would have been hailed as the highest virtues in a sovereign.

But Robert was wanting in that combination of qualities which could alone have enabled him to bring these higher principles into action; and this is explained in a single word, when it has been said he was unwarlike. The sceptre required to be held in a firm hand; and to restrain the outrages of a set of nobles so haughty as those who then domineered over Scotland, it was absolutely necessary that the king should possess somewhat of that fierce energy which distinguished themselves. Irresolution, timidity, and an anxious desire to conciliate the affection of all parties, induced him to abandon the most useful designs, because they opposed the selfishness, or threatened to abridge the power, of his barons; and this weakness of character was ultimately productive of fatal effects in his own family, and throughout the kingdom. It happened also, unfortunately for the peace of the community, that his father had delegated the chief power of the state to his brothers, the Earls of Fife and of Buchan, committing the general management of all public affairs, with the title of Governor, to the first;* and permitting the Earl of Buchan to rule over the northern parts of the kingdom, with an authority little less than regal. The first of these princes had long evinced a restless ambition, which had been increased by the early possession of power; but his character began now to discover those darker shades of crime, which grew deeper as he advanced in years. The Earl of Buchan, on the other

* Chamberlain Accounts, vol. ii. pp. 165, 192.

hand, was little less than a cruel and ferocious savage, a species of Celtic Attila, whose common appellation of the "Wolf of Badenoch," is sufficiently characteristic of the dreadful attributes which composed his character, and who issued from his lair in the north, like the devoted instrument of the divine wrath, to scourge and afflict the nation.

On the morning after the coronation, a little incident occurred, which is indicative of the gentle character of the king, and illustrates the simple manners of the times. The fields and inclosures round the monastery had been destroyed by the nobles and their retinue; and as it happened during the harvest, when the crops were ripe, the mischief fell heavily on the monks. A canon of the order, who filled the office of storekeeper, demanded an audience of the king, for the purpose of claiming some compensation; but on announcing his errand the chamberlain dismissed him with scorn. The mode in which he revenged himself was whimsical and extraordinary. Early on the morning after the coronation, before the king had awoke, the priest assembled a motley multitude of the farm-servants and villagers belonging to the monastery, who, bearing before them an image stuffed with straw, and armed with the drums, horns, and rattles which they used in their rustic festivals, took their station under the windows of the royal bedchamber, and at once struck up such a peal of yells, horns, rattles, and dissonant music, that the court awoke in terror and dismay. The priest who led the rout was instantly dragged before the king, and asked what he meant. "Please your majesty," said he, "what you have just heard are our rural carols, in which we indulge when our corps are brought in; and as you and your nobles have spared us the trouble and expense of cutting them down this season, we thought it grateful to give

you a specimen of our harvest jubilee." The freedom
and sarcasm of the answer would have been instantly
punished by the nobles; but the king understood and
pardoned the reproof, ordered an immediate inquiry
into the damage done to the monastery, and not only
paid the full amount, but applauded the humour and
courage of the ecclesiastic.*

It was a melancholy proof of the gentle and indolent
character of this monarch that, after his accession to
the throne, the general management of affairs, and
even the name of Governor,† were still intrusted to
the Earl of Fife, who for a while continued to pursue
such measures as seemed best calculated for the preservation of the public prosperity. The truce of
Leilinghen, which had been entered into between
France and England, in 1389, and to which Scotland
had become a party, was again renewed,‡ and at the
same time it was thought expedient that the league
with France, concluded between Charles the Sixth and
Robert the Second, in 1371, should be prolonged and
ratified by the oath of the King,§ so that the three
countries appeared to be mutually desirous of peace.
Upon the part of England, every precaution seems to
have been taken to prevent any infractions of the truce.
The Scottish commerce was protected; all injuries
committed upon the Borders were directed to be inves-
tigated and redressed by the Lords Wardens; safe
conducts to the nobles, the merchants, and the students
of Scotland, who were desirous of residing in or travelling through England, were readily granted; and
every inclination was shown to pave the way for the

---

* Fordun a Hearne, vol. iv. pp. 1111, 1112.
† Chamberlain Accounts, vol. ii. p. 165. "Et Comiti de Fyf: Custodi regni pro officio Custodis percipient: mille marcas per annum." Ibid. pp. 261, 267.
‡ Rymer, Fœdera, vol. vii. p. 622. Rotuli Scotiæ, vol. ii. pp. 103, 105.
§ Records of the Parliament of Scotland, sub anno 1390, p. 136, Rotuli Scotiæ, vol. ii. p. 98.

settlement of a lasting peace.* Upon the part of Scotland, these wise measures were met by a spirit equally conciliatory; and for eight years, the period for which the truce was prolonged, no important warlike operations took place: a blessed and unusual cessation, in which the country began to breathe anew, and to devote itself to the pursuits of peace.

So happy a state of things was first interrupted by the ferocity of the "Wolf of Badenoch," and the disorders of the northern parts of the kingdom. On some provocation given to Buchan by the Bishop of Moray, this chief descended from his mountains, and, after laying waste the country, with a sacrilege which excited unwonted horror, sacked and plundered the cathedral of Elgin, carrying off its chalices and vestments, polluting its shrines with blood, and, finally, setting fire to the noble pile, which, with the adjoining houses of the canons, and the neighbouring town, were burnt to the ground.† This exploit of the father, was only a signal for a more serious incursion, conducted by his natural son, Duncan Stewart, whose manners were worthy of his descent, and who, at the head of a wild assemblage of ketherans, armed only with the sword and target, broke across the range of hills which divide the counties of Aberdeen and Forfar, and began to destroy the country, and murder the inhabitants, with reckless and indiscriminate cruelty. Sir Walter Ogilvy, then Sheriff of Angus, along with Sir Patrick Gray, and Sir David Lindsay of Glenesk, instantly collected their power, and, although far inferior in numbers, trusting to the temper of their armour,

---

* Rotuli Scotiæ, vol. ii. pp. 99, 100, 101, 103, 105.
† Winton, vol. ii. p. 363. Keith's Catalogue, p. 83. See Chamberlain Accounts, vol. ii. p. 355.

attacked the mountaineers at Gasklune, near the Water of Ila.* But they were almost instantly overwhelmed, the Highlanders fighting with a ferocity, and a contempt of life, which seem to have struck a panic into their steel-clad assailants. Ogilvy, with his brother, Wat of Lichtoune, Young of Ouchterlony, the Lairds of Cairncross, Forfar, and Guthry, were slain, and sixty men-at-arms along with them; whilst Sir Patrick Gray and Sir David Lindsay were grievously wounded, and with difficulty carried off the field. The indomitable fierceness of the mountaineers is strikingly shown by an anecdote preserved by Winton. Lindsay had pierced one of these, a brawny and powerful man, through the body with his spear, and thus apparently pinned him to the earth; but although mortally wounded, and in the agonies of death, he writhed himself up by main strength, and, with the weapon in his body, struck Lindsay a desperate blow with his sword, which cut him through the stirrup and steel-boot into the bone, after which his assailant instantly sunk down and expired.†

These dreadful excesses, committed by a brother and nephew of the king, called for immediate redress; and it is a striking evidence of the internal weakness of the government, that they passed unheeded, and were succeeded by private feuds amongst the nobility, with whom the most petty disputes became frequently the causes of cruel and deadly revenge. A quarrel of this kind had occurred between the Lady of Fivy, wife to Sir David Lindsay, and her nephew Robert

---

* Winton, Chron. vol. ii. pp. 368, 369. Fordun a Goodal, vol. ii. p. 420. Glenbreret, where this writer affirms the battle to have been fought, is Glenbrierachan, about eleven miles north of Gasklune. Macpherson's Notes on Winton, p. 517.

† Winton, vol. ii. p. 369. Extracta ex Chronicis Scotiæ, MS. folio 240

Keith, a baron of great power. It arose from a trifling misunderstanding between some masons and the servants of Keith regarding a water-course, but it concluded in this fierce chief besieging his aunt in her castle; upon which Lindsay, who was then at court, flew to her rescue, and encountering Keith at Garvyach, compelled him to raise the siege, with the loss of sixty of his men, who were slain on the spot.*

Whilst the government was disgraced by the occurrence of such deliberate acts of private war in the low country, the Highlanders prepared to exhibit an extraordinary spectacle. Two numerous clans, or septs, known by the names of the clan Kay, and the clan Quhete,† having long been at deadly feud, their mutual attacks were carried on with that ferocity, which at this period distinguished the Celtic race from the more southern inhabitants of Scotland. The ideas of chivalry, the factitious principles of that system of manners from which we derive our modern code of honour, had hitherto made little progress amongst them; but the more intimate intercourse between the northern and southern portions of the kingdom, and the residence of the lowland barons amongst them, appear to have introduced a change; and the notions of the Norman knights becoming more familiar to the mountaineers, they adopted the singular idea of deciding their quarrel by a combat of thirty against thirty. This project, instead of discouragement, met with the approval of the government, who were happy that a scheme should have suggested itself, by which there was some prospect of the leaders in those fierce and

---

* Winton, vol. ii. p. 372.
† Clan Quete or clan Chattan. The clan Kay is thought to have been the clan Dhai—the Davidsons, a sept of the M'Pherson.

endless disputes being cut off. A day having been appointed for the combat, barriers were raised in the level ground of the North Inch of Perth, and in the presence of the king and a large concourse of the nobility, sixty tall athletic Highland soldiers, armed in the fashion of their country, with bows and arrows, sword and target, short knives and battle-axes, entered the lists, and advanced in mortal array against each other; but at this trying moment the courage of one of the clan Chattan faltered, and, as the lines were closing, he threw himself into the Tay, swam across the river, and fled to the woods. All was now at a stand: with the inequality of numbers the contest could not proceed; and the benevolent monarch, who had suffered himself to be persuaded against his better feelings, was about to break up the assembly, when a stout burgher of Perth, an armourer by trade, sprung within the barriers, and declared, that for half a mark he would supply the place of the deserter. The offer was accepted, and a dreadful contest ensued. Undefended by armour, and confined within a narrow space, the Highlanders fought with a ferocity which nothing could surpass; whilst the gashes made by the daggers and battle-axes, and the savage yells of the combatants, composed a scene altogether new and appalling to many French and English knights, who were amongst the spectators, and to whom, it may be easily imagined, the contrast between this cruel butchery, and the more polished and less fatal battles of chivalry, was striking and revolting. At last a single combatant of the clan Kay alone remained, whilst eleven of their opponents, including the bold armourer, were still able to wield their weapons; upon which the king threw down his gage, and the victory was awarded to the clan Quhete.

The leaders in this savage combat, are said to have been Shaw, the son of Farquhard, who headed the clan Kay, and Cristijohnson, who headed the victors;* but these names, which have been preserved by our contemporary chroniclers, are in all probability corrupted from the original Celtic. After this voluntary immolation of their bravest warriors, the Highlanders for a long time remained quiet within their mountains; and the Earl of Moray and Sir James Lindsay, by whom this expedient for allaying the feuds is said to have been encouraged, congratulated themselves on the success of their project. Soon after this, the management of the northern parts of the kingdom† was committed to the care of David earl of Carrick, the king's eldest son, who, although still a youth in his seventeenth year, and with the faults incident to a proud and impatient temper, evinced an early talent for government, which, under proper cultivation might have proved a blessing to the country.

For some years after this, the current of events is of that quiet character which offers little prominent or interesting. The weakness of the government of Richard the Second, the frenzy of the French King, the pacific disposition of the Scottish monarch, and the character of the Earl of Fife, his chief minister, who, although ambitious and intriguing, was unwarlike, all contributed to secure to Scotland the blessing of peace. The truce with England was renewed from year to year, and the intercourse between the two countries warmly encouraged; the nobility, the merchants, the students

---

* Winton, vol. ii. pp. 373, 374, and Notes p. 518. Fordun a Goodal, vol. ii. p. 420.

† Chamberlain Accounts, vol. ii. p. 349. "Et Duo. Comiti de Carrick de donacione regis pro expensis suis factis in partibus borealibus per tempus compoti: ut patet per literas regis concessas super has, testante clerico probacionis, 40 li."

of Scotland, received safe conducts, and travelled into England for the purposes of pleasure, business, or study, or to visit the shrines of the most popular saints; and the rivalry between the two nations was no longer called forth in mortal combats, but in those less fatal contests, by which the restless spirits of those times, in the absence of real war, kept up their military experience by an imitation of it in tilts and tournaments. An enthusiastic passion for chivalry now reigned in both countries, and, unless we make allowance for the universal influence of this singular system, no just estimate can be formed of the manners of the times. Barons who were sage in council, and high in civil or military office, would leave the business of the state, and interrupt the greatest transactions, to set off upon a tour of adventures, having the king's royal letters, permitting them to " perform points of arms, and manifest their prowess to the world." Wortley, an English knight of great reputation, arrived in Scotland; and, after a courteous reception at court, published his cartel of defiance, which was taken up by Sir James Douglas of Strathbrock, and the trial of arms appointed to be held in presence of the king at Stirling; but after the lists had been prepared, some unexpected occurrence appears to have prevented the duel from taking place.* Sir David Lindsay of Glenesk, who was then reputed one of the best soldiers in Scotland, soon after the accession of Robert the Third sent his cartel to the Lord Wells, an English knight of the court of Richard the Second, which having been accepted, the duel was appointed to take place in London in presence of the king. So important did Lindsay consider the affair, that he

* Chamberlain Accounts, vol. ii. p. 366. Fordun a Goodal, vol. ii. p. 421.

freighted a vessel belonging to Dundee* to bring him from London a new suit of armour; and, when the day arrived, at the head of a splendid retinue he entered the lists, which were crowded by the assembled nobles and beauties of the court. In the first course the English knight was borne out of his saddle; and Lindsay, although rudely struck, kept his seat so firmly, that a cry rose amongst the crowd, who insisted he was tied to his steed, upon which he vaulted to the ground, and, although encumbered by his armour, without touching the stirrup, again sprung into the saddle. Both the knights, after the first course, commenced a desperate foot combat with their daggers, which concluded in the total discomfiture of Lord Wells. Lindsay, who was a man of great personal strength, having struck his dagger firmly into one of the lower joints of his armour, lifted him into the air, and gave him so heavy a fall, that he lay at his mercy. He then, instead of putting him to death, a privilege which the savage laws of these combats at outrance conferred upon the victor, courteously raised him from the ground, and, leading him below the ladies' gallery, delivered him as her prisoner to the Queen of England.†

Upon another occasion, in one of those tournaments, an accomplished baron, named Piers Courtney, made his appearance, who bore upon his surcoat a falcon, with the distich,—" I bear a falcon fairest in flycht, whoso prikketh at her his death is dicht, in graith." To his surprise he found in the lists an exact imitation of himself in the shape of a Scottish knight, with the exception, that instead of a falcon, his surcoat bore a jay, with

---

* Rotuli Scotiæ, vol. ii. p. 104.
† Winton, vol. ii. pp. 355, 356, 357. Fordun a Goodal, vol. ii. p. 422. Lindsay, in gratitude for his victory, founded an altar in the parish church of Dundee. Extracta ex Chronicis Scotiæ, MS. fol. 243.

an inscription ludicrously rhyming to the defiance of Courtney,—" I bear a pyet peikand at ane pees,* qnhasa pykkis at her I sall pyk at his nees,† in faith." The challenge could not be mistaken; and the knights ran two courses against each other, in each of which the helmet of the Scot, from being loosely strapped, gave way, and foiled the attaint of Courtney, who, having lost two of his teeth by his adversary's spear, loudly complained of the occurrence, and insisted that the laws of arms made it imperative on both knights to be exactly on equal terms. " I am content," said the Scot, " to run six courses more on such an agreement, and let him who breaks it forfeit two hundred pounds." The challenge was accepted; upon which he took off his helmet, and, throwing back his thick hair, showed that he was blind of an eye, which he had lost by a wound in the battle of Otterburn. The agreement made it imperative on Courtney to pay the money, or to submit to lose an eye; and it may readily be imagined that Sir Piers, a handsome man, preferred the first to the last alternative.‡

The title of duke, a dignity originally Norman, had been brought from France into England; and we now find it for the first time introduced into Scotland in a parliament held by Robert the Third at Perth, on the 28th of April, 1398.§ At this meeting of the Estates, the king, with great pomp, created his eldest son David earl of Carrick, Duke of Rothesay, and at the same time bestowed the dignity of Duke of Albany upon the Earl of Fife, to whom, since his accession, he had intrusted almost the whole management of public affairs.‖ The

* Pees—piece. † Nees—nose. ‡ Fordun a Goodal, vol. ii. p. 423.
§ Fordun a Goodal, vol. ii. p. 422.
‖ Chamberlain Accounts, vol. ii. p. 421. Et libat: Clerico libacionis, domus Dni nostri Regis, ad expensas ipsius domus " factas apud Sconam, et apud Perth tempore quo tentum fuit Scaccarium, quo eciam tempore tentum

age of the heir-apparent rendered any further continuance of his delegated authority suspicious and unnecessary. Rothesay was now past his twentieth year; and his character, although exhibiting in an immoderate degree the love of pleasure natural to his time of life, was yet marked by a vigour which plainly indicated that he would not long submit to the superiority of his uncle Albany. From his earliest years he had been the darling of his father, and, even as a boy, his household and establishment appear to have been kept up with a munificence which was perhaps imprudent; yet the affectionate restraints imposed by his mother the queen, and the control of William de Drummond, the governor to whose charge his education seems to have been committed, might have done much for the formation of his character, had he not been deprived of both at an early age. It is a singular circumstance, also, that the king, although he possessed not resolution enough to shake off his imprudent dependence upon Albany, evidently dreaded his ambition, and had many misgivings for the safety of his favourite son, and the dangers by which he was surrounded. This may be inferred from the repeated bands or covenants for the support and defence of himself and his son and heir the Earl of Carrick, which were entered into between this monarch and his nobles, from the time the prince had reached his thirteenth year.*

These bands, although in themselves not unknown to the feudal constitution, yet were new in so far as they were agreements, not between subject and subject, but

---

fuit consilium Reg: ibidem super multis punctis et articulis necessariis pro negotiis regni, et reipublicæ, £119, 6s. 4d." The account goes on to notice the creation of the Earl of Carrick as Duke of Rothesay, of Fife as Duke of Albany, and of David Lindsay as Earl of Crawford.

* Chamberlain Accounts, vol. ii. p. 197.

between the king and those great vassals who ought to have been sufficiently bound to support the crown and the heir-apparent by the ordinary oaths of homage. It is in this light that these frequent feudal covenants, by which any vassal of the crown, for a salary settled upon him and his heirs, becomes bound to give his "service and support" to the sovereign and his eldest son the Earl of Carrick, are to be regarded as a new feature in the feudal constitution of the country, importing an increase in the power of the aristocracy, and a proportional decrease in the strength of the crown. There seems, in short, throughout the whole reign of David the Second and his successor, to have been a gradual dislocation of the parts of the feudal government, which left the nobles, far more than they had ever yet been, in the condition of so many independent princes, whose support the king could no longer compel as a right, but was reduced to purchase by pensions. In this way, there was scarce a baron of any power or consequence whom Robert had not attempted to bind to his service, and that of his son. The Duke of Albany, Lord Walter Stewart of Brechin his brother, Lord Murdoch Stewart, eldest son of Albany, and afterwards regent of the kingdom; Sir John Montgomery of Eaglesham, Sir William de Lindsay, Sir William Stewart of Jedburgh, and Sir John de Ramorgny, were all parties to agreements of this nature, in which the king, by a charter, grants to them, and in many instances to their children, for the whole period of their lives, certain large sums in annuity, under the condition of their defending the king and the Earl of Carrick, in time of peace as well as war.*

* Chamberlain Accounts, vol. ii. pp. 281, 310, 332, 197, 206, 207, 370, 495 219.

We shall soon have an opportunity of observing how feeble were such agreements to ensure to the crown the support and loyal attachment of the subjects, where they happened to counteract any schemes of ambition and individual aggrandizement.

In the meantime, the character of that prince, for whose welfare and security these alliances were undertaken, had begun to exhibit an increasing impatience of control, and an eager desire of power. Elegant in his person, with a sweet and handsome countenance, excelling in all knightly accomplishments, courteous and easy in his manners, and a devoted admirer of beauty, Rothesay was the idol of the populace; whilst a fondness for poetry, and a considerable acquaintance with the literature of the age, gave a superior refinement to his character, which, as it was little appreciated by a fierce nobility, probably induced him, in his turn, to treat their savage ignorance with contempt. He had already, at an early age, been familiarized to the management of public business, and had been engaged in the settlement of the disturbed northern districts, and employed as a commissioner for composing the differences on the Borders.* His mother, the queen, a woman of great sense and spirit, united her influence to that of her son; and a strong party was formed for the purpose of reducing the power of Albany, and compelling him to retire from the chief management of affairs, and resign his power into the hands of the prince.

It was represented to the king, and with perfect truth, that the kingdom was in a frightful state of anarchy and disorder; that the administration of the laws was suspended; those who loved peace, and were

* Chamberlain Accounts, vol. ii. p. 349. Winton, vol. ii. pp. 376, 377.

friends to good order, not knowing where to look for support; whilst, amid the general confusion, murder, robbery, and every species of crime, prevailed to an alarming and dreadful excess. All this had taken place, it was affirmed, in consequence of the misplaced trust which had been put into the hands of Albany, who prostituted his office of governor to his own selfish designs, and purchased the support of the nobles by offering them an immunity for their offences. "If," said the friends of the prince, "if it is absolutely necessary, from the increasing infirmities of the king, that he should delegate his authority to a governor or lieutenant, let his power be transferred to him to whom it is justly due, the heir-apparent to the throne; so that the country be no longer torn and endangered by the ambition of two contending factions, and shocked by the indecent and undignified spectacle of perpetual disputes in the royal household." These representations, and the increasing strength of the party of the prince, convinced Albany that it would be prudent for the present to give way to the secret wishes of the king and the open ambition of Rothesay, and to resign that office of governor, which he could no longer retain with safety.

A parliament was accordingly held at Perth on the 27th of January, 1398, of which the proceedings are interesting and important; and it is fortunate that a record has been lately discovered,* which contains a full account of this meeting of the three Estates. It is declared, in the first place, that the "misgovernance

* This valuable manuscript Record of the Parliament 1398, was politely communicated to me by Mr Thomson, Deputy-clerk Register, to whom we owe its discovery. It will be printed in the first volume of the Acts of the Parliaments of Scotland. It appears not to be an original record, but a contemporaneous translation from the Latin original, now lost.

of the realm, and the defaults in the due administration of the laws, are to be imputed to the king and his ministers;* and, if, therefore, the king chooses to excuse his own mismanagement, he is bound to be answerable for his officers, whom he must summon and arraign before his council, whose decision is to be given after they have made their defence, seeing no man ought to be condemned before he is called and openly accused."

After this preamble, in which it is singular at this early period to see clearly announced the principle of the king's responsibility through his ministers, it is declared, that since the king, for sickness of his person, is not able to labour in the government of the realm, nor to restrain "tresspassours," the council have judged it expedient that the Duke of Rothesay should be the king's lieutenant generally throughout the land for the term of three years, having full power in all things, equally as if he were himself the king, under the condition that he is to be obliged, by his oath, to administer the office according to the directions of the Council General; or, in absence of the parliament, with the advice of a council of experienced and faithful men, of whom the principal are to be the Duke of Albany, and Walter Stewart lord of Brechin, the Bishops of St Andrews, Glasgow, and Aberdeen, and the Earls of Douglas, Ross, Moray, and Crawford. To these were added, the Lord of Dalkeith, the Constable Sir Thomas Hay, the Marshal Sir William Keith, Sir Thomas Erskine, Sir Patrick Graham, Sir John Levingston, Sir William Stewart, Sir John of Ramorgny, Adam Forester, along with the Abbot of

---

* Skene, in his statutes of Robert the Third, p. 59, has suppressed the words, " sulde be imputyt to the kyng." His words are, " sulde be imput to the king's officiars."

Holyrood, the Archdean of Lothian, and Mr Walter Forester. It was next directed, that the different members of this council should take an oath to give to the young regent " lele counsail, for the common profit of the realm, nocht havande therto fede na frendschyp;" and that the duke himself be sworn to fulfil everything which the king, in his coronation oath, had promised to Holy Kirk and the people. These duties of the king were summarily explained to consist in the upright administration of the laws; the maintenance of the old manners and customs for the people; the restraining and punishing of all manslayers, reifars, brennars, and generally all strong and masterful misdoers; and more especially in the seizing and putting down of all cursed or excommunicated men and heretics.

Such being the full powers committed to the regent, provision was made against an abuse very common in those times: The king, it was declared, shall be obliged not to "let or hinder the prince in the execution of his office by any counter orders, as has hitherto happened; and, if such were given, the lieutenant was not to be bound either to return an answer, or to obey them. It was next directed by the parliament, that whatever measures were adopted, or orders issued, in the oxecution of this office, should be committed to writing, with the date of the day and place, and the names of the councillors by whose advice they were adopted; so that each councillor may be ready to answer for his own deed, and, if necessary, submit to the punishment, which, in the event of its being illegal, should be adjudged by the council-general. It was determined in the same parliament, that the prince, in the discharge of his duties as lieutenant, was to have the same salary allowed him as that given to the Duke of Albany, his predecessor, in the office of Regent, at the last council-general held at Stirling. With regard to the relations with foreign powers, it was resolved that an embassy, or, as it is singularly called, "a great message," be despatched to France; and that commissioners should be appointed to treat at Edinburgh of the peace with England, to determine whether the truce of twenty-eight years should be accepted or not.

On the subject of finance, a general contribution of eleven thousand pounds was raised for the common necessities of the kingdom, of which the clergy agreed to contribute their share, under protestation that it did not prejudice them in time to come; and the said contribution was directed to be levied upon all goods, cattle, and lands, as well demesne as other lands, excepting white sheep, riding-horses, and oxen for labour. With regard to the burgesses who were resident beyond the Forth, it was stated that they must contribute to this tax, as well as those more opulent burghers who dwelt in the south, upon protestation that their ancient laws and free customs should be preserved; that they should be required to pay only the same duties upon wool, hides, and skins, as in the time of King Robert last deceased, and be free from all tax upon salmon. The statutes which were passed in the council held at Perth, in April last, regarding the payment of duties upon English and Scots cloth, salt, flesh, grease, and butter, as well as horse and cattle, exported to England, were appointed to be continued in force; and the provisions of the same parliament went on to declare, that, considering the "great and horrible destructions, herschips, burning, and slaughter, which disgraced the kingdom, it was ordained, by consent of the three Estates, that every sheriff should make proclamation, that no man riding or going through the country be accompanied with more attendants than they are able to pay for; and that, under penalty of the loss of life and goods, no man disturb the country by such slaughters, burnings, raids, and destructions, as had been common under the late governor." The act also declared, that, " after such proclamation has been made, the sheriff shall use all diligence to discover and arrest the offenders, and shall bind them over to appear and stand their trial at the next Justice ayre: if unable to find bail, they were immediately to be put to the knowledge of an assize; and, if found guilty, instantly executed."

With regard to those higher and more daring offenders, whom the power of the sheriff, or his inferior officers, was altogether unable to arrest, (and there can be little doubt that this class included the greater portion of the nobles,) it was provided, that this officer " should publicly declare the names of them that may not be arrested, enjoining them within fifteen days to come and find bail to appear and stand their trial, under the penalty, that all who do not obey this summons shall be put to the king's horn, and their goods and estate confiscated." The only other provision of this parliament regarded a complaint of the queen-mother, stating, that her pension of two thousand six hundred marks had been refused by the Duke of Albany, the chamberlain, and an order by the king that it be immediately paid: a manifest proof of the jealousy which existed between this ambitious noble and the royal family.*

Whilst such was the course of events in Scotland, and the ambition of Rothesay, in supplanting his uncle Albany, was crowned with success, an extraordinary event had taken place in England, which seated Henry

* MS. Record of Parliament 1398, ut supra.

of Lancaster upon the throne, under the title of Henry the Fourth, and doomed Richard the Second to a perpetual prison. It was a revolution having, in its commencement, perhaps no higher object than to restrain within the limits of law the extravagant pretensions of the king; but it was hurried on to a consummation by a rashness and folly upon his part, which alienated the whole body of his people, and opened up to his rival an avenue to the throne, which it was difficult for human ambition to resist. The spectacle, however, of a king deposed by his nobles, and a crown forcibly appropriated by a subject who possessed no legitimate title, was new and appalling, and created in Scotland a feeling of indignant surprise, which is apparent in the accounts of our contemporary historians. Nor was this at all extraordinary. The feudal nobility considered the kingdom as a fee descendible to heirs, and regarded the right to the throne as something very similar to their own right to their estates; so that the principle, that a kingdom might be taken by *conquest*, on the allegation that the conduct of the king was tyrannical, was one which, if it gave Henry of Lancaster a lawful title, might afford to a powerful neighbour just as good a right to seize upon their property. It was extraordinary for us to hear, says Winton, with much simplicity, that a great and powerful king, who was neither pagan nor heretic, should yet be deposed like an old abbot, who is superseded for dilapidation of his benefice;* and it is quite evident, from the terms of the address which Henry used at his coronation, and his awkward attempt to mix up the principle of the king having vacated the throne by setting himself above the laws, with a vague hereditary

* Winton. vol. ii. p. 386.

claim upon his own side, that the same ideas were present to his mind, and occasioned him uneasiness and perplexity.*

It is well known, that he was scarce seated on the throne, when a conspiracy for the restoration of the deposed monarch was discovered, which was soon after followed by the news that Richard had died in Pontefract castle, and by the removal of a body declared to be that of the late king from Pomfret to St Paul's, where, as it lay in state in its royal shroud, Henry himself, and the whole of the nobility, officiated in the service for the dead. A report, however, almost immediately arose, that this was not the body of the king, who, it was affirmed, was still alive, but that of Maudelain, his private chaplain, lately executed as one of the conspirators, and to whom the king bore a striking resemblance.† After the funeral service, it is certain that Henry did not permit the body to be deposited in the tomb which Richard had prepared for himself and his first wife, at Westminster, but had it conveyed to the church of the preaching friars at King's Langley, where it was interred with the utmost secrecy and despatch.‡

Not long after this an extraordinary story arose in Scotland. King Richard, it was affirmed, having escaped from Pontefract, had found means to convey himself, in the disguise of a poor traveller, to the Western, or out Isles of Scotland, where he was accidentally recognised by a lady who had known him in Ireland, and who was sister-in-law to Donald lord of the Isles. Clothed in this mean habit, the unhappy mon-

* Fordun a Goodal, vol. ii. p. 427.
† Metrical Hist. of the Deposition of Richard the Second. Archæologia, vol. xx. p. 220.
‡ Otterburn, p. 229. Walsingham, p. 363. Gough's Sepulchral Monuments, vol. i. p. 168.

arch sat down in the kitchen of the castle belonging to this island prince, fearful, even in this remote region, of being discovered and delivered up to Henry. He was treated, however, with much kindness, and given in charge to Lord Montgomery, who carried him to the court of Robert the Third, where he was received with honour. It was soon discovered, that whatever was the history of his escape, either misfortune for the time had unsettled his intellect, or that, for the purpose of safety, he assumed the guise of madness; for although recognised by those to whom his features were familiar, he himself denied that he was the king; and Winton describes him as half mad, or wild. It is certain, however, that during the continuance of the reign of Robert the Third, and, after his death, throughout the regency of Albany, a period of nineteen years, this mysterious person was treated with the consideration befitting the rank of a king, although detained in a sort of honourable captivity; and it was constantly asserted in England and France, and believed by many of those best able to obtain accurate information, that King Richard was alive, and kept in Scotland. So much, indeed, was this the case, that, as we shall immediately see, the reign of Henry the Fourth, and of his successor, was disturbed by repeated conspiracies, which were invariably connected with that country, and which had for their object his restoration to the throne. It is certain also, that in contemporary records of unquestionable authenticity, he is spoken of as Richard the Second king of England; that he lived and died in the palace of Stirling; and that he was buried with the name, state, and honours, of that unfortunate monarch.*

A cloud now began to gather over Scotland, which

* See Appendix, at the end of this volume.

threatened to interrupt the quiet current of public prosperity, and once more to plunge the country into war. It was thought proper that the Duke of Rothesay, the heir-apparent to the throne, should no longer continue unmarried; and the Earl of March, one of the most powerful nobles in the kingdom, proposed his daughter, with the promise of a large dowry, as a suitable match for the young prince. The offer was accepted; but, before the preliminaries were arranged, March found his designs traversed and defeated by the intrigues and ambition of a family now more powerful than his own. Archibald earl of Douglas loudly complained, that the marriage of the heir to the crown was too grave a matter to be determined without the advice of the three Estates, and, with the secret design of procuring the prince's hand for his own daughter, engaged in his interest the Duke of Albany, who still possessed a great influence over the character of the king. What were Rothesay's own wishes upon the occasion is not easily ascertained. It is not improbable, that his gay and dissipated habits, which unfortunately seem not to have been restrained by his late elevation, would have induced him to decline the proposals of both the earls; but he was overruled: the splendid dowry paid down by Douglas, which far exceeded the promises of March, was perhaps the most powerful argument in the estimation of the prince and the king; and it was determined that the daughter of Douglas should be preferred to Elizabeth of Dunbar.

In the meantime, the intrigue reached the ears of March, who was not of a temper to suffer tamely so disgraceful a slight; and, little able or caring to conceal his indignation, he instantly sought the royal presence, and upbraided the king for his breach of agreement, demanding redress, and the restoration of the sum which he had paid down. Receiving an evasive reply, his passion broke out into the most violent language; and he left the monarch with a threat, that he would either see his daughter righted, or take a revenge which should convulse the kingdom. The first part of the alternative, however, was impossible. It was soon discovered that Rothesay, with great speed and secrecy, had rode to Bothwell, where his marriage with Elizabeth Douglas had been precipitately concluded; and the moment that this intelligence reached him, March committed the charge of his castle of Dunbar to Maitland his nephew, repaired to the English court, and entered into a correspondence with the new king.

His flight was the signal for the Douglasses to wrest his castle out of the hands of the weak and irresolute youth to whom it had been intrusted, and to seize upon his noble estates; so that, to the insult and injustice with which he had already been treated, was added an injury which left him without house or lands, and compelled him to throw himself into the arms of England.*

On ascending the throne, the Duke of Lancaster, known henceforth by the title of Henry the Fourth, was naturally anxious to consolidate his power, and would willingly have remained at peace; but the expiration of the truce which had been concluded with his predecessor seems to have been hailed with mutual satisfaction by the fierce Borderers; and careless of the pestilence which raged in England, the Scots broke across the marches in great force, and stormed the castle of Wark, during the absence of Sir Thomas Gray, the

---

* Rotuli Scotiæ, vol. ii. p. 153. Rymer, Fœdera, vol. viii. p. 153.

governor,* who, hurrying back to defend his charge, found it razed to the foundation. These inroads were speedily revenged by Sir Robert Umfraville, who defeated the Scots in a skirmish at Fullhopelaw, which was contested with much obstinacy. Sir Robert Rutherford with his five sons, Sir William Stewart, and John Turnbull, a famous leader, commonly called "Out wyth Swerd," were made prisoners;† and, the ancient enmity and rivalry between the two nations being again excited, the Borderers, on both sides issued from their woods and marshes, and commenced their usual system of cruel and unsparing ravage.

For a while these mutual excesses were overlooked, or referred to the decision of the march-wardens; but Henry was well aware that the secret feelings both of the king and of Albany were against him: he knew they were in strict alliance with France, which threatened him with invasion; and the story of the escape of the real or pretended Richard, whom he of course branded as an impostor, while the Scots did not scruple to entertain him as king, was likely to rouse his keenest indignation. He accordingly received the Earl of March with distinguished favour; and this baron, whose remonstrances regarding the restoration of his castle and estates had been answered with scorn, renounced his allegiance to his lawful sovereign, and agreed to become henceforward the faithful subject of the King of England;‡ upon which that monarch publicly declared his intention of instantly invading the country, and prepared, at the head of an army, to chastise the temerity of his vassal in the assumed

* Walsingham, p. 362.
† Rymer, Fœdera, vol. viii. p. 162. "This expressive appellative" appears in Rymer, "Joannus Tournebull Out wyth Swerd."
‡ Rymer, Fœdera, vol. viii. p. 153.

character of Lord Superior of Scotland. In so ludicrous a light did the revival of this exploded claim appear, that, with the exception of a miserable pasquinade, it met with no notice whatever. March, in the meantime, in conjunction with Hotspur and Lord Thomas Talbot, at the head of two thousand men, entered Scotland through the lands which he could no longer call his own, and wasting the country as far as the village of Popil, twice assaulted the castle of Hailes, but found himself repulsed by the bravery of the garrison; after which, they burnt and plundered the villages of Traprain and Methill, and encamped at Linton, where they collected their booty, kindled their fires, and, as it was a keen and cold evening in November, proposed to pass the night. So carelessly had they set their watches, however, that Archibald Douglas, the earl's eldest son, by a rapid march from Edinburgh, had reached the hill of Pencrag before the English received any notice of his approach; upon which they took to flight in the utmost confusion, pursued by the Scots, who made many prisoners in the wood of Coldbrandspath, and continued the chase to the walls of Berwick, where they took the banner of Lord Talbot.*

Soon after this, Henry determined to make good his threats; and, at the head of an army far superior in number to any force which the Scots could oppose to him, proceeded to Newcastle; and from thence summoned Robert of Scotland to appear before him as his liegeman and vassal.† To this ridiculous demand no answer was returned, and the king advanced into Scotland, directing his march towards the capital. Rothe-

---

* Fordun a Goodal, vol. ii. p. 429.
† Rymer, Fœdera, vol. viii. pp. 157, 158.

say, the governor, now commanded the castle of Edinburgh, and, incensed at the insolence of Henry, sent him his cartel, publicly defying him as his adversary of England; accusing him of having invaded, for the sole love of plunder, a country to which he had no title whatever; and offering to decide the quarrel, and spare the effusion of Christian blood which must follow a protracted war, by a combat of one hundred, two hundred, or three hundred nobles on each side.* This proposal Henry evaded, and proceeded without a check to Leith, from which he directed a monitory letter to the king, which, like his former summons, was treated with silent scorn.

The continuance of the expedition is totally deficient in historical interest, and is remarkable only from the circumstance, that it was the last invasion which an English monarch ever conducted into Scotland. It possessed, also, another distinction highly honourable to its leader, in the unusual lenity which attended the march of the army, and the absence of that plunder, burning, and indiscriminate devastation, which had accompanied the last great invasion of Richard, and, indeed, almost every former enterprise of the English. After having advanced to Leith, where he met his fleet, and reprovisioned his army, Henry proceeded to lay siege to the castle of Edinburgh, which was bravely defended by the Duke of Rothesay. Albany, in the meantime, having collected a numerous army, pushed on, by rapid marches, towards the capital, with the apparent design of raising the siege, and relieving the heir to the throne from the imminent danger to which he was exposed. On reaching Calder-moor, however, he pitched his tents, and showed no inclina-

---

* Rymer, Fœdera, vol. viii. p. 158.

tion to proceed; whilst public rumour loudly accused him of an intention to betray the prince into the hands of the enemy, and clear for himself a passage to the throne. Yet, although the prior and subsequent conduct of Albany gave a plausible colour to such reproaches, it is not impossible that the Duke might have avoided a battle without any such base intentions. The season of the year was far advanced, and the numerous host of the English king was already suffering grievously, both from sickness and want of provisions. Rothesay, on the contrary, and his garrison, were well provisioned, in high spirits, and ready to defend a fortress of great natural strength to the last extremity. The event showed the wisdom of these calculations; for Henry, after a short experience of the strength of the castle, withdrew his army from the siege; and receiving, about the same time, intelligence of the rebellion of the Welsh, commenced his retreat into England.

It was conducted with the same discipline and moderation which had marked his advance. Wherever a castle or fortalice requested protection, it was instantly granted, and a pennon, with the arms of England, was hung over the battlements, which was sacredly respected by the soldiers. Henry's reply to two canons of Holyrood, who besought him to spare their monastery, was in the same spirit of benevolence and courtesy: "Never," said he, "while I live, shall I cause distress to any religious house whatever: and God forbid that the monastery of Holyrood, the asylum of my father when an exile, should suffer aught from his son! I am myself a Cumin, and by this side half a Scot; and I came here with my army, not to ravage the land, but to answer the defiance of certain amongst you who have branded me as a traitor, to see whether they dare to make good the opprobrious epithets with which I am loaded in their letters to the French king, which were intercepted by my people, and are now in my possession. I sought him" (he here probably meant the Duke of Albany) "in his own land, anxious to give him an opportunity of establishing his innocence, or proving my guilt; but he has not dared to meet me."*

That these were not the real motives which led to an expedition so pompous in its preliminaries, and so inglorious in its results, Henry himself has told us, in the revival of the claim of homage, the summons to Robert as his vassal, and his resolution to punish his contumacy, and to compel him to sue for pardon; but when he discovered that any attempt to effect this would be utterly futile, and the rumours of the rebellion of Glendower made him anxious to return, it was not impolitic to change his tone of superiority into more courteous and moderate language, and to represent himself as coming to Scotland, not as a king to recover his dominions, but simply as a knight to avenge his injured honour. He afterwards asserted, that, had it not been for the false and flattering promises of Sir Adam Forester, made to him when he was in Scotland, he should not have so readily quitted that country; but the subject to which the king alluded is involved in great obscurity.† It may, perhaps, have related to the delivery into his hands of the mysterious captive who is supposed to have been Richard the Second.

The condition of the country now called for the attention of the great national council; and, on the 21st

---

* Fordun a Goodal, vol. ii. p. 430.
† Parliamentary Hist. of England, vol. ii. p. 72.

of February, 1401, a parliament was held at Scone,* in which many wise and salutary laws were passed. To some of these, as they throw a strong and clear light upon the civil condition of the country, it will be necessary to direct our attention; nor will the reader, perhaps, regret that the stirring narrative of war is thus sometimes broken by the quiet pictures of peace. The parliament was composed of the bishops, abbots, and priors; with the dukes, earls, and barons, and the freeholders and burgesses, who held of the king in chief. Its enactments appear to have related to various subjects connected with feudal possession: such as the brief of inquest; the duty of the chancellor in directing a precept of seisin upon a retour; the prevention of distress to vassals from all improper recognition of their lands made by their overlords; the regulation of the laws regarding the succession to a younger brother dying without heirs of his body; and the prevention of a common practice, by which, without consent of the vassal, a new superior was illegally imposed upon him. Owing to the precarious condition of feudal property, which, in the confusions incident to public and private war, was constantly changing its master, and to the tyranny of the aristocracy of Scotland, it is not surprising that numberless abuses should have prevailed, and that, to use the expressive language of the record itself, " divers and sindrie our soverane lordis lieges should be many wayes unjustlie trubled and wexed in their lands and heritage be inquisitions taken favorably, and be ignorant persons." To remedy such malversation, it was enacted, that no sheriff or other judge should cause any brief of inquest to be served, except in his own open court; and that the inquest should be

* Statutes of King Robert the Third, p. 51. Regiam Majestatem.

composed of the most sufficient and worthy persons resident within his jurisdiction, whom he was to summon upon a premonition of fifteen days. When an inquest had made a retour, by which the reader is to understand the jury giving their verdict or judgment, the chancellor was prohibited from directing a precept of seisin, or a command to deliver the lands into the hands of the vassal, unless it appeared clearly stated in the retour that the last heir was dead, and the lands in the hands of the king or the overlord.

It was enacted, at the same time, that all barons and freeholders who held of the king, should provide themselves with a seal bearing their arms, and that the retour should have appended to it the seals of the sheriff, and of the majority of the persons who sat upon the inquest. It appears to have been customary in those unquiet times, when " strongest might made strongest right," for the great feudal barons, upon the most frivolous pretences, to resume their vassals' lands, and to dispose of them to some more favoured or more powerful tenant. This great abuse, which destroyed all the security of property, and thus interrupted the agricultural and commercial improvement of the country, called for immediate redress; and a statute was passed, by which all such " gratuitous recognitions or resumptions of lands which had been made by any overlord, are declared of none effect, unless due and lawful cause be assigned for such having taken place." It was provided, also, that no vassal should lose possession of his lands in consequence of such recognition, until after the expiration of a year, provided he used diligence to repledge his lands within forty days thereafter.* The mode in which this ceremony is to be performed, is

* Statutes of King Robert the Third, pp. 52, 55.

briefly but clearly pointed out: the vassal being commanded to pass to the principal residence of his overlord, and, before witnesses, to declare his readiness to perform all feudal services to which he is bound by law, requesting the restoration of his lands upon his finding proper security for the performance of his duties as vassal; and in order to the prevention of all concealed and illegal resumptions, it is made imperative on the overlord to give due intimation of them in the parish church, using the common language of the realm; whilst the vassal is commanded to make the same proclamation of any offer to repledge, in the same public manner. In the event of a younger brother dying without heirs of his body, it is declared that his "conquest lands,"—that is, those acquired not by descent, but by purchase, or other title,—should belong to the immediate elder brother, according to the old law upon the subject; and it is made illegal for any vassal holding lands of the king, to have a new superior imposed upon him by any grant whatever, unless he himself consent to this alteration.

In those times of violence, it is interesting to observe the feeble attempts of the legislature to introduce these restraints of the law. In the event of a baron having a claim of debt against any unfortunate individual, it seems to have been a common practice for the creditor, on becoming impatient, to have proceeded to his house or lands, and there to have helped himself to an equivalent, or, in the language of the statute-book, "to have taken his poynd." And in such cases, where a feudal lord, with his vassals at his heel, met with any attractive property, in the form of horses or cattle, or rich household furniture, it may easily be believed that he would stand on little ceremony as to the exact amount of the debt, but appropriate what pleased him without much compunction. This practice was declared illegal, "unless the seizure be made within his own dominions, and for his own proper debt:" an exception, proving the extreme feebleness of the government; and in truth, when we consider the immense estates possessed at this period by the great vassals of the crown, amounting almost to a total annulment of the law.* In somewhat of the same spirit of toleration, a law was made against any one attempting, by his own power and authority, to expel a vassal from his lands, on the plea that he is not the rightful heir; and it was declared, that, whether he be possessed of the land lawfully or unlawfully, he shall be restored to his possession, and retain the same until he lose it by the regular course of law; whilst no penalty was inflicted on him who thus dared, in the open defiance of all peace and good government, to take the execution of the law into his own hands.

It was next declared unlawful to set free upon bail certain persons accused of great or heinous crimes; and the offenders thus excepted were described to be those taken for manslaughter, breakers of prison, common and notorious thieves, persons apprehended for fire-raising or felony, falsifiers of the king's money, or of his seal; such as have been excommunicated, and seized by command of the bishop; those accused of treason, and bailies who are in arrears, and make not just accounts to their masters.† Any excommunicated person who complains that he has been unjustly dealt with, was empowered within forty days to appeal from his judge to the conservator of the clergy, who, being advised by his counsel, must reform the sentence; and, if

* Statutes of King Robert the Third, p. 54. † Ibid.

the party still conceived himself to be aggrieved, it was made lawful for him to carry his appeal, in the last instance, to the General Assembly of the Church. With regard to the trial of cases by "singular combat," a wise attempt seems to have been made in this parliament to limit the circumstances under which this savage and extraordinary mode of judgment was adopted; and it is declared, that there must be four requisites in every crime before it is to be so tried. It must infer a capital punishment—it must have been secretly perpetrated—the person appealed must be pointed out by public and probable suspicion as its author—and it must be of such a nature as to render a proof by written evidence or by witnesses impossible. It was appointed that the king's lieutenant, and others the king's judges, should be bound and obliged to hear the complaints of all churchmen, widows, pupils, and orphans, regarding whatever injuries may have been committed against them; and that justice should be done to them speedily, and without taking from them any pledges or securities. Strict regulation was made, that all widows, who, after the death of their husbands, had been violently expelled from their dower lands, should be restored to their possession, with the accumulated rents due since their husbands' death; and it was specially provided, that interest or usury should not run against the debts of a minor until he is of perfect age, but that the debt should be paid with the interest which was owing by his predecessor, previous to his decease.*

Some of the more minute regulations of the same parliament were curious: a fine of a hundred shillings was imposed on all who catch salmon within the forbidden time; a penalty of six shillings and eight pence

* Statutes of King Robert the Third, p. 56.

on all who slay hares in time of snow; and it was strictly enjoined, as a statute to be observed through the whole realm, that there should be no muir-burning, or burning of heath, except in the month of March; and that a penalty of forty shillings should be imposed upon any one who dared to infringe this regulation, which should be given to the lord of the land where the burning had taken place.* With regard to a subject of great importance, "the assize of weightis and measuris," it is to be regretted that the abridgment of the proceedings of this parliament, left by Skene, which is all that remains to us, is in many respects confused and unintelligible. The original record itself is unfortunately lost. The chapter upon weights and measures commences with the declaration, that King David's common elne, or ell, had been found to contain thirty-seven measured inches, each inch being equal to three grains of bear placed lengthways, without the tail or beard. The stone, by which wool and other commodities were weighed, was to contain fifteen pounds; but a stone of wax, only eight pounds: the pound itself being made to contain fifteen ounces, and to weigh twenty-five shillings. It is observed in the next section of this chapter, that the pound of silver in the days of King Robert Bruce, the first of that name, contained twenty-six shillings and four pennies, in consequence of the deterioration of the money of this king from the standard money in the days of David the First, in whose time the ounce of silver was coined into twenty pennies. The same quantity of silver under Robert the First was coined into twenty-one pennies; "but now," adds the record, "in our days, such has been the deteriora-

* Statutes of King Robert the Third, pp. 53, 54.

tion of the money of the realm, that the ounce of silver actually contains thirty-two pennies."

It was enacted, that the boll should contain twelve gallons, and should be nine inches in depth, including the thickness of the tree on both the sides. In the roundness or circumference above, it was to be made to contain threescore and twelve inches in the middle of the " ower tree;" but in the inferior roundness, or circumference below, threescore eleven inches. The gallon was fixed to contain twelve pounds of water, four pounds of sea water, four of clear running water, and four of stagnant water. Its depth was to be six inches and a half, its breadth eight inches and a half, including the thickness of the wood on both sides; its circumference at the top twenty-seven inches and a half, and at the bottom twenty-three inches.* Such were all the regulations with regard to this important subject which appear in this chapter, and they are to be regarded as valuable and venerable relics of the customs of our ancestors; but the perusal of a single page of the Chamberlain Accounts will convince us how little way they go towards making up a perfect table of weights and measures, and how difficult it is to institute anything like a fair comparison between the actual wealth and comfort of those remote ages, and the prosperity and opulence of our own times.

The parliament next turned its attention to the providing of checks upon the conduct and administration of judges: a startling announcement, certainly, to any one whose opinions are formed on modern experience, but no unnecessary subject for parliamentary interference during these dark times. It was enacted, that every sheriff should have a clerk appointed, not by the

* Statutes of King Robert the Third, p. 56.

sheriff, but by the king, to whom alone this officer was to be responsible; and that such clerk should be one of the king's retinue and household, and shall advise with the king in all the affairs which were intrusted to him.* The sheriffs themselves were to appear yearly, in person or by deputy, in the king's Court of Exchequer, under the penalty of ten pounds, and removal from office; their fees, or salaries, were made payable out of the escheats in their own courts, and were not due until an account had been given by them in the Exchequer; and it was specially ordained, that no sheriff should pass from the king's court to execute his various duties in the sheriffdom, without having along with him for his information the "Acts of Parliament, and certain instructions in writ, to be given him by the king's Privy Council." It was enacted, that justiciars should be appointed upon the south side and north side of the water of Forth; it was made imperative upon these high judges to hold their courts twice in the year in each sheriffdom within their jurisdiction; and if any justiciar omitted to hold his court without being able to allege any reasonable impediment, he was to lose a proportion of his salary, and to answer to the king for such neglect of duty.

The process of all cases brought before the justiciar was appointed to be reduced into writing by the clerk; and a change was introduced from the old practice with regard to the circumstances under which any person summoned before the justiciar should be judged and punished as contumacious for not appearing. Of old, the fourth court, that is, the court held on the fourth day, was peremptory in all cases except such as concerned fee and heritage; but it was now appointed that

* Statutes of King Robert the Third, p. 57.

the second court, or the court held on the second day, and on the last day, should be peremptory; and any person who, being lawfully summoned, neglected to appear on either of these days, was to be denounced a rebel and put to the horn, as was the custom in "auld times and courts."* The office of the coroner was to arrest persons thus summoned; and it was declared lawful for such officers to make such arrests at any time within the year, either before or after the proclamation of the Justice Ayre. All lords of regality—by which the reader is to understand such feudal barons as possessed authority to hold their own courts within a certain division of property, all sheriffs, and all barons, who have the power of holding criminal courts—were strictly enjoined to follow the same order of proceeding as that which has been laid down for the observance of the Justiciars. These supreme judges were also commanded, in their annual courts, to inquire rigidly into the conduct of the sheriffs and other inferior officers; to scrutinize the manner in which they have discharged the duties committed to them; and, if they found them guilty of malversation, to remove them from their offices until the meeting of the next parliament. Any sheriff or inferior officer thus removed, was to find security for his appearance before the parliament, who, according to their best judgment, were to determine the punishment due for his offence, whether a perpetual removal from his office, or only a temporary suspension; and, in the meanwhile, the person so offending was ordained to lose his salary for that year, and another to be substituted by the Justiciar in his place.

With regard to such malefactors as were found to

* Statutes of King Robert the Third, p. 57.

be common destroyers of the land, wasting the king's lieges with plundering expeditions, burning, and consuming the country in their ruinous passage from one part to another, the sheriffs were commanded to do all diligence to arrest them, and to bind them over to appear at the next court of the Justiciar on a certain day, under a penalty of twenty pounds for each offender, to be paid in case of contumacy, or non-appearance, by those persons who were his sureties; and it was strictly enjoined that no person, in riding through the country, should be attended by more persons than those for whom he makes full payment, under the penalty of loss of life and property. In all time coming, no one was to be permitted with impunity to commit any slaughter, burning, theft, or "herschip;" and if the offender guilty of such crimes be not able to find security for his appearance to stand his trial before the Justiciar, the sheriff was enjoined instantly to try him by an assize, and, if the crime be proved against him, take order for his execution. In the case of thieves and malefactors who escaped from one sheriffdom to another, the sheriff, within whose jurisdiction the crime had been committed, was bound to direct his letters to the sheriff in whose county the delinquent had taken refuge. It was made imperative on such officer, with the barons, freeholders, and others the king's lieges, to assist in the arrest of such fugitives, in order to their being brought to justice; and this in every case, as well against their own vassals and retinue as against others; whilst any baron or other person who disobeyed this order, and refused such assistance, was to pay ten pounds to the king, upon the offence being proved against him before a jury.

It was made lawful for any tenant or farmer, who possessed lands under a lease of a certain endurance, to sell or dispose of the lease to whom he pleased, any time before its expiry. Any vassal or tenant who was found guilty of concealing the charter by which he held his lands, when summoned by his overlord to exhibit it, was to lose all benefit he might claim upon it; and in the case of a vassal having lost such charter, or of his never having had any charter, a jury was to be impannelled, in the first event, for the purpose of investigating by witnesses whether the manner of holding corresponds with the tenor of the charter which had been lost; and, in the second case, to establish by what precise manner of holding the vassal was in future to be bound to his overlord, which determination of the assize was in future to stand for his charter. If any person, in consequence of the sentence of a jury, had taken seisin or possession of land which was then in the hands of another, who affirmed it to be his property, it was made lawful for this last to retain possession, and to break the seisin, by instituting a process for its reduction within fifteen days, if the lands be heritage, and forty days if they be conquest. If any pork or bacon, which was unwholesome from any cause, or salmon spoilt and foul from being kept too long, was brought to market, it was to be seized by the bailies, and sent immediately to the "lipper folk,"*—a species of barbarous economy which says little for the humanity of the age; the bailies, at the same time, were to take care that the money paid for it be restored, and "gif there are no lipper folk," the obnoxious provisions were to be destroyed.†

Such is an outline of the principal provisions of this

* Leprous folk.   † Statutes of King Robert the Third, p. 52.

parliament, which I have detailed at some length, as they are the only relics of our legislative history which we shall meet with, until the reign of the first James; a period when the light reflected upon the state of the country, from the parliamentary proceedings, becomes more full and clear. Important as these provisions are, and evincing no inconsiderable wisdom for so remote a period, it must be recollected, that in such days of violence and feudal tyranny, it was an easier thing to pass acts of parliament than to carry them into execution. In all probability, there was not an inferior baron, who, sitting in his own court, surrounded by his mail-clad vassals, did not feel himself strong enough to resist the feeble voice of the law; and as for the greater nobles, to whom such high offices as Justiciar, Chancellor, or Chamberlain, were committed, it is certain, that instead of the guardians of the laws, and protectors of the rights of the people, they were themselves often their worst oppressors, and, from their immense power and vassalage, able in frequent instances to defy the mandates of the crown, and to resist all legitimate authority.

Of this prevalence of successful guilt in the higher classes, the history of the country during the year in which this parliament assembled, afforded a dreadful example, in the murder of the Duke of Rothesay, the heir-apparent to the throne, by his uncle the Duke of Albany. Rothesay's marriage, which in all probability was the result of political convenience more than of inclination, does not appear to have improved his character. At an age when better things were to be expected, his life continued turbulent and licentious; the spirit of mad unbridled frolic in which he indulged, the troops of gay and dissipated companions with whom he associated, gave just cause of offence to his friends, and filled the bosom of his fond and weak father with anxiety and alarm. Even after his assuming the temporary government of the country, his conduct was wild and unprincipled; he often employed the power intrusted to him against, rather than in support of, the laws and their ministers; plundered the collectors of the revenue;* threatened and overruled the officers to whose management the public money was intrusted; and exhibited an impatience for uncontrolled dominion.

Yet amid all his recklessness, there was a high honour and a courageous openness about Rothesay, which were every now and then breaking out, and giving promise of reformation. He hated all that was double, whilst he despised, and delighted to expose, that selfish cunning which he had detected in the character of his uncle, whose ambition, however carefully concealed, could not escape him. Albany, on the other hand, was an enemy whom it was the extremity of folly and rashness to provoke. He was deep, cold, and unprincipled; his objects were pursued with a pertinacity of purpose, and a complete command of temper, which gave him a great superiority over the wild and impetuous nobility by whom he was surrounded; and when once in his power, his victims had nothing to hope for from his pity. Rothesay he detested, and there is reason to believe had long determined on his destruction, as the one great obstacle which stood in the path of his ambition, and as the detector of his deep-laid intrigues; but he was for a while controlled and overawed by the influence of the queen, and of her two principal friends and advisers, Trail bishop of St

* Chamberlain Accounts, vol. ii. pp. 512, 520, 476.

Andrews, and Archibald the Grim earl of Douglas. Their united wisdom and authority had the happiest effects in restraining the wildness of the prince; soothing the irritated feelings of the king, whose age and infirmity had thrown him into complete retirement; and counteracting the ambition of Albany, who possessed too great an influence over the mind of the monarch. But soon after this the queen died; the Bishop of St Andrews and the Earl of Douglas did not long survive her; and, to use the strong expression of Fordun, it was now said commonly through the land,* that the glory and the honesty of Scotland were buried with these three noble persons. All began to look with anxiety for what was to follow; nor were they long kept in suspense. The Duke of Rothesay, freed from the gentle control of maternal love, broke into some of his accustomed excesses; and the king, by the advice of Albany, found it necessary to subject him to a control which little agreed with his impetuous temper.

It happened, that amongst the prince's companions was a Sir John de Ramorgny, who, by a judicious accommodation of himself to his capricious humours, by flattering his vanity and ministering to his pleasures, had gained the intimacy of Rothesay. Ramorgny appears to have been one of those men in whom extraordinary, and apparently contradictory qualities were found united. From his education, which was of the most learned kind, he seems to have been intended for the church; but the profligacy of his youth, and the bold and audacious spirit which he exhibited, unfitted him for the sacred office, and he became a soldier and

* Fordun a Goodal, vol. ii. p. 431. Extracta ex Chronicis Scotiæ, MS. p. 248.

a statesman. His great talents for business being soon discovered by Albany, he was repeatedly employed in diplomatic negotiations both at home and abroad; and this intercourse with foreign countries, joined to a cultivation of those elegant accomplishments to which most of the feudal nobility of Scotland were still strangers, rendered his manners and his society exceedingly attractive to the young prince. But these polished and delightful qualities were superinduced upon a character of consummate villany, as unprincipled in every respect as that of Albany, but fiercer, more audacious, and, if possible, more unforgiving.

Such was the person whom Rothesay in an evil moment admitted to his confidence and friendship, and to whom, upon being subjected to the restraint imposed upon him by Albany and his father, he vehemently complained. Ramorgny, with all his acuteness, had in one respect mistaken the character of the prince; and, deceived by the violence of his resentment, he darkly hinted at a scheme for ridding himself of his difficulties, by the assassination of his uncle. To his astonishment, the proposal was met by an expression of scorn and abhorrence; and whilst Rothesay disdained to betray his profligate associate, he upbraided him in terms too bitter to be forgiven. From that moment Ramorgny was transformed into his worst enemy; and throwing himself into the arms of Albany, became possessed of his confidence, and turned it with fatal revenge against Rothesay.* It was unfortunate for this young prince, that his caprice and fondness for pleasure, failings which generally find their punishment in mere tedium and disappointment, had raised

* Extracta ex Chronicis Scotiæ, MS. Advocates' Library, Edinburgh, p. 248.

against him two powerful enemies, who sided with Albany and Ramorgny, and, stimulated by a sense of private injury, readily lent themselves to any plot for his ruin. These were, Archibald earl of Douglas the brother of Rothesay's wife, Elizabeth Douglas, and Sir William Lindsay of Rossy, whose sister he had loved and forsaken. Ramorgny well knew that Douglas hated the prince for the coldness and inconstancy with which he treated his wife, and that Lindsay had never forgiven the slight put upon his sister; and with all the dissimulation in which he was so great a master, he, assisted by Albany, contrived, out of these dark elements, to compose a plot which it would have required a far more able person than Rothesay to have defeated.

They began by representing to the king, whose age and infirmities now confined him to a distant retirement, and who knew nothing but through the representations of Albany, that the wild and impetuous conduct of his son required a more firm exertion of restraint, than any which had yet been employed against him. The bearers of this unwelcome news to the king were Ramorgny and Lindsay; and such was the success of their representations, that they returned to Albany with an order under the royal signet, to arrest the prince, and place him in temporary confinement. Secured by this command, the conspirators now drew their meshes more closely round their victim; and the bold and unsuspicious character of the prince gave them every advantage. It was the custom in those times, for the castle or palace of any deceased prelate to be occupied by the king, until the election of his successor; and although the triennial period of the prince's government was now expired, yet probably jealous of the resumption of his power by Albany, he determined to seize the castle of St Andrews, belonging to Trail the bishop, lately deceased, before he should be anticipated by any order of the king. The design was evidently illegal; and Albany, who had received intimation of it, determined to make it the occasion of carrying his purpose into execution. He accordingly laid his plan for intercepting the prince; and Rothesay, as he rode towards St Andrews, accompanied by a small retinue, was arrested near Stratyrum, by Ramorgny and Lindsay, and subjected to a strict confinement in the castle of St Andrews, until the duke and the Earl of Douglas should determine upon his fate.

This needed little time, for it had been long resolved on; and when once masters of his person, the catastrophe was as rapid as it was horrible. In a tempestuous day, Albany and Douglas, with a strong party of soldiers, appeared at the castle, and dismissed the few servants who waited on him. They then compelled him to mount a sorry horse, threw a coarse cloak over his splendid dress, and hurrying on, rudely and without ceremony, to Falkland, thrust him into a dungeon. The unhappy prince now saw that his death was determined, but he little anticipated its cruel nature. For fifteen days he was suffered to remain without food, under the charge of two ruffians named Wright and Selkirk,* whose task it was to watch the agony of their victim till it ended in death. It is said that, for a while, the wretched prisoner was preserved in a remarkable manner, by the kindness of a poor woman,

* John Wright and John Selkirk are the names, as given by Fordun a Goodal, vol. ii. p. 431. In the Chamberlain Accounts, vol. ii. p. 666, sub anno 1405, is the following entry, which perhaps relates to this infamous person: "Johanni Wright uni heredum quondam Ricardi Ranulphi, per infeodacionem antiquam regis Roberti primi percipienti per annum hereditarie quinque libras de firmis dicti burgi (Aberdeen.)"

who, in passing through the garden of Falkland, and attracted by his groans to the grated window of his dungeon, which was level with the ground, became acquainted with his story. It was her custom to steal thither at night, and bring him food by dropping small cakes through the grating, whilst her own milk, conducted through a pipe to his mouth, was the only way he could be supplied with drink. But Wright and Selkirk, suspecting from his appearance, that he had some secret supply, watched and detected the charitable visitant, and the prince was abandoned to his fate. When nature at last sunk, his body was found in a state too horrible to be described, but which showed that, in the extremities of hunger, he had gnawed and torn his own flesh. It was then carried to the monastery of Lindores, and there privately buried, while a report was circulated that the prince had been taken ill and died of a dysentery.*

The public voice, however, loudly and vehemently accused his uncle of the murder; the cruel nature of his death threw a veil over the folly and licentiousness of his life; men began to remember and to dwell upon his better qualities; and Albany found himself daily becoming more and more the object of scorn and detestation. It was necessary for him to adopt some means to clear himself of such imputations; and the skill with which the conspiracy had been planned was now apparent: he produced the king's letter commanding the prince to be arrested; he affirmed that everything which had been done was in consequence of the orders he had received, defying any one to prove that the slightest violence had been used; and he appealed to and demanded the judgment of the parliament.

* Fordun a Goodal, vol. ii. p. 431. Chamberlain Accounts, vol. ii. p. 511.

This great council was accordingly assembled in the monastery of Holyrood, on the 16th of May, 1402; and a solemn farce took place, in which Albany and Douglas were examined as to the causes of the prince's death. Unfortunately, no original record of the examination, or of the proceedings of the parliament, has been preserved. The accused, no doubt, told the story in the manner most favourable to themselves, and none dared to contradict them; so that it only remained for the parliament to declare themselves satisfied, and to acquit them of all suspicion of a crime which they had no possibility of investigating. Even this, however, was not deemed sufficient, and a public remission was drawn up, under the king's seal, declaring their innocence, in terms which are quite conclusive as to their guilt.*

The explanation of these unjust and extraordinary proceedings is to be found in the exorbitant power of Douglas and Albany, and the weakness of the unhappy monarch, who bitterly lamented the fate of his son, and probably well knew its authors, but dreaded to throw the kingdom into those convulsions which must have preceded their being brought to justice. Albany, therefore, resumed his situation of governor; and the fate of Rothesay was soon forgotten in preparations for continuing the war with England.

The truce, as was usual, had been little respected by the Borderers of either country; the Earl of Douglas being accused of burning Bamborough castle, and that baron reproaching Northumberland for the ravages committed in Scotland. The eastern marches especially were exposed to constant ravages by the

* This deed was discovered by Mr Astle, and communicated by him to Lord Hailes, who printed it in his Remarks on the History of Scotland.

Earls of March and the Percies; nor was it to be expected that so powerful a baron as March would bear to see his vast possessions in the hands of the house of Douglas, without attempting either to recover them himself, or by havoc and burning to make them useless to his enemy. These bitter feelings led to constant and destructive invasions; and the Scottish Border barons,—the Haliburtons, the Hepburns, Cockburns, and Lauders,—found it necessary to assemble their whole power, and intrust the leading of it by turns to the most warlike amongst them, a scheme which rendered every one anxious to eclipse his predecessor by some exploit, or successful point of arms, termed, in the military language of the times, *chevanches*. On one of these occasions, the conduct of the little army fell to Sir Patrick Hepburn of Hailes, whose father, a venerable soldier of eighty years, was too infirm to take his turn in command. Hepburn broke into England and laid waste the country; but his adventurous spirit led him too far on, and Percy and March had time to assemble their power, and to intercept the Scots at Nesbit Moor, in the Merse, where a desperate conflict took place. The Scots were only four hundred strong, but they were admirably armed and mounted, and had amongst them the flower of the warriors of the Lothians; the battle was for a long time bloody and doubtful, till the Master of Dunbar, joining his father and Northumberland, with two hundred men from the garrison at Berwick, decided the fortune of the day.* Hepburn was slain, and his bravest knights either shared his fate or were taken prisoners. The spot where the conflict took place, is

* Fordun a Goodal, vol. ii. p. 423.

still known by the name of Slaughter Hill.* So important did Henry consider this success, probably from the rank of the captives, that, in a letter to his privy council, he informed them of the defeat of the Scots; complimented Northumberland and his son on their activity; and commanded them to issue their orders for the array of the different counties, as their indefatigable enemies, in great strength, had already ravaged the country round Carlisle, and were meditating a second invasion.

Nor was this inaccurate intelligence; for the desire of revenging the loss sustained at Nesbit Moor, and the circumstance of the King of England being occupied in the suppression of the Welsh rebellion under Glendower, encouraged the Earl of Douglas to collect his whole strength; and Albany, the governor, having sent his eldest son, Murdoch, to join him with a strong body of archers and spearmen, their united force was found to amount to ten thousand men. The Earls of Moray and Angus; Fergus Macdowall, with his fierce and half-armed Galwegians; the heads of the noble houses of Erskine, Grahame, Montgomery, Seton, Sinclair, Lesley, the Stewarts of Angus, Lorn, and Durisdeer, and many other knights and esquires, embracing the greater part of the chivalry of Scotland, assembled under the command of the Earl of Douglas; and, confident in their strength, and eager for revenge, pushed on, without meeting an enemy, to the gates of Newcastle. But although Henry was himself personally engaged in his Welsh war, he had left the veteran Earl of Northumberland, and his son Hotspur, in charge of the Borders; and the Scottish Earl of March, who had renounced his fealty to his sovereign, and

† Hume's Douglas and Angus, vol. i. p. 218.

become the subject of England, joined the Percies, with his son, Gawin of Dunbar.

Douglas, it may be remembered, had risen upon the ruins of March, and possessed his castle and estates; so that the renegade earl brought with him, not only an experience in Scottish war, and an intimate knowledge of the Border country, but that bitter spirit of enmity which made him a formidable enemy. It was probably by his advice that the Scots were allowed to advance without opposition through the heart of Northumberland; for the greater distance they were from home, and the longer time allowed to the English to collect their force, it was evidently the more easy to cut off their retreat, and to fight them at an advantage.

The result showed the correctness of this opinion. The Scottish army, loaded with plunder, confident in their own strength, and secure in the apparent panic of the enemy, retreated slowly and carelessly, and had encamped near Wooler, when they were met by the intelligence that Hotspur, with a strong army, had occupied the pass in their front, and was advancing to attack them. Douglas immediately drew up his force in a deep square, upon a neighbouring eminence, called Homildon Hill; an excellent position, had his sole object been to repel the attacks of the English cavalry and men-at-arms, but in other respects the worst that could have been chosen, for the bulk of Percy's force consisted of archers, and there were many eminences round Homildon by which it was completely commanded, the distance being within arrow-flight. Had the Scottish knights and squires, and the rest of their light-armed cavalry, who must have composed a body of at least a thousand men, taken possession of the rising ground in advance, they might have charged the

English archers before they came within bowshot, and the subsequent battle would have been reduced to a close-hand encounter, in which the Scots, from the strong ground which they occupied, must have fought to great advantage; but from the mode in which it was occupied by Douglas, who crowded his whole army into one dense column, the position became the most fatal that could have been selected.

The English army now rapidly advanced, and on coming in sight of the Scots, at once occupied the opposite eminence, which, to their surprise, they were permitted to do, without a single Scottish knight or horseman leaving their ranks; but at this crisis, the characteristic impetuosity of Hotspur, who, at the head of the men-at-arms, proposed instantly to charge the Scots, had nearly thrown away the advantage. March, however, instantly seized his horse's reins and stopt him. His eye had detected, at the first glance, the danger of Douglas's position; he knew from experience the strength of the long-bow of England; and, by his orders, the precedence was given to the archers, who, slowly advancing down the hill, poured their volleys as thick as hail upon the Scots, whilst, to use the words of an ancient manuscript chronicle, they were so closely wedged together, that a breath of air could scarcely penetrate their files, making it impossible for them to wield their weapons. The effects of this were dreadful, for the cloth-yard shafts of England pierced with ease the light armour of the Scots, few of whom were defended by more than a steel-cap and a thin jack, or breast-plate, whilst many wore nothing more than the leather acton, or quilted coat, which afforded a feeble defence against such deadly missiles. Even the better-tempered armour of the knights was found utterly unequal to resistance, when, owing to the gradual advance of their phalanx, the archers took a nearer and more level aim, whilst the Scottish bowmen drew a wavering and uncertain bow, and did little execution.* Numbers of the bravest barons and gentlemen were mortally wounded, and fell down on the spot where they were first drawn up, without the possibility of reaching the enemy; the horses, goaded and maddened by the increasing showers of arrows, reared and plunged, and became altogether unmanageable; whilst the dense masses of the spearmen and naked Galwegians presented the appearance of a huge hedgehog, (I use the expression of a contemporary historian,) bristled over with a thousand shafts, whose feathers were red with blood. This state of things could not long continue. "My friends," exclaimed Sir John Swinton, "why stand we here to be slain like deer, and marked down by the enemy? Where is our wonted courage? Are we to be still, and have our hands nailed to our lances? Follow me, and let us at least sell our lives as dearly as we can."†

Saying this, he couched his spear, and prepared to gallop down the hill; but his career was for a moment interrupted by a singular event. Sir Adam de Gordon, with whom Swinton had long been at deadly feud, threw himself from his horse, and kneeling at his feet, begged his forgiveness, and the honour of being knighted by so brave a leader. Swinton instantly consented; and, after giving him the accolade, tenderly embraced him. The two warriors then remounted, and at the head of their followers, forming a body of a hundred

---

* Walsingham, p. 366. Otterburn, p. 237. Fordun and Winton do not even mention the Scottish archers.
† Fordun a Goodal, vol. ii. p. 434. Winton, vol. ii. p. 401.

horse, made a desperate attack upon the English, which, had it been followed by a simultaneous charge of the great body of the Scots, might still have retrieved the fortune of the day. But such was now the confusion of the Scottish lines, that Swinton and Gordon were slain, and their men struck down or dispersed, before the Earl of Douglas could advance to support them; and when he did so, the English archers, keeping their ranks, fell back upon the cavalry, pouring in volley after volley, as they slowly retreated, and completing the discomfiture of the Scots by an appalling carnage. If we may believe Walsingham, the armour worn by the Earl of Douglas on this fatal day was of the most exquisite workmanship and temper, and cost the artisan who made it three years' labour; yet he was wounded in five places, and made prisoner along with Lord Murdoch Stewart, and the Earls of Moray and Angus. In a short time the Scottish army was utterly routed; and the archers, to whom the whole honour of the day belonged, rushing in with their knives and short swords, made prisoners of almost every person of rank or station.

The number of the slain, however, was very great; and multitudes of the fugitives—it is said nearly fifteen hundred—were drowned in an attempt to ford the Tweed. Amongst those who fell, besides Swinton and Gordon, were Sir John Levingston of Calendar, Sir Alexander Ramsay of Dalhousie, Sir Roger Gordon, Sir Walter Scott, and Sir Walter Sinclair, with many other knights and esquires, whose followers mostly perished with their masters. Besides the leaders, Douglas and Lord Murdoch, eighty knights were taken prisoners, and a crowd of esquires and pages, whose names and numbers are not ascertained. Among the first were three French knights, Sir Piers de Essars,

Sir James de Helsey, and Sir John Darni;* Sir Robert Erskine of Alva, Lord Montgomery, Sir James Douglas master of Dalkeith, Sir William Abernethy of Salton, Sir John Stewart of Lorn, Sir John Seton, Sir George Lesley of Rothes, Sir Adam Forester of Corstorphine, Sir Walter Bickerton of Luffness, Sir Robert Stewart of Durisdeer, Sir William Sinclair of Hermandston, Sir Alexander Home of Dunglas, Sir Patrick Dunbar of Bele, Sir Robert Logan of Restalrig, Sir Lawrence Ramsay, Sir Helias Kinmont, Sir John Ker, and Fergus Macdowall of Galloway, with many others whose names have not been ascertained.†

The fatal result of this day completely proved the dreadful power of the English bowmen; for there is not a doubt that the battle was gained by the archers. Walsingham even goes so far as to say, that neither earl, knight, nor squire, ever handled their weapons, or came into action, but remained idle spectators of the total destruction of the Scottish host; nor does there seem any good reason to question the correctness of this fact, although, after the Scots were broken, the English knights and horsemen joined in the pursuit. It was in every way a most decisive and bloody defeat, occasioned by the military incapacity of Douglas, whose pride was probably too great to take advice, and his judgment and experience in war too confined to render it unnecessary. Hotspur might now rejoice that the shame of Otterburn was effectually defaced; and March, if he could be so base as to enjoy the triumph, must have been amply satiated with revenge: for his rival, Douglas, was defeated, cruelly wounded, and a captive.‡

* Walsingham, pp. 407, 408. Otterburn, pp. 236, 7, 8.
† Fordun a Goodal, vol. ii. pp. 434, 435.
‡ Ibid. vol. ii. pp. 434, 435. Rymer, Fœdera, vol. ix. p. 26. Walsingham, p. 366. Extracta ex Chronicis Scotiæ, MS. p. 250.

The battle was fought on the day of the Exaltation of the Holy Cross, being the 14th September, in the year 1402; and the moment that the news of the defeat was carried to Westminster, the King of England directed his letters to the Earl of Northumberland, with his son Henry Percy, and also to the Earl of March, commanding them, for certain urgent causes, not to admit to ransom any of their Scottish prisoners, of whatever rank or station, or to suffer them to be at liberty under any parole or pretext, until they should receive further instructions upon the subject. To this order, which was highly displeasing to the pride of the Percies, as it went to deprive them of an acknowledged feudal right which belonged to the simplest esquire, the monarch subjoined his pious thanks to God for so signal a victory, and to his faithful barons for their bravery and success; but he commanded them to notify his orders regarding the prisoners to all who had fought at Homildon, concluding with an assurance, that he had no intention of ultimately depriving any of his liege subjects of their undoubted rights in the persons and property of their prisoners; a declaration which would not be readily believed.* If Henry thus defeated the objects, which the victory might have secured him, by his precipitancy and imprudence, Hotspur stained it by an act of cruelty and injustice. Teviotdale, it may perhaps be remembered, after having remained in the partial possession of the English for a long period, under Edward the Third, had at last been entirely wrested from them by the bravery of the Douglases; and as the Percies had obtained large grants of land in this district, upon which many fierce contests had taken place, their final expulsion from the country they called

* Rymer, Fœdera, vol. viii. p. 278.

their own, was peculiarly irritating. It happened, that amongst the prisoners was Sir William Stewart of Forrest, a knight of Teviotdale, who was a boy at the time the district "was Anglicised," and, like many others, had been compelled to embrace a virtual allegiance to England, by a necessity which he had neither the power nor the understanding to resist. On the miserable pretence that he had forfeited his allegiance, Hotspur accused him of treason, and had him tried by a jury; but the case was so palpably absurd and tyrannical, that he was acquitted. Percy, in great wrath, impannelled a second jury, and a second verdict of acquittal showed their sense and firmness; but the fierce obstinacy of feudal revenge was not to be so baffled, and these were not the days when the laws could check its violence. A third jury was summoned, packed, and overawed, and their sentence condemned Sir William Stewart to the cruel and complicated death of a traitor. It was instantly executed; and his quarters, with those of his squire, Thomas Ker, who suffered along with him, were placed on the gates of York; the same gates upon which, within a year, were exposed the mangled remains of Percy himself.* The avidity with which Hotspur seems to have thirsted for the blood of this unhappy youth, is only to be accounted for on the supposition of some deadly feud between the families; for on no other occasion did this celebrated soldier show himself naturally cruel, or unnecessarily severe.†

The events which followed the defeat of the Scots at Homildon are of an interesting nature, and merit particular attention. Not long after the victory, the

* Winton, vol. ii. p. 403.
† Fordun a Hearne, pp. 1150, 1151.

Percies began to organize that celebrated conspiracy against Henry the Fourth, the monarch whom their own hands had placed on the throne, which ended in the battle of Shrewsbury, and the defeat and death of Hotspur; but as the plot was yet in its infancy, an immediate invasion of Scotland was made the pretext for assembling an army, and disarming suspicion; whilst Percy, in conjunction with the Earl of March, talked boldly of reducing the whole of the country as far as the Scottish sea.* It is probable, indeed, that previous to this, the defeat at Homildon had been followed by the temporary occupation of the immense Border estates of the Earl of Douglas by the Earl of Northumberland; as, in a grant of the earldom of Douglas, which was about this time made to Northumberland by the King of England, the districts of Eskdale, and Liddesdale, with the forest of Ettrick and the Lordship of Selkirk, are noticed as being in the hands of the Percies; but so numerous were the vicissitudes of war in these Border districts, that it is difficult to ascertain who possessed them with precision;† and it is certain, that the recovery of the country by the Scots was almost simultaneous with its occupation. In the meantime, the combined army of March and the Percies took its progress towards Scotland; and commenced the siege of the tower of Cocklaws, commanded by John Greenlaw, a simple esquire,‡ and situated on the Borders. The spectacle of a powerful army, commanded by the best soldier in

---

* The Firth of Fourth usually went by this name.
† Rotuli Scotiæ, vol. ii. p. 163.
‡ Ibid. vol. ii. p. 172. It appears by a MS. letter of the Earl of Northumberland, that on 30th May, he and his son had indentures for the delivery of *Ormiston* Castle on the 1st of August, if not delivered by battle. Pinkerton's History, vol. i. p. 77.

England, proceeding to besiege a paltry march-tower, might have been sufficient to convince Henry, that the real object of the Percies was not the invasion of Scotland; and their subsequent proceedings must have confirmed this opinion. Assaulted by the archers, and battered by the trebuchets and mangonels, the little tower of Cocklaws not only held its ground, but its master, assuming the air of the governor of a fortress, entered into a treaty with Hotspur, by which he promised to surrender at the end of six weeks, if not relieved by the King of Scotland, or Albany the governor.* A messenger was despatched to Scotland with the avowed purpose of communicating this agreement to Albany, but whose real design was evidently to induce him to become a party to the conspiracy against Henry, and to support the Percies, by an immediate invasion of England. Nor was the mission unsuccessful; for Albany, anxious to avenge the loss sustained at Homildon, and irritated by the captivity of his eldest son, at once consented to the proposal, and assembled a numerous army, with which he prepared to enter England in person.† In the meantime, the Earl of Douglas, Sir Robert Stewart of Durisdeer, and the greater part of the barons and men-at-arms, who were made prisoners at Homildon, eagerly entered into the conspiracy, and joined the insurgents with a large force; but the Earl of March continued faithful to the King of England, actuated more, perhaps, by his mortal enmity to the Douglases, than by any great affection for Henry. Another alarming branch of the rebellion was in Wales, where Owen Glendower had raised an army of ten thousand men, and besides this,

* Fordun a Goodal, vol. ii. pp. 435, 436.
† Ibid. vol. ii. p. 436.

many of the English barons had entered into a correspondence with Percy, and bound themselves to join him with their power, although at the last most deserted him, and thus escaped his ruin.

All things being thus prepared, Henry Percy and the Earl of Douglas at once broke off the prosecution of their Scottish expedition; and, having joined the Earl of Worcester, began their march towards Wales, giving out at first that it was their design to assist the king in putting down .the rebel Glendower. Henry, however, was no longer to be deceived; and the representations of the Earl of March convinced him of the complicated dangers with which he was surrounded. It was his design to have delayed proceeding against the insurgents, until he had assembled such an overwhelming force as he thought gave a certainty of victory; but the Scottish earl vehemently opposed all procrastination, maintaining the extreme importance of giving battle to Percy before he had formed a junction with Glendower; and the king, following his advice, pushed on by forced marches, and entered Shrewsbury at the moment that the advance of Percy and Douglas could be seen marching forward to occupy the same city. On being anticipated by their opponent, they retired, and encamped at Hartfield, within a mile of the town. Henry immediately drew out his army by the east gate; and after a vain attempt at treaty, which was broken off by Percy's uncle the Earl of Worcester, the banners advanced, cries of St George and Esperance, the mutual defiances of the king and Percy, rent the air; and the archers on both sides made a pitiful slaughter, even with the first discharge. As it continued, the ranks soon became encumbered with the dead, "who lay as thick," says Walsingham, "as leaves in autumn;" and the knights and men-at-arms getting impatient, Percy's advance, which was led by Douglas, and consisted principally of Scottish auxiliaries, made a desperate charge upon the king's party, and had almost broken their array, when it was restored by the extreme gallantry of Henry, and his son the Prince of Wales, afterwards Henry the Fifth. After this, the battle continued for three hours to be obstinately contested, English fighting against English, and Scots against Scots, with the utmost cruelty and determination. It could not indeed be otherwise. The two armies were fourteen thousand strong on each side, and included the flower not only of the English chivalry, but of the English yeomen. Hotspur and Douglas were reckoned two of the bravest knights then living, and if defeated, could hope for no mercy; whilst Henry felt that, on his part, the battle must decide whether he was to continue a king, or to have the diadem torn from his brow, and be branded as a usurper. At one time he was in imminent danger; for Hotspur and Douglas, during the heat of the battle, coming opposite to the royal Standard, made a desperate attempt to become masters of the person of the king; and had so nearly succeeded, that the Scottish Earl slew Sir Walter Blunt, the standard-bearer, struck down the Earl of Stafford, and had penetrated within a few yards of the spot where Henry stood, when the Earl of March rushed forward to his assistance, and prevailed on him not to hazard himself so far in advance. On another occasion, when unhorsed, he was rescued by the Prince of Wales, who this day gave promise of his future military genius; but with all his efforts, seconded by the most determined courage in his soldiers, the obstinate endurance of the Scots, and the unwearied gallantry and military skill of Hotspur were gradually gaining ground, when this brave leader, as he raised his visor for a moment to get air, was pierced through the brain by an arrow, and fell down dead on the spot. His fall, which was seen by both sides, seems to have at once turned the fortune of the day. The rebels were broken and dispersed, the Scots almost entirely cut to pieces, Sir Robert Stewart slain, and the Earl of Douglas once more a captive, and severely wounded.*

In the meantime, whilst the rebellion of the Percies was thus successfully put down, Albany, the governor, assembled the whole strength of the kingdom; and, at the head of an army of fifty thousand men, advanced into England. His real object, as discovered by his subsequent conduct, was to second the insurrection of Hotspur; but, ignorant as yet that the rebellion had openly burst forth, he concealed his intention, and gave out to his soldiers that it was his intention to give battle to the Percies, and to raise the siege of Cocklaws.† On arriving before this little Border strength, instead of finding Hotspur, he was met by the news of his entire defeat and death in the battle of Shrewsbury; and, after ordering a herald to proclaim this to the army, he at once quietly retired into Scotland. Discouraged by the inactivity of the Welsh, by the death of Percy, the captivity of Douglas, and the submission of the Earl of Northumberland, Albany judiciously determined that this was not the most favourable crisis to attack the usurper, and for the present resumed a pacific line of policy. In their account of the rebellion of the Percies, and the expedition

* Walsingham, pp. 368, 369.
† Fordun a Hearne, pp. 1158, 1159, 1160.

of Albany, our ancient Scottish historians exhibit a singular instance of credulity in describing the investing of the Border fortalice by Hotspur, and the subsequent progress of Albany to raise the siege, as really and honestly engaged in by both parties; and it is difficult not to smile at the importance which the tower of Cocklaws and its governor assume in their narrative.

If Albany's government seemed destined to be inglorious in war, his civil administration was weak and vacillating, disgraced by the impunity, if not by the encouragement, of feudal tyranny and unlicensed oppression. Of this a striking instance occurred a little prior to the rebellion of the Percies. Sir Malcolm Drummond, brother to the late Queen of Scotland, had married Isabella countess of Mar in her own right, whose estates were amongst the richest in Scotland. When resident in his own castle, this baron was attacked by a band of armed ruffians, overpowered, and cast into a dungeon, where the barbarous treatment he experienced ended in his speedy death. The suspicion of this lawless act rested on Alexander Stewart, a natural son of the Earl of Buchan, brother to the king, who emulated the ferocity of his father, and became notorious for his wild and unlicensed life. This chief, soon after the death of Drummond, appeared before the strong castle of Kildrummie, the residence of the widowed countess, with an army of *ketherans*, stormed it in the face of every resistance, and, whether by persuasion or by violence is not certain, obtained her in marriage. To murder the husband, to marry the widow, and carry off the inheritance from her children, were deeds which, even under the misgovernment of Albany, excited the horror of the people, and called loudly for redress; but before this could be obtained, an extraordinary scene was acted at Kildrummie. Stewart presented himself at the outer gate of the castle, and there, in presence of the Bishop of Ross and the assembled tenantry and vassals, was met by the Countess of Mar, upon which, with much feudal pomp and solemnity, he surrendered the keys of the castle into her hands, declaring that he did so freely and with a good heart, to be disposed of as she pleased. The lady then, who seems to have forgotten the rugged nature of the courtship, holding the keys in her hands, declared that she freely chose Alexander Stewart for her lord and husband, and that she conferred on him the earldom of Mar, the castle of Kildrummie, and all other lands which she inherited. The whole proceedings were closed by solemn instruments or charters being taken on the spot; and this remarkable transaction, exhibiting in its commencement and termination so singular a mixture of the ferocity of feudal manners and the formality of feudal law, was legalized and confirmed by a charter of the king, which ratified the concession of the countess, and permitted Stewart to assume the titles of Earl of Mar, and Lord of Garvyach.* Yet he who was murdered, to make way for this extraordinary intrusion of the son of Buchan, was the king's brother-in-law; and there seems to have been little doubt that the successful wooer, and the assassin of Drummond, were one and the same person. Nothing could give us a more striking proof of the pusillanimity of the sovereign, the weakness of the law, and the gross partialities of Albany.

The unquiet and suspicious times of Henry the Fourth, whose reign was marked by an almost uninterrupted succession of conspiracies, rendered it an

---

* Sutherland Case, by Lord Hailes, chap. v. p. 43. Winton, vol. ii. p. 404

object of great moment with him to keep at peace with Scotland; and it was evidently the interest of that kingdom to cultivate an amicable relation with England. Its present danger consisted not so much in any fears of invasion, or any serious attempts at conquest, as in the dread of civil commotion and domestic tyranny under the partial administration of Albany. The murder of the Duke of Rothesay, and the impunity permitted to the worst crimes committed by the nobles, clearly proved that the governor would feel no scruples in removing any further impediment which stood in the way of his ambition; and that he looked for indulgence from the favour with which he treated similar crimes and excesses in the barons who composed his court, and with whom he was ready to share the spoils or the honours which he had wrested from their legitimate possessors.

Under a government like this, the king became a mere shadow. Impelled by his natural disposition, which was pacific and contemplative, he had at first courted retirement, and willingly resigned much of the management of the state to his brother; and now that the murder of Rothesay had roused his paternal anxieties, that the murmurs of the people loudly accused this brother of so dreadful a crime, and branded him as the abettor of all the disorders which distracted the country, he felt, yet dreaded, the necessity of interference; and, while he trembled for the safety of his only remaining son, he found himself unequal to the task of instituting proper measures for his security, or of reassuming, in the midst of age and infirmities, those toils of government, to which, even in his younger years, he had experienced an aversion. But although the unfortunate monarch, thus surrounded with difficulties, found little help in his own energy or resources, friends were still left who pitied his condition, and felt a just indignation at the successful tyranny of the governor. Of these, the principal was Henry Wardlaw bishop of St Andrews, a loyal and generous prelate, nephew to the Cardinal Wardlaw, and, like him, distinguished for his eminence as a scholar, and his devotion to literature. To his charge was committed the heir of the throne, James earl of Carrick, then a boy in his fourteenth year, who was educated in the castle of St Andrews, under the immediate eye of the prelate, in the learning, and accomplishments befitting his high rank, and already promising abilities.

In the meantime, the captivity of so many of the nobles and gentry, who had been recently taken at Nesbit Moor, and in the battles of Homildon Hill and Shrewsbury, had a manifest effect in quieting Scotland, encouraging its pacific relations, and increasing its commercial enterprise. The years which succeeded these fatal conflicts, were occupied with numerous expeditions of the Scottish captives, who, under the safe conducts of Henry, travelled into their own country, and returned either with money, or with cargoes of wool, fish, or live stock, with which they discharged their ransom and procured their liberty.* The negotiations also, concerning the ransom of Murdoch the son of Albany, the Earl of Douglas, and other eminent prisoners, promoted a constant intercourse; whilst the poverty of Scotland in its agricultural produce, is seen in the circumstance, that any English captives are generally redeemed in grain, and not in money. Some Norfolk fishermen, who had probably

* Rotuli Scotiæ, vol. ii. pp. 164, 166, 167, 172, 173, 177.

been pursuing their occupation upon the Scottish coast, having been captured and imprisoned, Henry permitted two mariners of Lynne to carry six hundred quarters of grain into Scotland for their redemption; and, at the same time, granted a license to an Irish merchant to import corn, flour, and other victuals and merchandise, into that country, during the continuance of the truce.* Upon the whole, the commercial intercourse between the two countries appears to have been prosecuted with great activity, although interrupted at sea by the lawless attacks of the English cruisers,† and checked by the depredations of the Borderers, and broken men of both nations.

One cause, however, for jealousy and dissatisfaction upon the part of Henry still remained, in the perpetual reports which proceeded from Scotland, with regard to Richard the Second being still alive in that country, where, it was said, he continued to be treated with kindness and distinction. That these assertions, as to the reappearance of the dethroned monarch, long after his reputed death, had some foundation in truth, there seems reason to believe;‡ but, whether true or not, it was no unwise policy in Albany to abstain from giving any public contradiction to the rumour, and at times even to encourage it, as in this manner he essentially weakened the government of Henry; and, by affording him full employment at home, rendered it difficult for him to engage in any schemes for the annoyance of his neighbours.

In 1404, a gentleman named Serle, who had formerly

---

* Rotuli Scotiæ, vol. ii. p. 172.
† Fœdera, vol. viii. pp. 411, 420, 450; and MS. Bibl. Cot. F. vii. No. 22, 89, 116, 117, 118, quoted in M'Pherson's Annals of Commerce, vol. i. p. 615.
‡ See Appendix, at the end of the volume.

been of Richard's bedchamber, repaired secretly to Scotland, and, on his return, positively affirmed that he had seen the king. The old Countess of Oxford, mother to Robert de Vere duke of Ireland, the favourite of Richard, eagerly gave credit to the story; and, by the production of letters, and the present of little silver harts, the gifts which the late king had been fond of distributing amongst his favourites, she had already contrived to persuade many persons to credit the report, when her practices were discovered, and the execution and confession of Serle put an end to the rumour for the present. It was asserted, that Serle had actually been introduced, when in Scotland, to a person whom he declared to bear so exact a resemblance to Richard the Second, that it was not astonishing many should be deceived by it; and it was evident, that if Albany had not lent himself in any open manner to encourage, he had not, on the other hand, adopted any means to expose or detect the alleged impostor.*

But this plot of Serle and the Countess of Oxford was followed by a conspiracy of greater moment, in which Scotland was deeply concerned, yet whose ramifications, owing to the extreme care with which all written evidence, in such circumstances, was generally concealed or destroyed, were extremely difficult to be detected. Its principal authors appear to have been the Earl of Northumberland the father of Hotspur, Scrope the Archbishop of York, whose brother Henry had beheaded, and the Earl Marshal of England, with the Lords Hastings, Bardolf, and Faulconbridge; but it is certain that they received the cordial concurrence of some party in the Scottish state, as Northumberland engaged to meet them at the general rendezvous

* Walsingham, p. 371.

at York, not only with his own followers, but with a large reinforcement of Scottish soldiers, and it was calculated that they would be able to take the field with an army of twenty thousand men.* Besides this, they had engaged in a correspondence with the French king, who promised to despatch an expedition, which, at the moment they took up arms in England, was to make a descent on Wales, where Owen Glendower, the fierce and indefatigable opponent of Henry, had promised to join them; and this formidable opposition was to be further strengthened by a simultaneous invasion of the Scots.

Northumberland's intentions in this conspiracy are very clearly declared, in an intercepted letter, which he addressed to the Duke of Orleans, and which is preserved in the Parliamentary Rolls. "I have embraced," says he, " a firm purpose, with the assistance of God, with your aid, and that of my allies, to sustain the just quarrel of my sovereign lord King Richard, if he is alive; and, if he is dead, to avenge his death; and, moreover, to sustain the right and quarrel, which my redoubted lady the Queen of England, your niece, may have to the kingdom of England; for which purpose I have declared war against Henry of Lancaster, at present Regent of England."†

A rebellion, so ably planned that it seemed almost impossible that it should not succeed, and hurl Henry from the throne, was ruined by the credulity of the Earl Marshal and the Archbishop, who became the victims of an adherent of the king's, Neville earl of Westmoreland. This nobleman, who had received intelligence

---

* Hall's Chronicle, p. 35. Edition 1809. London, 4to. Hardyng's Chronicle, p. 362. Edition 1812. London, 4to.
† Rolls of Parliament, vol. iii. p. 605. The original is in French.

of the plot, artfully represented himself as warmly interested in its success; and, having prevailed upon Scrope and Mowbray to meet him in a private conference, seized them both as they sat at his table, and hurried them to the king at Pontefract, by whose orders they were instantly beheaded. Northumberland, however, with his little grandson Henry Percy, and the Lord Bardolf, had the good fortune to escape into Scotland, where they were courteously received by Albany.

In this country, notwithstanding his advanced age and frequent failures, Percy continued to organize an opposition to the government of Henry; visiting, for this purpose, the court of France, and the Flemish States, and returning to stimulate the exertions of his Scottish friends. Although unsuccessful in his continental negotiations, it is evident, from the orders issued by Henry for the immediate array of the fighting men in the counties of York and Lancaster, as well as in Derby, Lincoln, and Nottingham, that Albany had been induced to assemble an army, and that the king had received intelligence of an intended invasion by the Scots, to be led, as the king expresses it, "by his common adversary, Robert duke of Albany, the pretended governor of Scotland."* Previous, however, to any such expedition, an event took place which effectually altered the relations between the governor and the English monarch, and introduced material changes into the state of the different parties in Scotland.

The continuance of his own power, and the adoption of every means by which the authority of the king, or the respect and affection due to the royal family, could be weakened or destroyed, was the principle of Albany's government: a principle which, although sometimes

* Rymer, Fœdera, vol. viii. p. 414.

artfully concealed, was never for a moment forgotten by this crafty statesman. In his designs, he had been all along supported by the Douglases: a family whom he attached to his interest by an ample share in the spoils with which his lawless government enabled him to gratify his creatures. Archibald earl of Douglas, the head of the house, we have seen become his partner in the murder of the Duke of Rothesay, and rewarded by the possession of the immense estates of the Earl of March,—a baron next to Douglas,—the most powerful of the Scottish aristocracy, but compelled, by the affront put upon his daughter, to become a fugitive in England, and a dependant upon the bounty of a foreign prince.

The battle of Homildon Hill made Douglas a captive; whilst many of his most powerful adherents shared his fate: and Albany, deprived of the countenance of his steadiest supporters, found the friends of the old king gradually gaining ground. A natural jealousy of the designs of the governor, against a youth who formed the only impediment between his own family and the succession to the crown, induced these persons to adopt measures for the security of the Earl of Carrick, now an only son. It was with this view that they had placed him under the charge of the Bishop of St Andrews, a man of uncorrupted honour and integrity; and, whilst the studies of the young prince were carefully conducted by this prelate, whose devotion to literature well fitted him for the task, the presence of the warlike Earl of Northumberland, who, with his grandson, young Henry Percy, had found an asylum in the castle of the bishop, was of great service to the young prince in his chivalrous exercises. It was soon seen, however, that, with all these advantages, Scotland was then no fit place for the residence of the youthful heir to the throne. The intrigues of Albany, and the unsettled state of the country, filled the bosom of the timid monarch with constant alarm. He became anxious to remove him for a season from Scotland; and, as France was at this time considered the best school in Europe for the education of a youth of his high rank, it was resolved to send the prince thither, under the care of the Earl of Orkney,[*] and Sir David Fleming of Cumbernauld, an intimate friend and adherent of the exiled Earl of Northumberland.

At this crisis, a secret negotiation took place between the English monarch and the Duke of Albany, regarding the delivery of Northumberland and Lord Bardolf; and it appears, that the party of the governor and the Douglases had embraced the treacherous plan of sacrificing the lives of two unfortunate exiles, who had found an asylum in Scotland, to procure in return the liberty of Murdoch, the son of the governor, the Earl of Douglas, and other captives who had been taken at Homildon. A baser project could not well be imagined; but it was accidentally discovered by Percy's friend, David Fleming, who instantly revealed it to the exiled noblemen, and advised them to consult their safety by flight.

This conduct of Albany, which afforded a new light into the treachery of his character, accelerated the preparations for the young prince's departure; and all being at length ready, the Earl of Carrick, then a boy in his fourteenth year, took his progress through Lothian to North Berwick, accompanied by the Earl of Orkney, Fleming of Cumbernauld, the Lords of Dirleton and Hermandston, and a strong party of the barons

[*] Rymer, Fœdera, vol. viii. p. 415.

of Lothian. The ship which was to convey him to France lay at the Bass; and having embarked along with the Earl of Orkney and a small personal suite, they set sail with a fair wind, and under no apprehensions for their safety, as the truce between England and Scotland was not yet expired, and the only vessels they were likely to meet were English cruisers. But the result showed how little was to be trusted to the faith of truces, or to the honour of kings; for the prince had not been a few days at sea, when he was captured off Flamborough Head, by an armed merchantman belonging to the port of Wye, and carried to London, where the king instantly committed him and his attendants to the Tower.*

In vain did the guardians of the young prince remonstrate against this cruelty, or present to Henry a letter from the king his father, which, with much simplicity, recommended him to the kindness of the English monarch, should he find it necessary to land in his dominions. In vain did they represent that the mission to France was perfectly pacific, and its only object, the education of the prince at the French court. Henry merely answered by a poor witticism, declaring that he himself knew the French language indifferently well, and that his father could not have sent him to a better master.†
So flagrant a breach of the law of nations, as the seizure and imprisonment of the heir-apparent during the time of truce, would have called for the most violent remonstrances from any government except that of Albany. But to this usurper of the supreme power, the capture of the prince was the most grateful event which could have happened; and to detain him in captivity became,

* Walsingham, p. 375. Winton, vol. ii. pp. 415, 416.
† Walsingham, p. 375. Extracta ex Chronicis Scotiæ, p. 253.

from this moment, one of the principal objects of his future life; we are not to wonder, then, that the conduct of Henry not only drew forth no indignation from the governor, but was not even followed by any request that the prince should be restored to liberty.

Whilst Albany's satisfaction was great at this unfortunate event, his indignation, and that of the Douglases, at the conduct of Sir David Fleming, in attempting to convey the heir apparent to a place of safety, and in facilitating the escape of Northumberland, was proportionably fierce and unforgiving; nor was it quenched until they had taken a bloody revenge. At the moor of Lang-Hermandston, the party which had accompanied the prince to North Berwick were attacked by James Douglas of Abercorn, second son of the Earl of Douglas, and Alexander Seton, where, after a fierce conflict, Fleming was slain, and the most of the barons who accompanied him made prisoners. A procession, which passed next day through Edinburgh, conveying to Holyrood the body of this noble knight, who was celebrated for his courage, tenderness, and fidelity, excited much commiseration; but the populace did not dare to rise against the Douglases, and Albany openly protected them. Those bitter feelings of wrath, and desires of revenge, which so cruel an attack excited, now broke out into interminable feuds and jealousies, and, ramifying throughout the whole line of the vassals of these two powerful families, continued for many years to agitate the minds of the people, and disturb the tranquillity of the country.[*]

The aged king, already worn out by infirmity, and now broken by disappointment and sorrow, did not

---

[*] Winton, vol. ii. p. 413. Fordun a Goodal, vol. ii. p. 439. Extracta ex Chronicis Scotiæ, p. 153.

long survive the captivity of his son. It is said, the melancholy news were brought him as he was sitting down to supper in his palace of Rothesay in Bute; and that the effect was such upon his affectionate but feeble spirit, that he drooped from that day forward, refused all sustenance, and died soon after of a broken heart. His death took place on the 4th of April, 1406, in the sixteenth year of his reign; and Albany, his brother, immediately succeeded to the prize which had so long been the paramount object of his ambition, by becoming the unfettered governor of Scotland. The character of this monarch requires little additional development. It was of that sweet, pacific, and indolent nature which unfitted him to subdue the pride, or overawe and control the fierce passions and resentments of his barons; and although the generosity and affectionate feelings of his heart inclined him, on every occasion, to be the friend of the poorer classes of his subjects, yet energy and courage were wanting to make these good wishes effectual; and it might almost be said, that in the dread of making any one his enemy, he made no one his friend. All the virtues of domestic life he possessed in a high degree; but these, as well as his devotion to intellectual accomplishments, were thrown away upon the rude times in which he lived. His wisdom, which was far before his age, saw clearly that the greatest blessing which could be conferred upon the country was peace; but it required firmness, and almost violence, to carry these convictions into the active management of the government, and these were qualities which Robert could not command. Had he been born in the rank of a subject, he would have been among the best and wisest men in his dominions; but as a king, his timidity and irresolution rendered all his virtues of none avail, and permitted the government to fall into the hands of an usurper, who systematically abused his power for the purposes of his own aggrandizement.

In person, Robert was tall, and of a princely presence; his countenance was somewhat florid, but pleasing and animated; whilst a beard of great length, and silvery whiteness, flowed down his breast, and gave a look of sanctity to his appearance. Humility, a deep conviction of the vanity of human grandeur, and aspirations for the happiness of a better world, were sentiments which he is said to have deeply felt, and frequently expressed; and nothing could prevail on him, in the custom of the age, and after the example of his father and grandfather, to provide a monument for himself. It is said, that his queen, Annabella, remonstrated with him on this occasion, when he rebuked her for speaking like one of the foolish women: "You consider not," said he, "how little it becomes a wretched worm, and the vilest of sinners, to erect a proud tomb for his miserable remains: let them who delight in the honours of this world so employ themselves. As for me, cheerfully would I be buried in the meanest shed on earth, could I thus secure rest to my soul in the day of the Lord."* He was interred, however, in the Abbey church of Paisley, before the high altar.

It has hitherto been believed by our Scottish historians, that there were born to him only two sons, David duke of Rothesay, and James earl of Carrick, who succeeded him in the throne. It is certain, however, that the king had a third son, Robert, who probably died very young, but whose existence is proved by a record of unquestionable authority.†

---

* Fordun a Goodal, vol. ii. p. 440.
† Chamberlain Accounts, vol. ii. p. 231. "Et Dno David Comiti de Car-

Upon the king's death, the three Estates of the realm assembled in parliament at Perth; and, having first made a solemn declaration that James earl of Carrick, then a captive in England, was their lawful king, and that the crown belonged of undoubted right to the heirs of his body, the Duke of Albany, being the next in succession, was chosen Regent;* and it was determined to send an embassy to the French court, for the purpose of renewing the league of mutual defence and alliance which had so long subsisted between the two countries. For this purpose, Sir Walter Stewart of Ralston, Lawder archdeacon of Lothian, along with two esquires, John Gil and John de Leth, were selected to negotiate with France; and their mission, as was to be expected from the exasperated feelings which were common to both countries with regard to their adversary of England, was completely successful. Charles the Sixth king of France, Louis his brother Duke of Anjou, and the Duke of Berry, by three separate deeds, each acting in his own name, ratified and confirmed the treaties formerly entered into between their country and the late King of Scotland; and assured the Duke of Albany, then regent of that kingdom, of their resolution to maintain the same firm and inviolate in all time to come.†

With regard to England, Albany now earnestly desired the continuance of peace; and it was fortunate that the principles which influenced his government, although selfish, and calculated for the preservation of his own power, proved, at this moment, the best for the interests of the country; whilst the English king,

---
rick percipienti pro se et heredibus suis de corpore suo legitime procreandis, quibus forte deficientibus, Roberto seneschallo fratri ipsius, et heredibus suis."
  * Winton, vol. ii. p. 418.
  † Records of the Parliament of Scotland, pp. 137, 138.

in the possession of the young heir to the throne, and master, also, of the persons of the chief nobility who had remained in captivity since the battle of Homildon Hill, was able to assume a decided tone in his negotiations, and exerted an influence over the governor, which he had not formerly enjoyed. A short time previous to the king's death, negotiations had been renewed for the continuance of the truce, and for the return of the Earl of Douglas to Scotland. The high value placed upon this potent baron, and the power of weakening Scotland which the English king possessed at this time, may be estimated from the circumstance, that he would not permit his return, until thirteen hostages, selected from the first families in the country, had repaired to Westminster and delivered themselves to the king.* It was one happy effect of the power and wealth which the capture of many noble prisoners necessarily conferred on those to whom they surrendered, that it softened the atrocities of war and diminished the effusion of blood. The only impediments to the continuance of peace arose out of the piracies of English cruisers and armed merchantmen, which, on the slightest provocation, were ready to make prize of any vessels they met,—French, Flemish, Genoese, or Scottish; and it is a singular circumstance, that, at this early period, we find the English ships beginning to insist on their superior right to the dominion of the seas, which they afterwards so proudly maintained. In 1402, a formal complaint was presented to Henry the Fourth by the magistrates of Bruges, which stated that two fishermen, one belonging to Ostend and the other to Briel, when engaged in the herring fishery of the North Sea, had been captured by the English and

* Rotuli Scotiæ, vol. ii. p. 177.

carried into Hull, although they lowered their sails the moment they were hailed.*

On the other hand, the Scots were not slow to make reprisals; although their power at sea, which we have seen so formidable during the reigns of Edward the Second and Third, appears to have experienced a sensible diminution. In 1404, the fishery on the coast of Aberdeenshire,—a source of considerable wealth,— had been invaded by the English: a small fleet of Scottish ships was immediately fitted out by Sir Robert Logan, who attacked and attempted to destroy some English vessels; but his force was insufficient, his ships were taken, and he himself carried prisoner into the port of Lynne in Norfolk.† Stewart earl of Mar, with whose singular courtship and marriage we are already acquainted, after amusing his taste for adventures in foreign war,‡ leading the life of a knight-errant, and dividing his time between real fighting and the recreations of tilts and tournaments, became latterly a pirate, and with a small squadron infested the coast between Berwick and Newcastle, destroying or making prizes of the English vessels.

These hostile invasions, which appear to have been mutually committed on each other by the English and the Scottish merchantmen, were not openly countenanced by either government. No regular maritime laws for the protection of trade and commerce had as yet been practically established in Europe; the vessels which traded from one country to another, were the property not of the nation, but of individuals, who, if their own gain or interest interfered, did not consider

* Rymer, Fœdera, vol. viii. p. 274, "quanquam ad primam vocem ipsorum Anglicorum idem Johannes Willes, velum suum declinavit." M'Pherson's Annals of Commerce, vol. i. p. 612.
† Walsingham, p. 364.
‡ Juvenal des Ursins, Histoire de Charles VI., p. 196.

themselves bound by treaties or truces; and when a ship of greater strength met a small merchantman richly laden, and incapable of resistance, the temptation to make themselves master of her cargo was generally too strong to be resisted.* Henry, however, showed himself willing to redress the grievances suffered by the Scottish merchants, as well as to put an end to the frequent infractions of the truce which were committed by the Borderers of both nations; and the perpetual grants of letters of safe conduct to natives of Scotland travelling through England on purposes of devotion, commerce, or pleasure, and eager to show their prowess in deeds of arms, or to seek for distinction in continental war, evinced a sincere anxiety to keep up an amicable relation between the two countries, and to pave the way for a lasting peace.†

The return to their country of the two most powerful barons in the state,—the Earls of Douglas and of March,—with the "stanching of that mortal feud which had long continued between them," was another event that promised the best effects. The immense estates of March, which during his exile had been occupied by Douglas, were restored to him, with the exception of the lordship of Annandale, and the castle of Lochmaben. These were retained by Douglas; and, in addition to the thirteen noble persons who were compelled to remain in England as hostages for his return, Henry extorted from him a ransom of a thousand marks before he consented to his departure.‡ Amongst the hostages were Archibald Douglas, eldest son of the

---

* Rymer, Fœdera, vol. viii. pp. 203, 420.
† Rotuli Scotiæ, pp. 176, 177, 178, 179, 180.   Rymer, vol. viii. pp. 416, 430, 445, 450.
‡ Rotuli Scotiæ, vol. ii. pp. 182, 184.   Harl. MS. 381. f. 212, quoted in Pinkerton's History, vol. i. p. 87.   Fordun a Goodal, vol. ii. p. 444.

earl, and James his son; James, the son and heir of James Douglas lord of Dalkeith; Sir William Douglas of Niddesdale, Sir John Seton, Sir Simon Glendinning, Sir John Montgomery, Sir John Stewart of Lorn, Sir William Graham, Sir William Sinclair of Hermandston, and others of the first rank and consequence.* The residence of these persons in England, and the care which Henry bestowed upon the education of their youthful monarch, who, though still retained in captivity, was provided with the best masters, treated with uniform kindness, and waited on with the honours due to his rank, contributed to increase the amicable intercourse between the two countries, and to give to both a short and happy interval of peace.

It was in the midst of this pacific period that the doctrines of Wickliff for the first time appeared in Scotland; and the flames of war had scarcely ceased, when the more dreadful flames of religious persecution were kindled in the country. John Resby, an English priest of the school of this great reformer, in whose remarkable works are to be found the seeds of almost every doctrine of Luther, had passed into Scotland, either in consequence of the persecutions of Wickliff's followers, which arose after his death, or from a desire to propagate the truth. After having for some time remained unnoticed, the boldness, and the novelty of his opinions at length awakened the jealousy of the church; and it was asserted that he preached the most dangerous heresies. He was immediately seized by Laurence of Lindores, an eminent doctor in theology, and compelled to appear before a council of the clergy, where this inquisitor presided. Here he was accused of maintaining no fewer than forty heresies, amongst

* Rotuli Scotiæ, vol. ii. pp. 181, 182.

which the principal were, a denial of the authority of the pope, as the successor of St Peter ; a contemptuous opinion of the utility of penances and auricular confession ; and an assertion that an absolutely sinless life was necessary in any one who dared to call himself the Vicar of Christ.*

Although Resby was esteemed an admirable preacher by the common people, his eloquence, as may easily be supposed, had little effect upon the bench of ecclesiastical judges before whom he defended himself. Laurence of Lindores was equally triumphant in his confutation of the written conclusions, and in his answers to the spoken arguments by which their author attempted to support them ; and the brave but unfortunate inquirer after the truth, was barbarously condemned to the flames, and delivered over to the secular arm. The cruel sentence was carried into immediate execution ; and he was burnt at Perth in the year 1407, his books and writings being consumed in the same fire with their master. It is probable that the church was stimulated to this unjustifiable severity by Albany the governor, whose bitter hatred to all Lollards and heretics, and zeal for the purity of the Catholic faith, are particularly recorded by Winton.†

And here, in the first example of persecution for religious opinions which is recorded in our history, the inevitable effects of such a course were clearly discernible in the increased zeal and affection which were evinced for the opinions which had been sealed by the blood of the preacher. The conclusions and little pamphlets of this early reformer were carefully concealed and preserved by his disciples ; and any who

* Fordun a Goodal, vol. ii. pp. 442, 443.
† Winton's Chronicle, vol. ii. p. 419.

had imbibed his opinions evinced a resolution and courage in maintaining them, which resisted every attempt to restore them to the bosom of the church. They did not dare, indeed, to disseminate them openly, but they met, and read, and debated in secret; and the doctrines which had been propagated by Resby, remained secretly cherished in the hearts of his disciples, and reappeared after a few years in additional strength, and with a spirit of more active and determined proselytism.* It is not improbable also, that amongst Resby's forty heretical conclusions were included some of those doctrines regarding the origin and foundation of the power of the civil magistrate and the rights of the people, which, being peculiar to the Lollards, were regarded with extreme jealousy by the higher orders in the state; and Albany's persecution of the heretics may have proceeded as much upon civil as on religious grounds.

Since the fatal battle of Durham, the castle of Jedburgh had been kept by the English. In its masonry, it was one of the strongest built fortresses in Scotland; and its garrison, by their perpetual attacks and plundering expeditions, had given great annoyance to the adjacent country. The moment the truce expired the Teviotdale Borderers recommenced the war, by reducing this castle; but on attempting to destroy the fortifications, it was found, that such was the induration and tenacity of the mortar, that the whole walls and towers seemed one mass of solid stone; and that the expense of razing and levelling the works would be great. In a parliament held at Perth, a proposal was made to raise the sum required by a

* Fordun a Goodal, vol. ii. p. 442. Appendix to Dr M'Crie's Life of Melville, vol. i. p. 418.

general tax of two pennies upon every hearth in the kingdom. But this the governor opposed, observing, that during the whole course of his administration, no such tax ever had been, or ever should be, levied; and that they who countenanced such an abuse, merited the maledictions of the poor. He concluded by giving orders that the sum required should be paid to the lords marchers out of the royal customs,—a liberality which was much extolled, and gained him high credit with the people.*

In the following year, a violent remonstrance was addressed by the English monarch to the Duke of Albany, complaining of the delay of the Earl of Douglas to fulfil his knightly word, by which he had solemnly engaged to return to his captivity; and threatening to use his hostages according to the laws of war, and to pursue the earl himself as a perjured rebel, if within a month he did not re-enter his person in ward. Douglas had, in truth, delayed his return to England a year beyond the stipulated period; and as the castle of Jedburgh was situated within his territories, it was naturally supposed by Henry that he had not been over scrupulous in observing the strict conditions of amity, and adherence to the "party of the King of England," to which he had set his hand and seal before regaining his liberty. Matters, however, were amicably composed between the offended monarch and his prisoner; and Douglas, having permanently purchased his liberty by the payment of a high ransom, once more returned to assume his wonted authority in the councils of the country.†

For some time after the reduction of Jedburgh, the war presented few features of interest or importance.

* Fordun a Goodal, vol. ii. p. 444.   † Rymer, Fœdera, vol. viii. p. 478

Fast castle, a strength considered impregnable from its peculiar situation, had been occupied, during the convulsions of the times, by an English adventurer named Holder, who, combining the avocations of a freebooter on shore and a pirate at sea, became the terror of the country round his retreat. For such purposes the castle was admirably adapted. It was built upon a high rock overhanging the German ocean, so rugged and precipitous, that all attack on that side was impossible; and it communicated with the adjoining country by a narrow neck of land, defended by a barbican, where a handful of resolute men could have defied an army. Notwithstanding these difficulties, Patrick Dunbar, son of the Earl of March, made himself master of the castle, and delivered the country from the depredations of its ferocious lord; but the particulars of the enterprise are unfortunately lost, and we only know that it was distinguished by the utmost address and courage.*

About the same time Gawin Dunbar, March's second son, and Archibald Douglas of Drumlanrig, attacked and gave to the flames the town of Roxburgh, then in possession of the English; but these partial successes were more than counterbalanced by the losses sustained by the Scots. Sir Robert Umfraville, vice-admiral of England, with a squadron of ten ships of war, broke into the Forth, ravaged the country on both sides, and collected an immense booty, after which he swept the seas with his fleet, and made prizes of fourteen Scottish merchantmen. At the time of Umfraville's invasion, there happened to be a grievous dearth of grain in England, and the quantity of corn which he carried off from Scotland so materially re-

* Fordun a Goodal, vol. ii. p. 444. " Non minus subtiliter quam viriliter."

duced the prices of provisions, that it procured him the popular surname of Robin Mendmarket. On another occasion, the same experienced leader, who had charge of the military education of Gilbert Umfraville, titular Earl of Angus, determined to hold a military array in honour of his youthful pupil, who had just completed his fourteenth year. His banner, accordingly, was raised for the first time amidst the shouts of his vassals; and the festivities were concluded by a Border "raid," in which Jedburgh was sacked during its public fair, and reduced to ashes.

But the attention of the country was soon after this diverted from such brief and insulated hostilities to an event of a more serious and formidable nature, which shook the security of the government, and threatened to dismember a portion of the kingdom. This was the rebellion of Donald lord of the Isles, of which the origin and the effects merit particular consideration. The ancient line of barons, which for a long period of years had succeeded to the earldom of Ross, ended at length in a female, Euphemia Ross, married to Sir Walter Lesley. Of this marriage there were two children: Alexander, afterwards Earl of Ross, and Margaret, married to Donald lord of the Isles. Alexander earl of Ross, married a daughter of the Duke of Albany, and had by her an only daughter, Euphemia countess of Ross, who became a nun, and resigned the earldom of Ross in favour of her uncle, John earl of Buchan. This destination of the property, the Lord of the Isles steadily and haughtily resisted. He contended, that by Euphemia taking the veil, she became civilly dead; and that the earldom of Ross belonged lawfully to him, in right of Margaret his wife.* His

* Sutherland Case, by Lord Hailes, chap. v. § 7.

plea was at once repelled by the governor; and this noble territory, which included the Isle of Skye, and a district in the mainland equal in extent to a little kingdom, was declared to be the property of the Earl of Buchan. But the island prince, who had the pride and the power of an independent monarch, derided the award of Albany, and, collecting an army of ten thousand men, prepared not only to seize the disputed county, but determined to carry havoc and destruction into the heart of Scotland. Nor, in the midst of these ferocious designs, did he want somewhat of a statesmanlike policy, for he engaged in repeated alliances with England; and, as the naval force which he commanded was superior to any Scottish fleet which could be brought against him, his co-operation with the English in their attacks upon the Scottish commerce, was likely to produce very serious effects.*

When his preparations were completed, he at once broke in upon the earldom at the head of his fierce multitudes, who were armed after the fashion of their country, with swords fitted both to cut and thrust, pole-axes, bows and arrows, short knives, and round bucklers formed of wood, or strong hide, with bosses of brass or iron. The people of the country readily submitted to him—to have attempted opposition, indeed, was impossible; and these northern districts had for many centuries been more accustomed to pay their allegiance to the Norwegian yarls, or pirate kings, whose power was at their door, than to acknowledge the remote superiority of the Scottish crown. At Dingwall, however, he was encountered by a formidable opponent in Angus Dhu, or Black Angus, who attacked him with great fierceness, but was over-

* Rymer, Fœdera, vol. viii. pp. 418, 527.

powered and made prisoner, after his brother Roderic Gald and the greater part of his men had been cut to pieces.

The Lord of the Isles then ordered a general rendezvous of his army at Inverness, and sent his summons to levy all the fighting men in Boyne and Enzie, who were compelled to follow his banner and to join the soldiers from the Isles; with this united force, consisting of the best levies in the islands and the north, he swept through Moray, meeting with none, or the most feeble resistance; whilst his soldiers covered the land like locusts, and the plunder of money, arms, and provisions, daily gave them new spirits and energy. Strathbogie was next invaded; and the extensive district of Garvyach, which belonged to his rival the Earl of Mar, was delivered up to cruel and indiscriminate havoc. It had been the boast of the invader that he would burn the rich burgh of Aberdeen, and make a desert of the country to the shores of the Tay; and as the smoke of his camp-fires was already seen on the banks of the Don, the unhappy burghers began to tremble in their booths, and to anticipate the realization of these dreadful menaces.* But their spirits soon rose when the Earl of Mar, whose reputation as a military leader was of the highest order, appeared at the head of an army, composed of the bravest knights and gentlemen in Angus and the Mearns, and declared his resolution of instantly advancing against the invader. Mar had the advantage of having been bred up in the midst of highland war, and at first distinguished himself, as we have seen, by his predatory expeditions at the head of the highlanders. But his marriage with the Countess of Mar, and his reception

* Fordun a Goodal, vol. ii. p. 445.

at court, appear to have effectually changed his character: the savage habits of his early life were softened down, and left behind them a talent for war, and an ambition for renown, which restlessly sought for employment wherever there was a chance of gaining distinction. When on the continent, he had offered his services to the Duke of Burgundy; and the victory at Liege was mainly ascribed to his skill and courage, so that his reputation abroad was as distinguished as at home. In a short time he found himself at the head of the whole power of Mar and Garvyach, in addition to that of Angus and the Mearns; Sir Alexander Ogilvy sheriff of Angus, Sir James Scrymgeour constable of Dundee and hereditary standard-bearer of Scotland, Sir Alexander Irvine, Sir Robert Melville, Sir William de Abernethy, nephew to Albany, and many other barons and esquires, with their feudal services, joined him with displayed banner; and Sir Robert Davidson, the provost of Aberdeen, and a troop of the stoutest burgesses, came forward to defend their hearths and their stalls from the ravages of the Lord of the Isles.

Mar immediately advanced from Aberdeen, and, marching by Inverury, came in sight of the highlanders at the village of Harlaw, on the water of Ury, not far from its junction with the Don. He found that his little army was immensely outnumbered, it is said, by nearly ten to one; but it consisted of the bravest barons in these parts; and his experience had taught him to consider a single knight in steel as a fair match against a whole troop of *ketherans*. Without delay, therefore, he intrusted the leading of the advance to the Constable of Dundee and Ogilvy the sheriff of Angus, who had with them a small, but compact, battalion of men-at-arms; whilst he himself followed with the rearward, composed of the main strength of his army, including the Irvings, the Maules, the Morays, the Straitons, the Lesleys, the Stirlings, the Lovels, headed by their chiefs, and with their banners and penoncelles waving amid their grove of spears. Of the islesmen and highlanders, the principal leaders were the Lord of the Isles himself, with Macintosh and Maclean, the heads of their respective septs, and innumerable other chiefs and chieftains, animated by the old and deep-rooted hostility between the Celtic and Saxon race.*

The shock between two such armies may be easily imagined to have been dreadful: the highlanders, who were ten thousand strong, rushing on with the fierce shouts and yells which it was their custom to raise in coming into battle, and the knights meeting them with levelled spears, and ponderous maces and battle-axes. In his first onset, Scrymgeour, and the men-at-arms who fought under him, with little difficulty drove back the mass of Islesmen, and, cutting his way through their thick columns, made a cruel slaughter. But, though hundreds fell around him, thousands poured in to supply their place, more fierce and fresh than their predecessors; whilst Mar, who had penetrated with his main army into the very heart of the enemy, found himself in the same difficulties, becoming every moment more tired with slaughter, more encumbered with the numbers of the slain, and less able to resist the increasing and reckless ferocity of the masses that still yelled and fought around him. It was impossible that this

* In one of the Macfarlane MSS., preserved in the Advocates' Library, entitled, "A Geographical Description of Scotland," (vol. i. pp. 7, 20,) will be found a minute description of the locality of this battle. See Illustrations, B.

should continue much longer without making a fatal impression on the Scots; and the effects of fatigue were soon seen. The Constable of Dundee was slain; and the highlanders, encouraged by his fall, wielded their broadswords and Lochaber axes with murderous effect; seizing and stabbing the horses, and pulling down their riders, whom they despatched with their short daggers. In this way were slain some of the best soldiers of these northern districts. Sir Robert Davidson, with the greater part of the burgesses who fought around him, were amongst the number; and many of the families lost not only their chief, but every male in the house. Lesley of Balquhain, a baron of ancient lineage, is said to have fallen with six of his sons slain beside him. The Sheriff of Angus, with his eldest son George Ogilvy, Sir Alexander Irving of Drum,* Sir Robert Maule, Sir Thomas Moray, William Abernethy, Alexander Straiton of Lauriston, James Lovel, Alexander Stirling, and above five hundred men-at-arms, including the principal gentry of Buchan, shared their fate; † whilst Mar himself, and a small number of the survivors, still continued the battle till nightfall. The slaughter then ceased; and it was found in the morning that the island lord had retreated by Inverury and the hill of Benochie, checked and broken certainly by the desperate contest, but neither conquered nor very effectually repulsed. Mar, on the contrary, although he passed the night on the field, did so, not in the

---

* There is a tradition in the family of Irving of Drum, that the Laird of Maclean was slain by Sir Alexander Irving. Genealogical Collections, MS. Adv. Library, Jac. V. 4, 16. vol. i. p. 180. Irving was buried on the field, where in ancient times a cairn marked the place of his interment, which was long known by the name of Drum's Cairn. Kennedy's Annals of Aberdeen, vol. i. p. 51.

† Fordun a Hearne, pp. 1175, 6. Extracta ex Chronicis Scotiæ, MS. fol. 257.

triumphant assertion of victory, but from the effects of wounds and exhaustion: the best and bravest of his friends were stretched around him; and he found himself totally unable to pursue the retreat of the islesmen. Amongst those of the highlanders who fell were the chiefs of Maclean and Macintosh, with upwards of nine hundred men: a small loss compared with that sustained by the lowlanders. The battle was fought on St James's Eve, the twenty-fourth of July; and from the ferocity with which it was contested, and the dismal spectacle of civil war and bloodshed exhibited to the country, it appears to have made a deep impression on the national mind. It fixed itself in the music and the poetry of Scotland. A march, called the Battle of Harlaw, continued to be a popular air down to the time of Drummond of Hawthornden; and a spirited ballad, on the same event, is still repeated in our own age, describing the meeting of the armies, and the deaths of the chiefs, in no ignoble strain.* Soon after the battle, a council-general was held by the governor, in which a statute was passed, in favour of the heirs of those who had died in defence of the country, exempting them from the feudal fines usually exacted before they entered upon possession of their estates, and permitting them, although minors, immediately to serve heirs to their lands. It will, perhaps, be recollected, that Bruce, on the eve of the battle of Bannockburn, encouraged his troops by a promise of the like nature.†

It was naturally suspected by Albany, that the chief of the Isles, who was crippled rather than conquered,

---

* Battle of Harlaw. Laing's Early Metrical Tales, p. 229.
† History, supra, vol. i. p. 268. The fact mentioned in the text is proved by a Retour in the Cartulary of Aberdeen, fol. 121, in favour of Andrew de Tulidef, whose father, William de Tulidef, was slain at Harlaw. It was pointed out to me by my friend Mr Thomson, Deputy Clerk-Register, to whom this volume is under repeated obligations. See Illustrations, letter C.

had only fallen back to refresh his men and procure reinforcements from Ross-shire and the Hebrides; and as the result of the battle had shown that, however inferior in arms or in discipline, the highlanders could make up for these disadvantages in numbers and ferocity, a renewal of the invasion was anticipated with alarm; and Albany determined to prevent it by an unwonted display of military spirit and activity. He collected an army in the autumn; marched in person to Dingwall, one of the principal castles of the ancient Earls of Ross, situated at the west end of the Cromarty Firth; and, having made himself master of it, appointed a governor, and proceeded to repossess himself of the whole county of Ross. Donald, however, fell back upon his island strengths, and during the winter defied his enemies; but as soon as the summer permitted the resumption of hostilities, Albany again attacked him; and, after a war conducted with various success, the island king was compelled to lay down his assumed independence, and give up all claim to the earldom of Ross; to consent to become a vassal of the Scottish crown; and to deliver hostages for his future good behaviour. The treaty was concluded at Polgilbe or Polgillip, now Loch Gilp, an arm of the sea running into the district of Knapdale in Argyle.* This successful termination of a rebellion, which appeared so formidable in its commencement, was followed by a truce with England, in which it was declared, that from the river Spey in Scotland to the mount of St Michael in Cornwall, all hostilities between the two countries should cease after the 17th of May, 1412, for the period of six years.†

* Fordun a Hearne, p. 1177. Macpherson's Geographical Illustrations, voce Polgylbe.
† Rymer, Fœdera, vol. viii. p. 737.

Albany now became impatient for the return of his eldest son, who had remained a captive in England since the battle of Homildon. As he felt the approach of age, he was desirous of making a quiet transfer of his power in the government into the hands of his own family; and various negotiations regarding the hostages to be delivered for Murdoch, and the ransom which was claimed, had already taken place, but without success; whilst the total indifference evinced by the governor to the prolonged captivity of the sovereign, clearly showed, that if age had impaired his strength, it had in no degree awakened his remorse, or stifled his ambition. It was evident that he intended his son to succeed him in the high authority which he had so long usurped; and Sir Walter Stewart of Ralston, and John de Leith, were engaged in a final treaty for the return of the future governor, when their proceedings were suddenly interrupted by the death of Henry the Fourth, and the accession of a new sovereign to the English throne.*

The uncertain tenure by which the crown had been held by Henry the Fourth, and his consequent anxiety to ward off all foreign attack when his attention was required in suppressing conspiracy at home, had contributed greatly to preserve the peace with Scotland; and under his successor, Henry the Fifth, the great designs of this youthful conqueror against France, and his subsequent invasion of that kingdom, rendered it as materially his interest, as it had been that of his predecessor, to maintain pacific relations with that country. In this view, the possession of the King of Scotland, and the eldest son of the Regent, gave him a hold over the politics of the country, which he employed with great skill and effect in weakening the enmity and neu-

* Rymer, Fœdera, vol. viii. pp. 708, 735; 775.

tralising the hostile schemes of those parties which were opposed to his wishes, and inclined to renew the war.

But it is necessary here, for a moment, to interrupt the narrative, in order to fix our attention upon a spectacle, which, amid the gloomy pictures of foreign or domestic war, offers a refreshing and pleasing resting place to the mind. This was the establishment of the University of St Andrews, by Henry Wardlaw, the bishop of that see, to whom belongs the unfading honour of being the founder of the first university in Scotland, the father of the infant literature of his country. Before this time, the generosity of the Lady Devorguilla, the wife of John Baliol, had established Baliol College in Oxford, in the end of the thirteenth century; and we have seen the munificence of a Scottish prelate, the Bishop of Moray, distinguishing itself by the institution of the Scottish College of Paris in 1326; but it was reserved for the enlightened spirit of Wardlaw to render unnecessary the emigration of our Scottish youth to these and other foreign seminaries, by opening the wells of learning at home; and, in addition to the various schools which were connected with the monasteries, by conferring upon his country the distinction of a university, protected by papal sanction, and devoted to the cultivation of what were then esteemed the higher branches of science and philosophy. The names of the first professors in this early institution have been preserved. The fourth book of the Sentences of Peter Lombard was explained by Laurence of Lindores: a venerable master in theology, whose zeal for the purity of the Catholic faith had lately been displayed in the condemnation of John Resby the Wickliffite at Perth. The importance then attached to an education in the canon law, was shown by its being taught and expounded by four different masters, who conducted their pupils from its simplest elements to its most profound reasonings. These were Richard Cornel archdeacon of Lothian, John Litstar canon of St Andrews, John Shevez official of St Andrews, and William Stevens afterwards bishop of Dumblane; whilst in philosophy and logic the lectures were delivered by John Gill, William Fowlis, and William Crosier. These learned persons commenced their prelections in 1410, immediately after the feast of Pentecost, and continued their labours for two years and a half. But although a communication with Rome had taken place, the establishment was yet unsanctioned by that authority, without which all such institutions were then considered imperfect.*

At length, on the 3d of February, 1413, Henry Ogilvy, master of arts, made his entry into the city, bearing the papal bulls, which endowed the infant seminary with the high and important privileges of a university; and his arrival was welcomed by the ringing of bells from the steeples, and the tumultuous joy of all classes of the inhabitants. On the following day, being Sunday, a solemn convocation of the clergy was held in the refectory; and the papal bulls having been read in presence of the bishop, the chancellor of the university, they proceeded in procession to the high altar, where *Te Deum* was sung by the whole assembly; the bishops, priors, and other dignitaries, being arrayed in their richest canonicals, whilst four hundred clerks, besides novices and lay-brothers, prostrated themselves before the altar, and an immense multitude of spectators, bent their knees in gratitude and adoration. High mass was then celebrated; and

* Fordun a Goodal, vol. ii. pp. 445, 446.

when the service was concluded, the remainder of the day was devoted to mirth and festivity. In the evening, bonfires in the streets, peals of bells, and musical instruments, processions of the clergy, and joyful assemblies of the people, indulging in the song, the dance, and the wine-cup, succeeded to the graver ceremonies of the morning; and the event was welcomed by a boisterous enthusiasm, more befitting the brilliant triumphs of war, than the quiet and noiseless conquests of science and philosophy.

The first act of Henry the Fifth which affected Scotland, seemed to indicate an extremity of suspicion, or a promptitude of hostility, which were equally alarming. His father died on the twentieth of March, and on the succeeding day the king issued orders, that James king of Scotland, and Murdoch earl of Fife, should be committed to the Tower.* It would appear, however, by the result, that this was more a measure of customary precaution, enforced upon all prisoners upon the death of the sovereign to whom their parole had been given, than of any individual hostility. It was believed that the prisoners might avail themselves of a notion, that during the interval between the death of one king and the accession of another, they were not bound by their parole, but free to escape; and this idea is confirmed by the circumstance of their being liberated from the Tower within a short time after their commitment.

Henry's great designs in France rendered it, as we have already remarked, absolutely necessary for him to preserve his pacific relations with Scotland; and, under a wise and patriotic governor, the interval of rest which his reign afforded to that country might

---

* Fœdera, vol. ix. p. 2.

have been improved to the furtherance of its best interests. But Albany, had he even been willing, did not dare to employ in this manner the breathing time allowed him. As a usurper of the supreme power, he was conscious that he continued to hold it only by the sufferance of the nobles; and in return for their support, it became necessary for him to become blind to their excesses, and to pass over their repeated delinquencies. Dilapidation of the lands and revenues of the crown, invasions of the rights of private property, frequent murders arising from the habit of becoming the avengers of their own quarrel, and a reckless sacrifice of the persons and liberties of the lower classes in the community, were crimes of perpetual recurrence, which not only escaped with impunity, but whose authors were often the very dignitaries to whom the prosecution and the punishment belonged; whilst the conduct of the governor himself, in his unremitting efforts for the aggrandizement of his own family, increased the evil by the weight of his example; and the pledge which it seemed to furnish that no change for the better would be speedily attempted.

During the few remaining years of Albany's administration, two objects are seen to be constantly kept in view: the restoration of his son, Murdoch Stewart, and the retention of his sovereign, James the First, in captivity; and in both, his intrigues were successful. It was impossible for him, indeed, so effectually to keep down the hereditary animosity between the two nations, as to prevent it from breaking forth in Border inroads and insulated acts of hostility; but a constant succession of short truces, and a determination to discourage every measure which might have the effect of again plunging the country into war, succeeded in conciliating the English king, and rendering him willing to agree to the return of his son to Scotland. In consequence of this an exchange was negotiated: young Henry Percy, the son of the illustrious Hotspur, who, since the rebellion and death of his grandfather the Earl of Northumberland, had remained in Scotland, returned to England, and was reinstated in his honours; whilst Murdoch Stewart was finally liberated from his captivity, and restored to the desires rather of his father than of his country. It was soon, however, discovered that his character was of that unambitious and feeble kind, which unfitted him for the purposes which had made his return so anxiously expected by the governor.

In his attempts to accomplish his second object, that of detaining his sovereign a prisoner in England, Albany experienced more serious difficulties. James's character had now begun to develop those great qualities, which during his future reign so highly distinguished him. The constant intercourse with the court of Henry the Fourth, which was permitted to Scottish subjects, had enabled many of his nobility to become acquainted with their youthful sovereign; these persons he found means to attach to his interest; and, upon their return, they employed their utmost efforts to traverse the designs of Albany. Owing to their influence, a negotiation for his return to his dominions took place in 1416, by the terms of which the royal captive was to be permitted to remain for a certain time in Scotland, upon his leaving in the hands of the English king a sufficient number of hostages to secure the payment of a hundred thousand marks, in the event of his not delivering himself within the stipulated period.* To the Bishop of Durham, and the

* Rymer, Fœdera, vol. ix. pp. 341, 417.

Earls of Northumberland and Westmoreland, was intrusted the task of receiving the oaths of the Scottish king and his hostages; whilst the treaty had been so far successful, that letters of safe conduct were granted to the Bishops of St Andrews and Glasgow, the Earls of Crawford, Douglas, and Mar, Murdoch Stewart, Albany's eldest son, and John his brother, Earl of Buchan, to whom the final adjustment was to be committed. But from what cause cannot now be discovered, the treaty, when on the eve of being concluded, mysteriously broke off. Whether it was owing to the intrigues of the governor, or the jealousy of Scottish influence in the affairs of France, Henry became suddenly cool, and interrupted the negotiation, so that the unfortunate prince saw himself at one moment on the eve of regaining his liberty, and being restored to the kingdom which was his rightful inheritance, and the next remanded back to his captivity, and condemned to the misery of that protracted hope which sickens the heart. Are we to wonder that his resentment against the man whose base and selfish intrigues he well knew to be the cause of the failure of the negotiation, should have assumed a strength and a violence which, at a future period, involved not only himself but his whole race in utter ruin?

In the meantime, however, the power of the state was fixed too firmly in the hands of Albany for the friends of the young king to defeat his schemes; and as the governor began to suspect that a continuance of peace encouraged intrigues for the restoration of James and his own deposition, he determined, as soon as the last short truce had expired, not only to invade England, but to send over an auxiliary force to the assistance of France. The object of all this was apparent:

a war gave immediate employment to the restless spirits of the nobility; it at once interrupted their intercourse with their captive sovereign; it necessarily incensed the English monarch; put an end to that kind and conciliatory spirit with which he had conducted his correspondence with that country; and rendered it almost certain that he would retain the royal captive in his hands.

The baseness of Albany in pursuing this line of policy cannot be too severely condemned. If ever there was a period in which Scotland could have enjoyed peace with security and with advantage, it was the present. The principles upon which Henry the Fifth acted with regard to that country were those of perfect honour and good faith. All those ideas of conquest, so long and so fondly cherished by the English kings since the days of Edward the First, had been renounced, and the integrity and independence of the kingdom completely acknowledged. In this respect, the reigns of Edward the Third and Henry the Fifth offer as striking a contrast in the conduct pursued by these two monarchs towards Scotland, as they present a brilliant parallel in their ambitious attacks upon France. The grasping and gigantic ambition of Edward the Third was determined to achieve the conquest of both countries, and it must be allowed that he pursued his object with great political ability; but his failure in this scheme, and the unsuccessful result of the last invasion by Henry the Fourth, appear to have convinced his warlike son that two such mighty designs were incompatible, and that one of the first steps towards ultimate success in his French war must be the complete restoration of amity with Scotland.

It was now, therefore, in the power of that country

to enjoy a permanent peace, established on the basis of independence. The King of England was ready to deliver to her a youthful sovereign of great talents and energy, who, although a captive, had been educated at his father's court with a liberality which had opened to him every avenue to knowledge; and under such a reign, what might not have been anticipated, in the revival of good order, the due execution of the laws, the progress of commerce and manufactures, the softening the harshness and tyranny of the feudal aristocracy, and the gradual amelioration of the middle and lower classes of the community? Yet Albany hesitated not to sacrifice all this fair prospect of national felicity to his individual ambition; and once more plunged the country into war, for the single purpose of detaining his sovereign in captivity, and transferring the power which he had so long usurped into the hands of his son. For a while he succeeded; but he little anticipated the dreadful reckoning to which those who now shared his guilt and his triumph were so soon to be called.

His talents for war, however, were of a very inferior description. An expedition which he had meditated against England in a former year, in which it was commonly reported that he was to besiege Berwick at the head of an army of sixty thousand men, and that the cannon and warlike machines to be employed in the enterprise had already been shipped on board the fleet, concluded in nothing, for neither army nor artillery ever appeared before Berwick.* Nor was his second invasion much more successful. He laid siege indeed to Roxburgh, and the miners had commenced their operations, when news was brought to

* Walsingham, p. 399. Fordun a Goodal, vol. ii. p. 449.

his camp, that the Duke of Bedford, to whom Henry, during his absence in France, had intrusted the protection of the Borders, was advancing, by rapid marches, at the head of an army of forty thousand men. Albany had foolishly imagined that the whole disposable force of England was then in France with the king; but, on discovering his mistake, he precipitately abandoned the siege; and, without having achieved anything in the least degree correspondent to his great preparations, retreated into Scotland. The invasion, from its inglorious progress and termination, was long remembered in the country by the contemptuous appellation of "The Foul Raid."*

But if the war was carried on in this feeble manner by Albany, the English cannot be accused of any such inglorious inactivity. On the contrary, Henry had left behind him as guardians of the marches, some of his bravest and most experienced leaders; and amongst these, Sir Robert Umfraville governor of Berwick, eager to emulate the exploits of his countrymen in France, invaded Scotland by the east marches, and committed dreadful havoc and devastation. The whole country was reduced into one wide field of desolation, and the rich Border towns of Hawick, Selkirk, Jedburgh, Lauder, Dunbar, with the numerous villages, hamlets, and granges of Teviotdale and Liddesdale, were burnt to the ground; whilst the solitary success upon the part of Scotland seems to have been the storming of Wark castle by William Haliburton, which, however, was soon afterwards retaken by Sir Robert Ogle, and the whole of the Scottish garrison put to the sword.†

* Rymer, Fœdera, vol. ix. p. 307. A. D. 1415.
† Fordun a Goodal, vol. ii. p. 458. Hardyng's Chronicle, p. 382.

It was not long after this that the Dauphin despatched the Duke of Vendome on an embassy to the Scottish court. Its object was to request assistance against the English; and a parliament having been immediately assembled, it was determined by the governor to send into France a large auxiliary force, under the conduct of his second son, Sir John Stewart earl of Buchan, and the Earl of Wigtown. The vessels for the transport of these troops were to be furnished by France; and the King of Castile, with the Infanta of Arragon, who were in alliance with the Scots, had promised to fit out forty ships for the emergency. Alarmed at a resolution which might produce so serious a diversion in favour of his enemies, Henry instantly despatched his letters to his brother the Duke of Bedford, on whom, during his absence in France, he had devolved the government, directing him to seize and press into his service, in the various seaports where they could be found, a sufficient number of ships and galleons, to be armed and victualled with all possible despatch, for the purpose of intercepting the Scottish auxiliaries; but the command was either disregarded, or came too late; for an army of seven thousand troops, amongst whom were the flower of the Scottish nobles, were safely landed in France, and were destined to distinguish themselves in a signal manner in their operations against the English.*

For a year, however, they lay inactive, and during this period important changes took place in Scotland. Albany the governor, at the advanced age of eighty, died at the palace of Stirling, on the 3d of September, 1419. If we include the period of his management of the state under his father and brother, he may be said

* Extracta ex Chronicis Scotiæ, MS. p. 262. See Illustrations, D.

to have governed Scotland for thirty-four years; but his actual regency, from the death of Robert the Third to his own decease, did not exceed fourteen years.* So effectually had he secured the interest of the nobility, that his son succeeded, without opposition, to the power which his father had so ably and artfully consolidated. No meeting of the parliament, or of any council of the nobility, appears to have taken place; and the silent assumption of the authority and name of governor by Duke Murdoch, during the continued captivity of the king, was nothing else than a bold act of treason.† It was soon apparent, however, that the dangerous elevation was rather thrust upon him by his party than chosen by himself; and that he possessed neither the talents nor the inclination to carry on that system of usurpation, of which his father had raised the superstructure, and no doubt flattered himself that he had secured the foundations. Within four years, under the weak, gentle, and vacillating administration of Murdoch, it crumbled away, and gave place to a state of rude and unlicensed anarchy. The nobility, although caressed and flattered by Albany, who, in his desire to attain popularity, had divided amongst them the spoils of the crown lands, and permitted an unsafe increase of individual power, had yet been partially kept within the limits of authority; and if the laws were not conscientiously administered, they were not openly outraged. But under the son all became, within a short time, one scene of rude unlicensed anarchy; and it was evident that, to save the country

---

* Fordun & Goodal, vol. ii. p. 466. Extracta ex Chronicis Scotiæ, p. 263, MS.
† In Macfarlane's Genealogical Collections, MS. vol. i. p. 3, is a precept of sasine by Duke Murdoch to the Laird of Balfour, in which he styles himself "Regni Scotiæ Gubernator."

from ruin, some change must speedily take place. In the meantime, Henry the Fifth, alarmed at the success of the strong auxiliary force which the Earls of Buchan and Wigtown had conducted to France, insisted upon his royal captive James the First accompanying him in his expedition to renew the war in that country, having first entered into an engagement with that prince, by which he promised to permit him to revisit his dominions for a stipulated period, and under the condition of his delivering into the hands of England a sufficient number of hostages for his return.*

Archibald earl of Douglas, the most powerful noble in Scotland, appears at this time to have deeply interested himself in the return of James to his dominions. He engaged to assist Henry in his French war with a body of two hundred knights and squires, and two hundred mounted archers; and that prince probably expected that the Scottish auxiliaries would be induced to detach themselves from the service of the Dauphin, rather than engage in hostilities with their rightful sovereign. According to the English historians, the Scottish king, when requested by Henry to command his subjects on their allegiance to leave the service of France, replied, that as long as he remained a prisoner it neither became him to issue, nor them to obey such an order. But he added, that to win renown as a private knight, and to be instructed in the art of war under so great a captain, was an opportunity he willingly embraced. Of the particulars of his life at this period, no account remains, but there is ample evidence that he was in constant communication with Scotland. His private chaplain William de Mirton, Alexander de Seton lord of Gordon, William Fowlis secretary to

* Rymer. Fœdera, vol. x. pp. 19, 125.

the Earl of Douglas, and in all probability many others, were engaged in secret missions, which informed him of the state of parties in his dominions, of the weak administration of Murdoch, the unlicensed anarchy which prevailed, and the earnest wishes of all good men for the return of their sovereign.*

It was at this crisis, that Henry the Fifth closed his heroic career, happier than Edward the Third in his being spared the mortification of outliving those brilliant conquests, which, in the progress of years were destined to be as effectually torn from the hand of England. The Duke of Bedford, who succeeded to the government of France, and the Duke of Gloucester, who assumed the office of Regent in England, during the minority of Henry the Sixth, appear to have been animated with favourable dispositions towards the Scottish king; and within a few months after the accession of the infant sovereign, a negotiation took place, in which Alexander Seton lord of Gordon, Thomas de Mirton, the chaplain of the Scottish monarch, Sir John Forester, Sir Walter Ogilvy, John de Leith, and William Fowlis, had a meeting with the privy council of England upon the subject of the king's return to his dominions.† It was determined, that on the twelfth of May, 1423, James should be permitted to meet at Pontefract with the Scottish ambassadors, who should be empowered to enter into a negotiation upon this subject with the ambassadors of the King of England; and such a conference having accordingly taken place, the final treaty was concluded at London between the Bishop of Glasgow chancellor of Scotland, the Abbot of Balmerinoch, George Borthwick arch-

---

* Rymer, Fœdera, vol. x. pp. 166, 227. Ibid. pp. 174, 296.
† Ibid. vol. x. p. 266.

deacon of Glasgow, and Patrick Howston licentiate in the laws, ambassadors appointed by the Scottish governor;* and the Bishop of Worcester and Stafford the treasurer of England, William Alnwick keeper of the privy seal, the Lord Cromwell, Sir John Pelham, Robert Waterton, Esq., and John Stokes doctor of laws, commissaries appointed by the English regency.

It will be recollected that James had been seized by the English during the time of truce, and to have insisted on a ransom for a prince, who by the law of nations was not properly a captive, would have been gross injustice. The English commissioners accordingly declared that they should only demand the payment of the expenses of the King of Scotland which had been incurred during the long period of his residence in England; and these they fixed at the sum of forty thousand pounds of good and lawful money of England, to be paid in yearly sums of ten thousand marks, till the whole was discharged. It was determined that the king should not only promise, upon his royal word and oath, to defray this sum, but that certain hostages from the noblest families in the country should be delivered into the hands of the English king, to remain in England at their own expense till the whole sum was paid; and that, for further security, a separate obligation should be given by the four principal towns of Edinburgh, Perth, Dundee, and Aberdeen,† by which they promised to defray the sum to the English treasury, in the event of its not being paid by their own sovereign.

In addition to this, the ambassadors of both countries were empowered to treat of a marriage between

* Rymer, Fœdera, vol. x. p. 298. The commission by the governor is dated Inverkeithing, August 19, 1423.
† Ibid. vol. x. p. 303.

the Scottish king and some English lady of noble birth; and as James, during his captivity, had fallen in love with the daughter of the Earl of Somerset, a lady of royal descent by both parents, and of great beauty and accomplishments, this part of their negotiation was without difficulty concluded. Johanna Beaufort had already given her heart to the royal captive; and the marriage was concluded with the customary feudal pomp in the church of St Mary Overy, in Southwark,* after which the feast was held in the palace of her uncle, the famous Cardinal Beaufort, a man of vast wealth and equal ambition.† Next day, James received as the dower of his wife, a relaxation from the payment of ten thousand marks of the original sum which had been agreed on.‡ A truce of seven years was concluded; and, accompanied by his queen and a brilliant cortege of the English nobility, to whom he had endeared himself by his graceful manners and deportment, he set out for his own dominions. At Durham, he was met by the Earls of Lennox, Wigtown, Moray, Crawford, March, Orkney, Angus, and Strathern, with the Constable and Marshal of Scotland, and a train of the highest barons and gentry of his dominions, amounting altogether to about three hundred persons; from whom a band of twenty-eight hostages were selected, comprehending some of the most noble and opulent persons in the country. In the schedule containing their names, the annual rent of their estates is also set down, which renders it a document of much interest, as illustrating the wealth and comparative influence of the Scottish aristocracy.§

* Rymer, Fœdera, vol. x. pp. 321, 323.
† Gough's Sepulchral Monuments, vol. ii. p. 127, plate 41, p. 148. Dugdale's Baronage, vol. ii. p. 122.
‡ Rymer, Fœdera, vol. x. p. 323, dated 12th Feb. 1424.
§ Ibid. vol. x. pp. 307, 309. See Illustrations, E.

From Durham, James, still surrounded by his nobles, and attended by the Earl of Northumberland, the sheriff of that county, and an escort under Sir Robert Umfraville, Sir William Heron, and Sir Robert Ogle, proceeded in his joyful progress, and halted, on reaching the Abbey of Melrose, for the purpose of fulfilling the obligation which bound him to confirm the treaty by his royal oath, upon the Holy Gospels, within four days after his entry into his own dominions.*

He was received by all classes of his subjects with expressions of tumultuous joy and undissembled affection; and the regent hastened to resign the government into the hands of a prince who was in every way worthy of the crown.

* Rymer, Fœdera, vol. x. pp. 333, 343. Dated April 5, 1425.

CHAP. III.

JAMES THE FIRST.

1424—1437.

CONTEMPORARY PRINCES.

King of England.	King of France.	Popes.
Henry VI.	Charles VII.	Martin V. Eugene IV.

In James the First, Scotland was at length destined to receive a sovereign of no common character and endowments. We have seen, that when a boy of fourteen, he was seized by the English, and from that time till his return in 1424, twenty years of his life embracing the period of all others the most important and decisive in the formation of future character, had been passed in captivity. If unjust in his detention, Henry the Fourth appears to have been anxious to compensate for his infringement of the law of nations by the care which he bestowed upon the education of the youthful monarch. He was instructed in all the warlike exercises, and in the high-bred observances and polished manners of the school of chivalry; he was generously provided with masters in the various arts and sciences; and as it was the era of the revival of learning in England, the age especially of the rise of poetic literature in Chaucer and Gower, his mind and imagination became deeply infected with a passion for those elegant pursuits. But James, during his long captivity, enjoyed far higher advantages. He was able to study the arts of government, to make his observations on the mode of administering justice in England, and to extract wisdom and experience from a personal acquaintance with the disputes between the sovereign and his nobility; whilst in the friendship and confidence with which he appears to have been uniformly treated by Henry the Fifth, who made him the partner of his campaigns in France, he became acquainted with the politics of both countries, received his education in the art of war from one of the greatest captains whom it has produced; and, from his not being personally engaged, had leisure to avail himself to the utmost of the opportunities which his peculiar situation presented. There were other changes also, which were then gradually beginning to manifest themselves in the political condition of the two countries, which, to his acute and discerning mind, must necessarily have presented a subject of thought and speculation—I mean the repeated risings of the commons against the intolerable tyranny of the feudal nobility, and the increased wealth and consequence of the middle classes of the state; events which, in the moral history of those times, are of deep interest and importance, and of which the future monarch of Scotland was a personal observer. The school, therefore, in which James was educated seems to have been eminently qualified to produce a wise and excellent king; and the history of his reign corroborates this observation.

On entering his kingdom, James proceeded to Edinburgh, where he held the festival of Easter; and on the twenty-first of May he and his queen were solemnly crowned in the Abbey church of Scone.

According to an ancient hereditary right, the king was placed in the royal seat by the late governor, Murdoch duke of Albany and earl of Fife, whilst Henry Wardlaw bishop of St Andrews, the same faithful prelate to whom the charge of his early education had been committed, anointed his royal master, and placed the crown upon his head, amid a crowded assembly of the nobility and clergy, and the shouts and rejoicings of the people. The king then proceeded to bestow the honour of knighthood upon Alexander Stewart, the younger son of the Duke of Albany; upon the Earls of March, Angus, and Crawford; William Hay of Errol constable of Scotland, John Scrymgeour constable of Dundee, Alexander Seton of Gordon, and eighteen others of the principal nobility and barons;* after which he convoked his parliament on the twenty-sixth of May, and proceeded to the arduous task of inquiring into the abuses of the government, and adopting measures for their reformation.

Hitherto James had been but imperfectly informed regarding the extent to which the government of Albany and his feeble successor had promoted, or permitted, the grossest injustice and the most unlicensed peculation. He had probably suspected that the picture had been exaggerated; and with that deliberate policy which constituted a striking part of his character, he resolved to conduct his investigations in person, before he gave the slightest hint of his ultimate intentions. It is said, indeed, that when he first entered the kingdom, the dreadful description given by one of his nobles of the unbridled licentiousness and contempt of the laws which everywhere prevailed,

* Extracta ex Chronicis Scotiæ, MS. fol. 269, 270. Fordun a Goodal, vol. ii. p. 474.

threw him for a moment off his guard. "Let God but grant me life," cried he, with a loud voice, "and there shall not be a spot in my dominions where the key shall not keep the castle, and the furze-bush the cow, though I myself should lead the life of a dog to accomplish it!"* This, however, was probably spoken in confidence, for the object of the king was to inform himself of the exact condition of his dominions without exciting alarm, or raising a suspicion which might foster opposition and induce concealment. The very persons who sat in this parliament, and through whose assistance the investigation must be conducted, were themselves the worst defaulters; an imprudent word escaping him, and much more a sudden imprisonment or a hasty, perhaps an unsuccessful, attempt at impeachment, would have been the signal for the nobles to fly to their estates and shut themselves up in their feudal castles, where they could have defied every effort of the king to apprehend them; and in this way all his plans might have been defeated or indefinitely protracted, and the country plunged into something approaching to a civil war.

The three Estates of the realm having been assembled, certain persons were elected for the determination of the "Articles" to be proposed to them by the king, leave of returning home being given to the other members of the parliament. Committees of parliament had already been introduced by David the Second, on the ground of general convenience, and the anxiety of the barons and landholders to be present on their estates during the time of harvest.† From this period to the present time, embracing an interval of more

---
* Fordun & Goodal, vol. ii. p. 511.
† Acts of the Parliament of Scotland, sub anno 1424, History, supra, vol. II. p. 234.

than half a century, the destruction of the records of the parliaments of Robert the Second and Third, and of the government of Albany and his son, renders it impossible to trace the progress of this important change, by which we now find the Lords of the Articles "*certe persone ad articulos*," an acknowledged institution, in the room of the parliamentary committees of David the Second; but it is probable that the king availed himself of this privilege to form a small body of the nobility, clergy, and burgesses, of whose fidelity he was secure, and who lent him their assistance in the difficult task upon which he now engaged.

The parliament opened with an enactment, commanding all men to honour the Church, declaring that its ministers should enjoy, in all things, their ancient freedom and established privileges, and that no person should dare to hinder the clergy from granting leases of their lands or tithes, under the spiritual censures commonly incurred by such prevention. A proclamation followed, directed against the prevalence of private war and feuds amongst the nobility, enjoining the king's subjects to maintain thenceforward a firm peace throughout the realm, and discharging all barons, under the highest pains of the law, from " moving or making war against each other; from riding through the country with a more numerous following of horse than properly belonged to their estate, or for which, in their progress, due payment was not made to the king's lieges and hostellars. All such riders or gangars," upon complaint being made, were to be apprehended by the officers of the lands where the trespass had been committed, and kept in sure custody till the king declared his pleasure regarding them; and in order to the due execution of this and other enactments, it was ordained that officers and ministers of the laws should be appointed generally throughout the realm, whose personal estate must be of wealth and sufficiency enough to be proceeded against, in the event of malversation, and from whose vigour and ability the "commons of the land" should be certain of receiving justice.*

The penalty of rebellion or treason against the king's person was declared to be the forfeiture of life, lands, and goods, whilst all friends or supporters of rebels were to be punished according to the pleasure of the sovereign. The enactments which followed regarding those troops of sturdy mendicants, who traversed the country, extorting charity where it was not speedily bestowed, present us with some curious illustrations of the manners of the times. The king commanded that no companies of such loose and unlicensed persons should be permitted to beg or insist on quarters from any husbandman or churchman, sojourning in the abbeys or on the farm granges, and devouring the wealth of the country. An exception was made in favour of "royal beggars," with regard to whom it is declared, that the king had agreed, by advice of his parliament, that no beggars or "thiggars" be permitted to beg, either in the burgh or throughout the country, between the ages of fourteen and threescore and ten years, unless it be first ascertained by the council of the burgh that they are incapacitated from supporting themselves in any other way. It was directed that they who were thus permitted to support themselves should wear a certain token, to be furnished them by the sheriff, or the alderman and bailies; and that proclamation be made, that all beggars having no such

---

* Acts of the Parliament of Scotland, vol. ii. p. 2. Statutes of the Realm, Rich. II., vol. ii. pp. 9, 10. Statutes against Bonds or Confederacies.

tokens, do immediately betake themselves to such trades as may enable them to win their own living, under the penalty of burning on the cheek and banishment from the country.* It is curious to discern, in this primitive legislative enactment, the first institution of the king's blue coats or bedesmen, a venerable order of privileged mendicants, whose existence has only expired within these few years.

During the weak administration of Robert the Second and Third, and still more under the unprincipled government of Albany, the "great customs," or the duties levied throughout the realm upon the exportation or importation of merchandise, had been diminished by various grants to private persons; and, in addition to this, the crown lands had been shamelessly alienated and dilapidated. It was declared by the parliament, that in all time coming the great customs should remain in the hands of the king for the support of his royal estate, and that all persons who made any claim upon such customs, should produce to the sovereign the deed or grant upon which such a demand was maintained.† With regard to the lands and rents which were formerly in possession of the ancestors of the king, it was provided, that special directions should be given to the different sheriffs throughout the realm, to make inquiries of the oldest and worthiest officers within their sheriffdom, as to the particular lands or annual rents which belonged to the king, or in former times were in the hands of his royal predecessors, David the Second, Robert the Second, and Robert the Third. In these returns by the sheriffs, the names of the present possessors of

* Acts of the Parliament of Scotland, vol. ii. pp. 2, 8.
† See a statute of Richard the Second on the same subject, pp. 41, 42, vol. ii. Statutes of the Realm.

these lands were directed to be included, and an inquest was then to be summoned, who, after having examined the proper evidence, were enjoined to return a verdict under their seals, adjudging the property to belong to the crown. To facilitate such measures, it was declared that the king may summon, according to his free will and pleasure, his various tenants and vassals to exhibit their charters and holdings, in order to discover the exact extent of their property.*

The next enactment related to a very important subject, the payment of the fifty thousand marks which were due to England, and the deliverance of the hostages who were detained in security. Upon this subject it was ordained, that a specific sum should be raised upon the whole lands of the kingdom, including regality lands as well as others, as it would be grievous and heavy upon the commons to raise the whole "*finance*" at once. For this purpose, an aid or donative, expressed in the statute by the old Saxon word a *zelde*, and amounting to the sum of twelve pennies in every pound, was directed to be raised upon all rents, lands, and goods, belonging to lords and barons within their domains, including both corn and cattle. From this valuation, however, all riding horses, draught oxen, and household utensils, were excepted. The burgesses, in like manner, were directed to contribute their share out of their goods and rents. In addition to this donative, the parliament determined that certain taxes should also be raised upon the cattle and the corn, the particulars of which were minutely detailed in the record. As to the tax upon all grain which was then housed, excepting the purveyance of the lords and barons for their own consumption, it was ordained that the boll

* Acts of the Parliament of Scotland, vol. ii. p. 4.

of wheat should pay two shillings; the boll of rye, bear, and pease, sixteen pence; and the boll of oats six pence. With regard to the green corn, all the standing crops were to remain untaxed until brought into the barn. As to cattle, it was determined that a cow and her calf, or quey of two years old, should pay six shillings and eight pence; a draught ox the same; every wedder and ewe, each at the rate of twelve pennies; every goat, gymmer, and dynmont, the same; each wild mare, with her colt of three year old, ten shillings; and lastly, every colt of three years and upwards, a mark.*

For the purpose of the just collection of this tax throughout the country, it was directed that every sheriff should within his own sheriffdom summon the barons and freeholders of the king, and by their advice select certain honest and discreet men, who should be ready to abide upon all occasions the scrutiny of the sovereign as to their faithful discharge of their office in the taxation; and to whom the task of making an "Extent," as it was technically called, or, in other words, of drawing up an exact inventory of the property of the country, should be committed. These officers, or "*extentours,*" are directed to be sworn as to the faithful execution of their office, before the barons of the sheriffdom; they are commanded, in order to insure a more complete investigation, to take with them the parish priest, who is to be enjoined by his bishop to inform them faithfully of all the goods in the parish; and having done so, they are then to mark down the extent in a book furnished for the purpose, in which the special names of every town in the kingdom, and of every person dwelling therein, with the exact amount of their property, was to be particularly enumerated;

* Acts of the Parliament of Scotland, p. 4.

all which books were to be delivered into the hands of the king's auditors at Perth, upon the twelfth day of July next. It is deeply to be regretted, that none of these records of the property of the kingdom have reached our time.

It was further declared upon this important subject, that all the lands of the kingdom should be taxed according to their present value, and that the tax upon all goods and gear should be paid in money of the like value with the coin then current in the realm. It was specially enjoined, that no one in the kingdom, whether he be of the rank of clerk, baron, or burgess, should be excepted from payment of this tax, and that all should have the money ready to be delivered within fifteen days after the taxation had been struck, the officers employed in its collection being empowered, upon failure, to take payment in kind, a cow being estimated at five shillings; a ewe or wedder, at twelve pence; a goat, gymmer, or dynmont, at eight pence; a three-year old colt at a mark; a wild mare and her foal at ten shillings; a boll of wheat at twelve pennies; of rye, bear, and pease, at eight pence; and of oats, at three pence.* If the lord of the land, where such payment in kind had been taken, chose to advance the sum for his tenants, the sheriffs were commanded to deliver the goods to him; if not, they were to be sold at the next market cross, or sent to the king.

It was next determined by the parliament, that the prelates should tax their rents and kirks in the same manner, and at the same rate, as the baron's land; every bishop in each deanery of his diocese being directed to cause his official and dean to summon all his tenants and freeholders before him, and to select tax-

* Acts of the Parliament of Scotland, vol. ii. p. 4.

gatherers, whose duty it was to "extend" the ecclesiastical lands in the same way as the rest of the property of the country; it being provided, in every instance where a churchman paid the whole value of his benefice, that the fruits of his kirk lands should next year be free from all imposition or exaction. In the taxation of the rents and goods of the burgesses, the sheriff was directed to send a superintendant to see that the tax-gatherers, who were chosen by the aldermen and bailies, executed their duty faithfully and truly; and it was directed, that the salary and expenses of the various collectors in baronies, burghs, or church lands, should be respectively determined by the sheriff, aldermen, and prelates, and deducted from the whole amount of the tax, when it was given into the hands of the "auditors" appointed by the king to receive the gross sum, on the twelfth day of July at Perth. The auditors appointed were the Bishops of Dunkeld and Dunblane, the Abbots of Balmerinoch and St Colm's Inch, Mr John Scheves, the Earl of Athole, Sir Patrick Dunbar, William Borthwick, Patrick Ogilvy, James Douglas of Balveny, and William Erskine of Kinnoul. I have been anxious to give the entire details of this scheme of taxation, as it furnishes us with many interesting facts illustrative of the state of property in the country at this early period of its history, and as it is not to be found in the ordinary edition of the Statutes of James the First.

After some severe enactments against the slayers of salmon within the forbidden time, which a posterior statute informs us was in the interval between the feast of the Assumption of Our Lady and the feast of St Andrew in the winter, it was declared, that all *yairs and cruves*, (meaning certain mechanical contrivances for the taking of fish by means of wattled traps placed between two walls in the stream of the river,) which have been built in fresh waters where the sea ebbs and flows, should be put down for three years, on account of the destruction of the spawn, or young fry, which they necessarily occasion. This regulation was commanded to be peremptorily enforced, even by those whose charters included a right of "cruve fishing," under the penalty of a hundred shillings; and the ancient regulation regarding the removal of the cruve on Saturday night, known by the name of "Saturday's Slap," as well as the rules which determined the statutory width of the "*hecks*," or wattled interstices, were enjoined to be strictly observed.* The extent to which the fisheries had been carried in Scotland, and the object which they formed even to the foreign fish-curers, appeared in the statutory provisions regarding the royal custom imposed upon all herring taken within the realm, being one penny upon every thousand fresh herring sold in the market. Upon every last of herring which were taken by Scottish fishermen and barrelled, a duty of four shillings, and on every last taken by strangers, a duty of six shillings was imposed; whilst, from every thousand red herrings made within the kingdom, a duty of four pennies was to be exacted.†

With regard to mines of gold or silver it was provided, that wherever such have been discovered within the lands of any lord or baron, if it can be proved that three half pennies of silver can be produced out of the pound of lead, the mine should, according to the established practice of other realms, belong to the king, a

---

* Acts of the Parliament of Scotland, vol. ii. p. 5.
† A last, according to Skene, contains twelve great barrels, or fourteen smaller barrels, pp. 139, 140.

species of property from which there is no evidence that any substantial wealth ever flowed into the royal exchequer. It was enacted, that no gold or silver should be permitted to be carried forth of the realm, except it pay a duty of forty pence upon every pound exported: and in the event of any attempt to contravene this provision, the defaulter was to forfeit the whole gold or silver, and to pay a fine of forty-one pennies to the king. It was moreover provided, that in every instance where merchant strangers have disposed of their goods for money, they should either expend the same in the purchase of Scottish merchandise, or in the payment of their personal expenses, for proof of which, they must bring the evidence of the host of the inn where they made their abode; or, if they wished to carry it out of the realm, they were to pay the duty upon exportation.*
It was determined, that the money in present circulation throughout the realm, which had been greatly depreciated from the original standard, should be called in, and a new coinage issued of like weight and fineness with the money of England.

It having been found that a considerable trade had been carried on in the sale and exportation of oxen, sheep and horses, it was provided, in the same spirit of unenlightened policy which distinguished the whole body of the statutes relative to the commerce of the country, that upon every pound of the price received in such transactions, a duty of twelve pennies should be levied by the king. Upon the same erroneous principle, so soon as it was discovered that a considerable trade was carried on in the exportation of the skins of

---

* In England, by a statute of Henry IV., merchant strangers were permitted to export one-half of the money received for their manufactures. Statutes of the Realm, vol. ii. p. 122.

harts and hinds, of martins, fumarts, rabbits, does, roes, otters, and foxes, it was provided, that a check should be given to this flourishing branch of trade, by imposing a certain tax or custom upon each of such commodities, in the event of their being purchased for exportation.* It appears that many abuses had crept into the ecclesiastical state of the country by the frequent purchase of pensions from the pope, against which practices a special statute was directed, declaring, that in all time coming, no person should purchase any pension payable out of any benefice, religious or secular, under the penalty of forfeiting the same to the crown; and that no clerk, without an express license from the king, should either himself pass over the sea, or send procurators for him upon any foreign errand.

A singular and primitive enactment followed regarding rookeries; in which, after a preamble stating the mischief to the corn which was occasioned by rooks building in the trees of kirkyards and orchards, it was provided, that the proprietors of such trees should, by every method in their power, prevent the birds from building; and, if this cannot be accomplished, that they at least take special care that the young rooks, or branchers, were not suffered to take wing, under the penalty, that all trees upon which the nests are found at Beltane, and from which it can be established, by good evidence, that the young birds have escaped, should be forfeited to the crown, and forthwith cut down, unless redeemed by the proprietor. No man, under a penalty of forty shillings, was to burn muirs from the month of March till the corn be cut down; and if any such defaulter was unable to raise the sum, he was commanded to be imprisoned for forty days.

* Acts of the Parliament of Scotland, vol. ii. p. 6.

The great superiority of the English archers has been frequently pointed out in the course of this history; and the importance of introducing a more frequent practice of the long-bow appears to have impressed itself deeply on the mind of the king, who had the best opportunity, under Henry the Fifth, of witnessing its destructive effects during his French campaigns. It was accordingly provided, that all the male subjects of the realm, after reaching the age of twelve years, "busk them to be archers;" that is, provide themselves with the usual arms of an archer; and that upon every ten-pound land bow-marks be constructed, especially in the vicinity of parish churches, where the people may practice archery, and, at the least, shoot thrice about, under the penalty of paying a wedder to the lord of the land, in the event of neglecting the injunction. To give further encouragement to archery, the pastime of foot-ball, which appears to have been a favourite national game in Scotland, was forbidden, under a severe penalty, in order that the common people might give the whole of their leisure time to the acquisition of a just eye and a steady hand, in the use of the long-bow.*

Such is an abstract of the statutory regulations of the first parliament of James; and it is evident that, making allowance for the different circumstances in which the two countries were situated, the most useful provisions, as well as those which imply the deepest ignorance of the true principles of commercial policy, were borrowed from England. Those, for instance, which imposed a penalty upon the exportation of sheep, horses, and cattle; which implied so deep a jealousy of the gold and silver being carried out of the realm; which

* Acts of the Parliament of Scotland, vol. ii. pp. 5, 6.

forbade the riding armed, or with too formidable a band of servants; which encouraged archery; which related to mendicants and vagabonds; to the duties and qualifications of bailies and magistrates; which extended to the privileges of the church, and forbade the interference of the pope with the benefices of the realm, are, with a few changes, to be found amongst the statutes of Richard the Second, and the fourth and fifth Henries; and prove that the king, during his long detention in England, had made himself intimately acquainted with the legislative policy of that kingdom.

It admits of little doubt, that during the sitting of this parliament, James was secretly preparing for those determined measures, by which, eight months afterwards, he effectually crushed the family of Albany, and compelled the fierce nobility, who had so long despised all restraint, to respect the authority of the laws, and tremble before the power of the crown. But in these projects it was necessary to proceed with extreme caution; and the institution of the Lords of the Articles seems to have furnished the king with an instrument well suited for the purpose he had in view, which, without creating alarm, enabled him gradually to mature his plans, and conduct them to a successful issue. Who were the persons selected for this committee it is, unfortunately, impossible to discover; but we may be certain that they enjoyed the confidence of the king, and were prepared to support him to the utmost of their power. With them, after the return of the rest of the most powerful lords and barons to their estates, who, from the warmth and cordiality with which they were received, had little suspicion of the secret measures meditated against them, James prepared and passed into laws many statutes, which, from the proud spirit of his nobles, he knew they would not hesitate to despise and disobey, and thus furnish him with an opportunity to bring the offenders within the power of the laws, which he had determined to enforce to the utmost rigour against them. Amongst the statutes which were evidently designed to be the future means of coercing his nobility, those which regarded the resumption of the lands of the crown, and the exhibition of the charters by which their estates were held, may be at once recognised; and to these may be added the enactments against the numerous assemblies of armed vassals with which the feudal nobility of the time were accustomed to traverse the country, and bid defiance to the local magistracy.

The loss of many original records, which might have thrown some certain light upon this interesting portion of our history, renders it impossible to trace the various links in the projects of the king. Some prominent facts alone remain; yet from these it is not difficult to discover at least the outline of his proceedings.

He suffered eight months to expire before he convoked that celebrated parliament at Perth, at which he had secretly resolved to exhibit his own strength, and to inflict a signal vengeance upon the powerful family of Albany. During this interval, he appears to have gained to his party the whole influence of the clergy, and to have quietly consolidated his own power amongst a portion of the barons. The Earl of Mar, and his son Sir Thomas Stewart, William Lauder bishop of Glasgow and Chancellor, Sir Walter Ogilvy the Treasurer, John Cameron provost of the Collegiate Church of Lincluden and private secretary to the king, Sir John Forester of Corstorphine chamberlain, Sir John Stewart and Sir Robert Lauder of the Bass, Thomas Somerville of Carnwath, and Alexander Levingston of Callendar, members of the king's council, were, in all probability, the only persons whom James admitted to his confidence, and intrusted with the execution of his designs;* whilst the utmost secrecy appears to have been observed with regard to his ultimate purposes.

Meanwhile Duke Murdoch and his sons, with the Earls of Douglas, March, and Angus, and the most powerful of the nobility, had separated without any suspicion of the blow which was meditated against them; and, once more settled on their own estates, and surrounded by their feudal retainers, soon forgot the statutes which had been so lately enacted; and with that spirit of fierce independence which had been nourished under the government of Albany and his son, dreamt little of producing their charters or giving up the crown lands or rents which they had received, of abridging their feudal state or dismissing their armed followers, or, indeed, of yielding obedience to any part of the laws which interfered with their individual importance and authority. They considered the statutes in precisely the same light in which there is reason to believe all parliamentary enactments had been regarded in Scotland for a long period before this: as mandates to be obeyed by the lower orders, under the strictest exactions of penalty and forfeitures; and to be attended to by the great and the powerful, provided they suited their own convenience, and did not offer any great violence to their feelings of pride or their possession of power. The weak and feeble government of Robert the Second and Third, with the indulgence to which

* See Hay's MS. Collection of Diplomata, vol. iii. p. 98, for a deed dated 30th of December, 1424, which gives the members of the king's privy council.

the aristocracy were accustomed under Albany, had riveted this idea firmly in their minds; and they acted upon it without the suspicion, that a monarch might one day be found not only with sagacity to procure the enactment of laws which should level their independence, but with a determination of character, and a command of means, which should enable him to carry these laws into execution.

On being summoned, therefore, by the king to attend a parliament, to be held at Perth on the twelfth of March, they obeyed without hesitation; and as the first subject which appears to have been brought before the three Estates was the dissemination of the heretical opinions of the Lollards, which began to revive about this time in the country, no alarm was excited, and the business of the parliament proceeded as usual. It was determined that due inquiry should be made by the ministers of the king, whether the statutes passed in his former parliament had been obeyed; and, in the event of its being discovered that they had been disregarded, orders were issued for the punishment of the offenders. All leagues or confederacies amongst the king's lieges were strictly forbidden; all assistance afforded to rebels, all false reports, or "leasing-makings," which tended to create discord between the sovereign and his people, were prohibited under the penalty of forfeiting life and lands; and in every instance where the property of the church was found to have been illegally occupied, restoration was ordered to be made by due process of law.*

The parliament had now continued for eight days, and as yet everything went on without disturbance; but on the ninth an extraordinary scene presented itself. Murdoch, the late governor, with Lord Alexander

* Acts of the Parliament of Scotland, vol. ii. p. 7.

Stewart, his younger son, were suddenly arrested, and immediately afterwards twenty-six of the principal nobles and barons shared the same fate. Amongst these were Archibald earl of Douglas, William Douglas earl of Angus, George Dunbar earl of March, William Hay of Errol constable of Scotland, Scrymgeour constable of Dundee, Alexander Lindesay, Adam Hepburn of Hailes, Thomas Hay of Yester, Herbert Maxwell of Caerlaverock, Alexander Ramsay of Dalhousie, Alan Otterburn secretary to the Duke of Albany, Sir John Montgomery, Sir John Stewart of Dundonald, commonly called the Red Stewart, and thirteen others. During the course of the same year, and a short time previous to this energetic measure, the king had imprisoned Walter, the eldest son of Albany, along with the Earl of Lennox and Sir Robert Graham: a man of a fierce and vindictive disposition, who from that moment vowed the most determined revenge, which he lived to execute in the murder of his sovereign.* The heir of Albany was shut up in the strong castle of the Bass, belonging to Sir Robert Lauder, a firm friend of the king; whilst Graham and Lennox were committed to Dunbar; and the Duke of Albany himself confined in the first instance in the castle of St Andrews, and afterwards transferred to that of Caerlaverock. At the same moment, the king took possession of the castles of Falkland, and of the fortified palace of Doune, the favourite residence of Albany.† Here he found Isabella, the wife of Albany, a daughter of the Earl of Lennox, whom he immediately committed to the castle of Tantallon; and with a success and a rapidity which can only be accounted for by the supposition of the

* Fordun a Hearne, vol. iv. p. 1269.
† Statistical Account of Scotland, vol. xx. pp. 57, 60.

utmost vigour in the execution of his plans, and a strong military power to overawe all opposition, he possessed himself of the strongest fortresses in the country; and, after adjourning the parliament, to meet within the space of two months at Stirling, upon the eighteenth of May,* he proceeded to adopt measures for inflicting a speedy and dreadful revenge upon the most powerful of his opponents.

In the palace of Stirling, on the twenty-fourth of May, a court was held with great pomp and solemnity for the trial of Walter Stewart, the eldest son of the Duke of Albany. The king, sitting on his throne, clothed with the robes and insignia of majesty, with the sceptre in his hand, and wearing the royal crown, presided as supreme judge of his people. The loss of all record of this trial is deeply to be regretted, as it would have thrown light upon an interesting, but obscure portion of our history. We know only from an ancient chronicle that the heir of Albany was tried for robbery, "*de roboria.*" The jury was composed of twenty-one of the principal nobles and barons; and it is a remarkable circumstance, that amongst their names which have been preserved, we find seven of the twenty-six barons whom the king had seized and imprisoned two months before at Perth, when he arrested Albany and his sons. Amongst these seven, were the three most powerful lords in the body of the Scottish aristocracy—the Earls of Douglas, March, and Angus; the rest were Sir John de Montgomery, Gilbert Hay of Errol the constable, Sir Herbert Herries of Terregles, and Sir Robert Cuningham of Kilmaurs.† Others who sat upon this jury

---

* Fordun a Hearne, vol. iv. p. 1270.
† Ibid. pp. 1269, 1270, 1271. See also Extracta ex Chronicis Scotiæ, MS. p. 272.

we know to have been the assured friends of the king, and members of his privy council. These were, Alexander Stewart earl of Mar, Sir John Forester of Corstorphine, Sir Thomas Somerville of Carnwath, and Sir Alexander Levingston of Callendar. It is probable that the seven jurymen above mentioned were persons attached to the party of Albany, and that the intention of the king, in their imprisonment, was to compel them to renounce all idea of supporting him, and to abandon him to his fate. In this result, whatever were the means adopted for its accomplishment, the king succeeded. The trial of Walter Stewart occupied a single day. He was found guilty, and condemned to death. His fate excited a deep feeling of sympathy and compassion in the breasts of the people; for the noble figure and dignified manners of the eldest son of Albany were peculiarly calculated to make him friends amongst the lower classes of the community.

On the following day, Duke Murdoch himself, with his second son Alexander, and his father-in-law the Earl of Lennox were tried before the same jury. What were the crimes alleged against the Earl of Lennox and Alexander Stewart, it is now impossible to determine; but it may be conjectured, on strong grounds, that the usurpation of the government and the assumption of supreme authority during the captivity of the king, offences amounting to high treason, constituted the principal charge against the late regent. His father undoubtedly succeeded to the regency by the determination of the three Estates assembled in parliament; but there is no evidence that any such decision was passed which sanctioned the high station assumed by the son; and if so, every act of his government was an act of treason, upon which the jury could have no difficulty in pronouncing their verdict. Albany was accordingly found guilty; the same sentence was pronounced upon his son, Alexander Stewart; the Earl of Lennox was next condemned; and these three noble persons were publicly executed on that fatal eminence, before the castle of Stirling, known by the name of the Heading Hill. As the condemnation of Walter Stewart had excited unwonted commiseration amongst the people, the spectacle now afforded was calculated to raise that feeling to a still higher pitch of distress and compassion. Albany and his two sons were men of almost gigantic stature,* and of so noble a presence, that it was impossible to look upon them without an involuntary feeling of admiration; whilst the venerable appearance and white hairs of Lennox, who had reached his eightieth year, inspired a sentiment of tenderness and pity, which, even if they admitted the justice of the sentence, was apt to raise in the bosom of the spectators a disposition to condemn the rapid and unrelenting severity with which it was carried into execution. Even in their days of pride and usurpation, the family of Albany had been the favourites of the people. Its founder, the regent, courted popularity; and although a usurper, and stained with murders, seems in a great measure to have gained his end. It is impossible indeed to reconcile the high eulogium of Bower and Winton† with the dark actions of his life; but it is evident, from the tone of these historians, that the severity of James did not carry along with it the feelings of the people. Yet,

---

* Albany and his sons were buried in the church of the Preaching Friars at Stirling, on the south side of the high altar, "figuris et armis eorundem depictis."—Extracta ex Chronicis Scotiæ, MS. p. 272. Fordun a Goodal, vol. ii. p. 483. "Homines giganteæ staturæ."

† Fordun a Hearne, p. 1228. Winton, vol. ii. pp. 419, 420. See Illustrations, F.

looking at the state of things in Scotland, it is easy to understand the object of the king. It was his intention to exhibit to a nation, long accustomed to regard the laws with contempt and the royal authority as a name of empty menace, a memorable example of stern and inflexible justice, and to convince them that a great change had already taken place in the executive part of the government.

With this view another dreadful exhibition followed the execution of the family of Albany. James Stewart, the youngest son of this unfortunate person, was the only member of it who had avoided the arrest of the king, and escaped to the Highlands. Driven to despair, by the ruin which threatened his house, he collected a band of armed freebooters, and, assisted by Finlay bishop of Lismore, and Argyle his father's chaplain, attacked the burgh of Dumbarton, with a fury which nothing could resist. The king's uncle, Sir John of Dundonald, called the Red Stewart, was slain, the town sacked and given to the flames, and thirty men murdered, after which the son of Albany returned to his fastnesses in the north. But so hot was the pursuit which was instituted by the royal vengeance, that he, and the ecclesiastical bandit who accompanied him, were dislodged from their retreats, and compelled to fly to Ireland.* Five of his accomplices, however, were seized, and their execution, which immediately succeeded that of Albany, was unpardonably cruel and disgusting. They were torn to pieces by wild horses, after which their warm and quivering limbs were suspended upon gibbets: a terrible warning to the people of the punishment which awaited those, who imagined

---

* Fordun a Hearne, vol. iv. p. 1270.

that the fidelity which impelled them to execute the commands of their feudal lord, was superior to the ties which bound them to obey the laws of the country.

These executions were followed by the forfeiture to the crown of the immense estates belonging to Albany and to the Earl of Lennox; a seasonable supply of revenue, which, amid the general plunder to which the royal lands had been exposed, was much wanted to support the dignity of the throne, and in the occupation of a considerable portion of which, there is reason to believe, the king only resumed what had formerly belonged to him. With regard to the conduct of the Bishop of Lismore, James appears to have made complaint to the pope, who directed a bull, addressed to the Bishops of St Andrews and Dunblane, by which they were empowered to inquire into the treason of the prelate, and other rebels against the king.*

The remaining barons, who had been imprisoned at the time of Albany's arrest, appear to have been restored to liberty immediately after his execution, and the parliament proceeded to the enactment of several statutes, which exhibit a singular combination of wisdom and ignorance, some being as truly calculated to promote, as others were fitted to retard, the improvement and prosperity of the country. It was ordained, that every man, of such simple estate, as made it reasonable that he should be a labourer or husbandman, should either combine with his neighbour to pay half the expense of an ox and a plough, or dig every day a portion of land seven feet in length and six feet in breadth. In every sheriffdom within the realm, "weaponschawings," or an armed muster of

---

* Innes' MS. Chronology, quoted by Chalmers in his Life of James the First, p. 14, prefixed to the Poetic Remains.

the whole fighting men in the county for the purpose of military exercise and an inspection of their weapons, were appointed to be held four times in the course of the year. Symptoms of the decay of the forest and green wood, or perhaps, more correctly speaking, proofs of the improved attention of the nobles to the enclosure of their parks and the ornamental woods around their castles, are to be discerned in the enactment, which declared it to be a part of the duty of the Justice Clerk to make inquiries regarding those defaulters, who steal green wood, or strip the trees of their bark under cover of night, or break into orchards to purloin the fruit; and provided, that where any man found his stolen woods in other lords' lands, it should be lawful for him on the instant to seize both the goods and the thief, and to have him brought to trial in the court of the baron upon whose lands the crime was committed.*

With regard to the commerce of the country, some regulations were now passed, dictated by the same jealous spirit which has been already remarked as pervading the whole body of our commercial legislation. It was strictly enjoined, that no tallow should be exported out of the country under the penalty of being forfeited to the king; that no horses were to be carried forth of the realm till they were past the age of three years, and that no merchant was to be permitted to pass the sea for the purposes of trade, unless he either possess in property, or at least in commission, three serplaiths of wool, or the value of such in merchandise, to be determined by an inquest of his neighbours, under a penalty of forty-one pounds to the king, if found guilty of disobeying the law.

* Acts of the Parliament of Scotland, vol. ii. pp. 7, 8.

Upon the subject of the administration of justice to the people in general, and more especially to such poor and needy persons who could not pay an advocate for conducting their cause, a statute was passed in this parliament which breathes a spirit of enlarged humanity. After declaring that all bills of complaints, which, for divers reasons, affecting the profit of the realm, could not be determined by the parliament, should be brought before the particular judge of the district to which they belong, to whom the king was to give injunction to distribute justice, without fraud or favour, as well to the poor as to the rich, in every part of the realm, it proceeded as follows, in language remarkable for its strength and simplicity: " And gif thar be ony pur creatur," it observes, " that for defalte of cunnyng or dispens, can nocht, or may nocht folow his caus ; the king, for the lufe of God, sall ordane that the juge before quhame the causs suld be determyt purway and get a lele and wyss advocate to folow sic creaturis caus. And gif sic caus be obtenyt, the wrangar sall assythe the party skathit, and ye advocatis costis that travale. And gif the juge refusys to doe the lawe evinly, as is befor saide, ye party plenzeand sall haf recours to ye king, ye quhilk sall sa rigorusly punyst sic jugis, yat it be ane ensampill till all utheris."*

It was declared to be the intention of the sovereign to grant a remission or pardon of any injury committed upon person or property in the Lowland districts of his dominions, where the defaulter made reparation, or, according to the Scottish phrase, " assythement," to the injured party, and where the extent of the loss had been previously ascertained by a jury of honest

* Acts of the Parliament of Scotland, vol. ii. p. 8.

and faithful men; but from this rule, the Highlands, or northern divisions of the country, were excepted, where, on account of the practice of indiscriminate robbery and murder which had prevailed, previous to the return of the king, it was impossible to ascertain correctly the extent of the depredation, or the amount of the assythement. The condition of his northern dominions, and the character and manners of his Highland subjects,—if indeed they could be called his subjects, whose allegiance was of so peculiar and capricious a nature,—had given birth to many anxious thoughts in the king, and led not long after this to a personal visit to these remote regions, which formed an interesting episode in his reign.

The only remaining matter of importance which came under the consideration of this parliament, was the growth of heresy, a subject which, in its connexion as with the first feeble dawnings of reformation, is peculiarly interesting and worthy of attention. It was directed that every bishop within his diocese should make inquisition of all Lollards and heretics, where such were to be found, in order that they be punished according to the laws of the holy Catholic church, and that the civil power be called in for the support of the ecclesiastical, if required.* Eighteen years had now elapsed since John Resby, a follower of the great Wickliff, was burnt at Perth. It was then known, that his preaching, and the little treatises which he or his disciples had disseminated through the country, had made a deep impression; and the ancient historian who informs us of the circumstance, observes, that even in his own day, these same books and conclusions were secretly preserved by some unhappy persons

* Acts of the Parliament of Scotland, vol. ii. pp. 7, 8.

under the instigation of the devil, and upon the principle that stolen waters are sweet.*

There can be no doubt, that at this period the consciences of not a few in the country were alarmed as to the foundations of a faith upon which they had hitherto relied, and that they began to judge and reason for themselves upon a subject of all others the most important which can occupy the human mind,— the grounds of a sinner's pardon and acceptance with God. An under current of reformation, which the church denominated heresy, was beginning gradually to sap the foundations upon which the ancient papal fabric had been hitherto securely resting; and the Scottish clergy, alarmed at the symptoms of spiritual rebellion, and possessing great influence over the mind of the monarch, prevailed upon him to interpose the authority of a legislative enactment, to discountenance the growth of the new opinions, and to confirm and follow up the efforts of the church, by the strength and terror of the secular arm. The education of James in England, under the direction of two monarchs, who had sullied their reign by the cruel persecution of the followers of Wickliff, was little calculated to open his mind to the convictions of truth, or to the principles of toleration; and at this moment he owed so much to the clergy, and was so engrossed with his efforts for the consolidation of the royal power, that he could neither refuse their request, nor inquire into the circumstances under which it was preferred. The statute, therefore, against Lollards and heretics was passed; the symptoms of rebellion, which ought to have stimulated the clergy to greater zeal, purity, and usefulness, were put down by a strong hand; and the

* Fordun a Hearne, vol. iv. p. 1169.

reformation was retarded only to become more resistless at the last.

In the destruction of our national records many links in the history of this remarkable parliament have been lost; but the success with which the king conducted this overthrow of the house of Albany, certainly gives us a high idea of his ability and courage; and in the great outlines enough has been left to convince us, that the undertaking was of a nature the most delicate and dangerous which could have presented itself to a monarch recently seated on a precarious throne, surrounded by a fierce nobility, to whom he was almost a stranger, and the most powerful of whom were connected by blood or by marriage with the ancient house whose destruction he meditated. The example indeed was terrible; the scaffold was flooded with royal and noble blood; and it is impossible not to experience a feeling of sorrow and indignation at the cruel and unrelenting severity of James. It seems as if his rage and mortification at the escape of his uncle, the prime offender, was but imperfectly satisfied with the punishment of the feeble Murdoch; and that his deep revenge almost delighted to glut itself in the extermination of every scion of that unfortunate house. But to form a just opinion, indeed, of the conduct of the king, we must not forget the galling circumstances in which he was situated. Deprived for nineteen years of his paternal kingdom, by a system of unprincipled usurpation; living almost within sight of his throne, yet unable to reach it; feeling his royal spirit strong within him, but detained and dragged back by the successful and selfish intrigues of Albany, it is not surprising that when he did at last escape from his bonds, his rage should be that of the chafed lion who has broken the toils, and that the principle of revenge, in those dark days esteemed as much a duty as a pleasure, should mingle itself with his more cool determination to inflict punishment upon his enemies.

But laying individual feelings aside, the barbarism of the times, and the precarious state in which he found the government, compelled James to adopt strong measures. Nothing but an example of speedy and inflexible severity could have made an impression upon the iron-nerved and ferocious nobles, whose passions, under the government of the house of Albany, had been nursed up into a state of reckless indulgence, and a contempt of all legitimate authority; and there seems reason to believe, that the conduct pursued by the king was deemed by him absolutely necessary to consolidate his own power, and enable him to carry into effect his ultimate designs for promoting the interests of the country. Immediately after the conclusion of the parliament, James despatched Lord Montgomery of Eliotston, and Sir Humphrey Cunningham, to seize the castle of Lochlomond,* the property of Sir James Stewart, the youngest son of Albany, who had fled to Ireland along with his father's chaplain, the Bishop of Lismore. Such was the terror inspired by the severity of James, that this fierce youth never afterwards returned, but died in banishment; so that the ruin of the house of Albany appeared to be complete.

In the course of the preceding year the queen had brought into the world a daughter, her first-born, who was baptized by the name of Margaret; and, as the policy of France led those who then ruled in her coun-

---

* "In the south end of the island Inchmurin, the ancient family of Lennox had a castle, but it is now in ruins." This is probably the castle alluded to, Stat. Acct. vol. ix. p. 16. Extracta ex Chronicis Scotiæ, fol. 273.

cils to esteem the alliance of Scotland of great importance in her protracted struggle with England, it was determined to negotiate a marriage between Louis of Anjou, the heir to the throne, and the infant princess. In that kingdom the affairs of Charles the Seventh were still in a precarious situation. Although the great military genius of Henry the Fifth no longer directed and animated the operations of the campaign, yet, under the Duke of Bedford, who had been appointed Regent of France, fortune still favoured the arms of the invaders; and the successive defeats of Crevant and Verneuil, in which the auxiliary forces of the Scots were almost entirely cut to pieces, had lent a vigour and confidence to the councils and conduct of the English, and imparted a proportionable despondency to the French, which seemed to augur a fatal result to the efforts of that brave people. It became necessary, therefore, to court every alliance from which effectual assistance might be expected; and the army of seven thousand Scottish men-at-arms, which had passed over under the command of the Earls of Buchan and Wigtown in 1420, with the additional auxiliary force which the Earl of Douglas led to join the army of Charles the Seventh, convinced that monarch that the assistance of Scotland was an object, to attain which no efforts should be spared. Accordingly, Stewart of Darnley, Lord of Aubigny and Constable of the Scottish army in France, along with the Archbishop of Rheims, the first prelate in the realm, were despatched in 1425 upon an embassy to negotiate the marriage between Margaret of Scotland and Louis the Dauphin, and to renew the ancient league which had so long connected the two countries with each other.*

* Fordun a Goodal, vol. ii. p. 484.

James received the ambassadors with great distinction, agreed to the proposed alliance, and despatched Leighton bishop of Aberdeen, with Lauder archdeacon of Lothian, and Sir Patrick Ogilvy justiciar of Scotland, to return his answer to the Court of France. It was determined, that in five years the parties should be betrothed, after which, the Scottish princess was to be conveyed with all honour to her royal consort. About the same time the king appears to have sent ambassadors to the Court of Rome, but it is difficult to discover whether they merely conveyed those general expressions of spiritual allegiance which it was usual for sovereigns to transmit to the Holy See after their coronation, or related to matters more intimately affecting the ecclesiastical state of the kingdom. If we may judge from the numbers and dignity of the envoys, the communication was one of importance, and may, perhaps, have related to those measures for the extirpation of heresy which we have seen occupying the attention of the legislature under James's second parliament. It was a principle of this enterprising monarch, in his schemes for the recovery and consolidation of his own power, to cultivate the friendship of the clergy, whom he regarded as a counterpoise to the nobles; and with this view he issued a commission to Leighton the Bishop of Aberdeen, authorizing him to resume all alienations of the lands of the church which had been made during the regencies of the two Albanys, commanding his justiciars and officers of the law to assist in all proper measures for the recovery of the property which had been lost, and conferring upon the prelate the power of anathema in case of resistance.*

During the same year there arrived in Scotland an

* MS. in Harleian Coll. quoted in Pinkerton's History, vol. i. p. 116.

embassy from the States of Flanders, upon a subject of great commercial importance. It appears that the Flemings, as allies of England, had committed hostilities against the Scottish merchants during the captivity of the king, which had induced him to order the staple of the Scottish commerce in the Netherlands to be removed to Middelburgh in Zealand. The measure had been attended with much loss to the Flemish traders; and the object of the embassy was to solicit the return of the trade. The king, who, at the period of its arrival, was engaged in keeping his birthday, surrounded by his barons at St Andrews, received the Flemish envoys with distinction; and, aware of the importance of encouraging the commercial enterprise of his people, seized the opportunity of procuring more ample privileges for the Scottish merchants in Flanders, in return for which, he agreed that the staple should be restored.*

At this period, besides the wealthy citizens and burghers, who adopted commerce as a profession, it was not uncommon for the richer nobles and gentry, and even for the sovereign, to embark in mercantile adventures. In 1408, the Earl of Douglas freighted a vessel, with one or two super-cargoes, and a crew of twenty mariners, to trade in Normandy and Rochelle; in the succeeding year the Duke of Albany was the proprietor of a vessel which carried six hundred quarters of malt, and was navigated by a master and twenty-four sailors; and, at a still later period, a vessel, the Mary of Leith, obtained a safe conduct from the English monarch to unship her cargo, which belonged to his dear cousin James, the King of Scotland, in the port of Lon-

* Fordun a Goodal, vol. ii. pp. 487, 509.

don, and expose the merchandise to sale.* At the same time the Lombards, esteemed, perhaps, the most wealthy and enterprising merchants in Europe, continued to carry on a lucrative trade with Scotland; and one of their large carracks, which, compared with the smaller craft of the English and Scottish merchants, is distinguished by the contemporary chronicler as an " enormous vessel," *navis immanissima*, was wrecked by a sudden storm in the Firth of Forth. The gale was accompanied by a high spring-tide, against which the mariners of Italy, accustomed to the Mediterranean navigation, had taken no precautions; so that the ship was driven from her anchors, and cast ashore at Granton, about three miles above Leith.†

The tax of twelve pennies upon every pound of rent, and other branches of income, which was directed to be levied in the first parliament held at Perth after the king's return, has been already mentioned. The sum to be thus collected was destined for the payment of the arrears which the king had become bound to advance to England, as the amount of expense incurred by his maintenance during his captivity; and it appears by the account of Walter Bower, the continuator of Fordun, who was himself one of the commissioners for this taxation, that during the first year, it amounted to fourteen thousand marks; which would give nearly two hundred and eighty thousand marks, or about three millions of modern sterling money, as the annual income of the people of Scotland in 1424.

It must be recollected, however, that this does not include the lands and cattle employed by landholders in their own husbandry, which were particularly ex-

* Rotuli Scotiæ, vol. ii. p. 257. Ibid. 1st Sept. 9 Henry IV., p. 187. 2d Dec. 11 Henry IV., p. 193.
† Fordun a Goodal, vol. ii. p. 487.

cepted in the collection. The tax itself was an innovation; and in the second year the zeal of the people cooled; they openly murmured against the universal impoverishment it occasioned; and the collection was far less productive. In those primitive times, all taxes, except in customs, which became a part of the apparent price of the goods on which they were charged, were wholly unknown in Scotland. The people were accustomed to see the king support his dignity, and discharge his debts, by the revenues of the crown lands, which, previous to the late dilapidations, were amply sufficient for that purpose; and with equal prudence and generosity, although supported by a resolution of the three Estates, James declined to avail himself of this invidious mode of increasing his revenue, and gave orders that no further efforts should be made to levy the imposition.*

Upon the eleventh of March, 1425, the king convoked his third parliament at Perth, and the institution of the Lords of the Articles appears to have been fully established. The various subjects upon which the decision of the great council was requested, were declared to be submitted by the sovereign to the determination of certain persons to be chosen by the three Estates from the prelates, earls, and barons then assembled; and the legislative enactments which resulted from their deliberations, convey to us an animated and instructive picture of the condition of the country. After the usual declaration, that the holy Catholic church and its ministers should continue to enjoy their ancient privileges, and be permitted without hindrance to grant leases of their lands, or of their teinds, there follows a series of

* Fordun a Goodal, vol. ii. p. 482. M'Pherson's Annals of Commerce, vol. i. p. 640.

regulations and improvements, both as to the laws themselves and the manner of their administration, which are well worthy of attention.

It was first announced, that all the subjects of the realm must be governed by the statutes passed in parliament, and not by any particular laws, or any spiritual privileges or customs of other countries; and a new court, known by the name of the SESSION, was instituted for the administration of justice to the people. It was declared, that the king, with the consent of his parliament, had ordained, that his chancellor, and along with him certain discreet persons of the three Estates, who were to be chosen and deputed by himself, should, from this day forth, sit three times in the year at whatever place the sovereign may appoint them, for the examination and decision of all causes and quarrels which may be determined before the king's council; and that these judges should have their expenses paid by the parties against whom the decision was given, out of the fines of court, or otherwise as the monarch may determine. The first session of this new court was appointed to be held the day after the feast of St Michael the Archangel, or on the thirtieth of September; the second on the Monday of the first week of Lent; and the third on the morning preceding the feast of St John the Baptist.*

A Register was next appointed, in which a record was to be kept of all charters and infeftments, as well as of all letters of protection, or confirmations of ancient rights or privileges, which, since the king's return, had been granted to any individuals; and within four months after the passing of this act, all such charters were to be produced by the parties to whom they have been

* Acts of the Parliament of Scotland, vol. ii. p. 11.

granted, and regularly marked in the book of record. Any person who was a judge or officer of justice within the realm, or any person who had prosecuted and summoned another to stand his trial, was forbidden, under a penalty of ten pounds, to sit upon his jury; and none were to be allowed to practise as attorneys in the justice-ayres, or courts held by the king's justiciars, or their deputies, who were not known to the justice and the barons as persons of sufficient learning and discretion. Six wise and able men, best acquainted with the laws, were directed to be chosen from each of the three Estates, to whom was committed the examination of the books of the law, that is to say, " Regiam Majestatem," and " Quoniam Attachiamenta;" and these persons were directed by parliament, in language which marked the simple legislation of the times, " to mend the lawis that nedis mendyng," to reconcile all contradictory, and explain all obscure enactments, so that henceforth fraud and cunning may assist no man in obtaining an unjust judgment against his neighbour.*

One of the greatest difficulties which at this early period stood in the way of all improvement introduced by parliamentary regulations, was the slowness with which these regulations were communicated to the more distant districts of the country; and the extreme ignorance of the laws which subsisted, not only amongst the subjects of the realm and the inferior ministers of justice, but even amongst the nobles and barons, who, living in their own castles in remote situations, rude and illiterate in their habits, and bigoted in their attachment to those ancient institutions under which they had so long tyrannised over their vassals, were little anxious to become acquainted with new laws; and frequently,

* Acts of the Parliament of Scotland, vol. ii. p. 11.

when they did penetrate so far, pretended ignorance, as a cover for their disobedience. To obviate, as far as possible, this evil, it was directed by the parliament, that all statutes and ordinances made prior to this, should be first transcribed in the king's register, and afterwards, that copies of them should be given to the different sheriffs in the country. The sheriffs were then strictly enjoined to publish and proclaim these statutes in the chief and most notable places in the sheriffdom, and to distribute copies of them to prelates, barons, and burghs of bailiery, the expense being paid by those who made the application. They were commanded, under the penalty of being deprived of their office, to cause all acts of the legislature to be observed throughout their county, and to inculcate upon the people, whether burghers or landholders, obedience to the provisions made by their sovereign since his return from England; so that, in time coming, no man should have cause to pretend ignorance of the laws.*

The defence of the country was another subject which came before this parliament. It was provided, that all merchants of the realm passing beyond seas should, along with their usual cargoes, bring home such a supply of harness and armour as could be stowed in the vessel, besides spears, spear-shafts, bows, and bowstrings; nor was this to be omitted upon any of their voyages: particular injunctions were added with regard to the regulation of "*weaponschawings*," or the annual county musters for the inspection of arms, and the encouragement of warlike exercises. Every sheriff was directed to hold them four times in the year within his county, upon which occasion it was his duty to see that every gentleman having ten pounds value in land,

* Acts of the Parliament of Scotland, vol. ii. p. 11.

should be sufficiently harnessed and armed with steel basnet, leg-harness, sword, spear, and dagger, and that all gentlemen of less property should be armed according to their estate. All yeomen of the realm, between the ages of sixteen and sixty, were directed to be provided with bows and a sheaf of arrows. With regard to the burghs, it was appointed that the weaponschawing should be held within them also, four times during the year, that all their inhabitants should be well armed, and that the aldermen and the bailies were to be held responsible for the due observance of this regulation; whilst certain penalties were inflicted on all gentlemen and yeomen who may be found transgressing these enactments.*

The regulations relating to the commercial prosperity of the country, and its intercourse with other nations, manifest the same jealousy and ignorance of the true prosperity of the realm, which influenced the deliberations of the former parliaments. Taxes were repeated upon the exportation of money, compulsory regulations promulgated against foreign merchants, by which they were compelled to lay out the money which they received for their commodities, upon the purchase of Scottish merchandise, directions were given to the sheriffs, and other ministers of the law, upon the coasts opposite to Ireland, to prevent all ships and galleys from sailing to that country without special license of the king's deputes, to be appointed for this purpose in every seaport; no merchant or shipman was to be allowed to give to any Irish subject a passage into Scotland, unless such stranger could show a letter or passport from the lord of the land from whence he came, declaring the business for which he desired to enter the realm,

* Acts of the Parliament of Scotland, vol. ii. pp. 9, 10.

and all such persons, previous to their being allowed to land, were to be examined by the king's deputy of the seaport where the ship had weighed anchor, so that it might be discovered whether the business they had in hand were to the profit or the prejudice of the king and his estate. These strict enactments were declared to proceed from no desire to break or interrupt the good understanding which had been long maintained between the King of Scotland "and his gud aulde frendis the Erschry of Irelande;" but because at that time the open rebels of the king had taken refuge in that country, and the welfare and safety of the realm might be endangered by all such unrestrained intercourse as should give them an opportunity of plotting with their friends, or afford facilities to the Irish of becoming acquainted with the private affairs of the government of Scotland.*

A quaint and amusing provision was introduced in this parliament, which is entitled, "Anent hostillaris in villagis and burowyis." It informs us that hostlers, or innkeepers, had made grievous complaints to the king against a villanous practice of his lieges, who, in travelling from one part of the country to another, were in the habit of taking up their residence with their acquaintances and friends, instead of going to the regular inns and hostelries; whereupon the sovereign, with counsel and consent of the three Estates, prohibited all travellers on foot or horseback from rendezvousing at any station except the established hostelry of the burgh or village; and interdicted all burgesses or villagers from extending to them their hospitality, under the penalty of forty shillings. The higher ranks of the nobles and the gentry would, however, have considered

* Acts of the Parliament of Scotland, vol. ii. p. 11.

this as an infringement upon their liberty; and it was accordingly declared, that all persons whose estate permitted them to travel with a large retinue in company, might quarter themselves upon their friends, under the condition that they sent their attendants and horses to be lodged at the common hostelries.*

The remaining enactments of this parliament related to the regulation of the weights and measures, and to the appointment of an established standard to be used throughout the realm; to the obligation of all barons or freeholders to attend the parliament in person; to the offering up of regular prayers and collects, by all priests religious and secular, throughout the kingdom, for the health and prosperity of the king, his royal consort, and their children; and, lastly, to the apprehension of all stout, idle vagabonds, who possess the ability, but not the inclination, to labour for their own living. These were to be apprehended by the sheriff, and compelled, within forty days, to bind themselves to some lawful craft, so that they should no longer devour and trouble the country. The regulation of the standard size of the boll, firlot, half firlot, peck, and gallon, which were to be used throughout the kingdom, was referred to the next parliament; whilst it was declared, that the water measures then in use should continue the same; that with regard to weights, there should be made a standard stone, which was to weigh exactly fifteen legal troy pounds, but to be divided into sixteen Scots pounds, and that, according to this standard, weights should be made, and used by all buyers and sellers throughout the realm.

James had already increased the strength and prosperity of his kingdom by various foreign treaties of

* Acts of the Parliament of Scotland, vol. ii. p. 10.

alliance and commercial intercourse: he was at peace with England; the ancient ties between France and Scotland were about to be more firmly drawn together by the projected marriage between his daughter and the Dauphin; he had re-established his amicable relations with Flanders; and the court of Rome, flattered by his zeal against heresy, and his devotedness to the Church, was disposed to support him with all its influence. To complete these friendly relations with foreign powers, he now concluded by his ambassadors, William lord Crichton his chamberlain, and William Fowlis provost of the collegiate church of Bothwell his almoner, a treaty with Eric king of Denmark, Norway, and Sweden, in which the ancient alliances entered into between Alexander the Third, Robert the First, and the princes who in their days occupied the northern throne, were ratified and confirmed; mutual freedom of trade agreed upon, saving the peculiar rights and customs of both kingdoms; and all damages, transgressions, and defaults on either side, cancelled and forgiven. James also consented to continue the annual payment of a hundred marks for the sovereignty of the little kingdom of Man and the Western Isles, which Alexander the Third had purchased in 1266 for the sum of four thousand marks.* Their allegiance, indeed, was of a precarious nature, and for a long time previous to this the nominal possession of the Isles, instead of an acquisition of strength and revenue, had proved a thorn in the side of the country; but the king, with that firmness and decision of character for which he was remarkable, had now determined, by an expedition conducted in person, to reduce within the control of the laws the northern parts of his dominions,

* Fordun a Hearne, vol. iv. pp. 1355, 1358.

and confidently looked forward to the time when these islands would be esteemed an acquisition of no common importance.

Meanwhile he prepared to carry his schemes into execution. Having summoned his parliament to meet him at Inverness, he proceeded, surrounded by his principal nobles and barons, and at the head of a force which rendered all resistance unavailing, to establish his residence for a season in the heart of his northern dominions.* It was their gloomy castles, and almost inaccessible fastnesses, which had given refuge to those fierce and independent chiefs, who neither desired his friendship, nor deprecated his resentment, and who were now destined at last to experience the same unrelenting severity, which had fallen upon the house of Albany. At this period the condition of the Highlands, so far as it is discoverable from the few authentic documents which have reached our times, appears to have been in the highest degree rude and uncivilized. There existed a singular combination of Celtic and of feudal manners. Powerful chiefs of Norman name and Norman blood had penetrated into the remotest districts, and ruled over multitudes of vassals and serfs, whose strange and uncouth appellatives proclaim their difference of race in the most convincing manner.† The tenure of lands by charter and seisin, the feudal services due by the vassal to his lord, the bands of friendship or of manrent which indissolubly united certain chiefs and nobles to each other, the baronial courts, and the complicated official pomp of feudal life, were all to be found in full strength and operation in the northern counties; but the dependence of the barons, who had

* Fordun a Goodal, vol. ii. p. 488.
† MS. Adv. Lib. Coll. Diplom. a Macfarlane, vol. i. p. 245. MS. Cart. Moray v. 263. See Illustrations. G.

taken up their residence in these wild districts, upon the king, and their allegiance and subordination to the laws, were far less intimate and influential, than in the lowland divisions of the country; and as they experienced less protection, we have already seen, that in great public emergencies, when the captivity of the sovereign, or the payment of his ransom, called for the imposition of a tax upon property throughout the kingdom, these great northern chiefs thought themselves at liberty to resist its collection within their mountainous principalities.*

Besides such Scoto-Norman barons, however, there were to be found in the Highlands and the Isles, those fierce aboriginal chiefs, who hated the Saxon and the Norman race, and offered a mortal opposition to the settlement of all intruders within a country which they considered their own. They exercised the same authority over the various clans or septs of which they were the heads or leaders, which the baron possessed over his vassals and their military followers; and the dreadful disputes and collisions which perpetually occurred between these distinct ranks of potentates, were accompanied by spoliations, ravages, imprisonments, and murders, which had at last become so frequent and so far extended, that the whole country beyond the Grampian range was likely to be cut off, by these abuses, from all regular communication with the more pacific parts of the kingdom.

This state of things called loudly for redress, and the measures of the king, on reaching Inverness, were of a prompt and determined character. He summoned the most powerful chiefs to attend his parliament; and this command, however extraordinary it may appear,

* History, supra, vol. ii. pp. 151, 153.

these ferocious leaders did not think proper to disobey. It may be that he employed stratagem, and held out the prospect of pardon and reconciliation; or perhaps a dreadful example of immediate execution, in the event of resistance, may have persuaded the Highland nobles, that obedience gave them a chance for their lives, whilst a refusal left them no hope of escape. But by whatever method their attendance was secured, they soon bitterly repented their facility; for instantly on entering the hall of parliament, they were arrested, ironed, and cast into separate prisons, where all communication with each other, or with their followers, was impossible. So overjoyed was James at the success of his plan, and the apparent readiness with which these fierce leaders seemed to rush into the toils which had been prepared for them, that Bower described him as turning triumphantly to his courtiers, whilst they tied the hands of the captives, and reciting some leonine or monkish rhymes, applauding the skill exhibited in their arrest, and the deserved death which awaited them. Upon this occasion, forty greater and lesser chiefs were seized, but the names of the highest only have been preserved: Alexander of the Isles; Angus Dow, with his four sons, who could bring into the field four thousand men from Strathnaver; Kenneth More, with his son-in-law, Angus of Moray and Makmathan, who could command a sept of two thousand strong; Alexander Makreiny of Garmoran, and John Macarthur, a potent chief, each of whom could muster a thousand men; along with John Ross, William Lesley, and James Campbell, are those enumerated by our contemporary historian; whilst the Countess of Ross, the mother of Alexander of the Isles, and heiress of Sir Walter Lesley, a rich and potent baron, was apprehended at the same time, and compelled to share the captivity of her son.*

Some of these, whose crimes had rendered them especially obnoxious, the king ordered to immediate execution. James Campbell was tried, convicted, and hanged, for his murder of John of the Isles; Alexander Makreiny and John Macarthur were beheaded, and their fellow-captives dispersed and confined in different prisons throughout the kingdom. Of these, not a few were afterwards condemned and executed; whilst the rest, against whom nothing very flagrant could be proved, were suffered to escape with their lives. By some, this clemency was speedily abused, and by none more than the most powerful and ambitious of them all, Alexander of the Isles.

This ocean lord, half prince and half pirate, had shown himself willing, upon all occasions, to embrace the friendship of England, and to shake himself loose of all dependence upon his sovereign; whilst the immense body of vassals whom he could muster under his banner, and the powerful fleet with which he could sweep the northern seas, rendered his alliance or his enmity a matter of no inconsiderable consequence. After a short confinement, the king, moved, perhaps, by his descent from the ancient family of Lesley, a house of high and hereditary loyalty, restored him to liberty, after an admonition to change the evil courses to which he had been addicted, and to evince his gratitude by a life of consistent attachment to the throne. Alexander, however, after having recovered his liberty, only waited to see the king returned to his lowland dominions, and then broke out into a paroxysm of fury and revenge. He collected the whole strength of Ross

* Fordun a Hearne, vol. iv. pp. 1283, 1284.

and of the Isles, and at the head of an army of ten thousand men, grievously wasted the country, directing his principal vengeance against the crown lands, and concluding his campaign by razing to the ground the royal burgh of Inverness.*

James, however, with an activity for which his enemy was little prepared, instantly collected a feudal force, and flew, rather than marched, to the Highlands, where, in Lochaber, he came up with the fierce, but confused and undisciplined army of the island chief. Although his army was probably far inferior in numbers, yet the sudden appearance of the royal banner, the boldness with which he confronted his enemy, and the terror of the king's name, gave him all the advantage of a surprise; and before the battle began, Alexander found himself deserted by the clan Chattan and the clan Cameron, who, to a man, went over to the royal army. It is deeply to be regretted that the account of this expedition should be so meagre, even in Bower, who was a contemporary. All those particular details, which would have given interest to the story, and individuality to the character of the persons who acted in it, and which a little pains might have then preserved, are now irrecoverably lost. We know only, that the Lord of the Isles, with his chieftains and ketherans, was completely routed, and so hotly pursued by the king, that he sent an embassy to sue for peace. This presumption greatly incensed the monarch; he derided the idea of an outlaw, who knew not where to rest the sole of his foot, and whom his soldiers were then hunting from one retreat to other, arrogating to himself the dignity of an independent prince, and attempting to open a correspon-

* Fordun a Hearne, vol. iv. p. 1285.

dence by his ambassadors; and sternly and scornfully refusing to enter into any negotiation, returned to his capital, after giving strict orders to his officers to exert every effort for his apprehension.

Driven to despair, and finding it every day more difficult to elude the vigilance which was exerted, Alexander resolved at last to throw himself upon the royal mercy. Having privately travelled to Edinburgh, this proud chief, who had claimed an equality with kings, condescended to an unheard-of humiliation. Upon a solemn festival, when the monarch and his queen, attended by their suite, and surrounded by the nobles of the court, stood in front of the high altar in the church of Holyrood, a miserable-looking man, clothed only in his shirt and drawers, holding a naked sword in his hand, and with a countenance and manner in which grief and destitution were strongly exhibited, suddenly presented himself before them. It was the Lord of the Isles, who fell upon his knees, and delivering up his sword to the king, implored his clemency. James granted him his life, but instantly imprisoned him in Tantallon castle, under the charge of William earl of Angus, his nephew. His mother, the Countess of Ross, was committed to close confinement in the ancient monastery of Inchcolm, situated in an island in the Firth of Forth.* She was released, however, after little more than a year's imprisonment; and the island lord himself soon after experienced the royal favour, and was restored to his lands and possessions.

This unbending severity, which in some instances approached the very borders of cruelty, was, perhaps, a necessary ingredient in the character of a monarch, who, when he ascended the throne, found his kingdom,

* Fordun a Hearne, vol. iv. p. 1286.

to use the expressive language of an ancient chronicle,* little else than a wide den of robbers. Two anecdotes of this period have been preserved by Bower, the faithful contemporary historian of the times, which illustrate, in a striking manner, both the character of the king, and the condition of the country. In the highland districts, one of those ferocious chieftains, against whom the king had directed an act of parliament already quoted, had broken in upon a poor cottager, and carried off two of her cows. Such was the unlicensed state of the country, that the robber walked abroad, and was loudly accused by the aggrieved party, who swore that she would never put off her shoes again till she had carried her complaint to the king in person. "It is false," cried he; "I'll have you shod myself before you reach the court;" and with a brutality scarcely credible, the monster carried his threat into execution, by fixing with nails driven into the flesh two horse shoes of iron upon her naked feet, after which he thrust her wounded and bleeding on the highway. Some humane persons took pity on her; and, when cured, she retained her original purpose, sought out the king, told her story, and showed her feet, still seamed and scarred by the inhuman treatment she had received. James heard her with that mixture of pity, kindness, and incontrollable indignation, which marked his character; and having instantly directed his writs to the sheriff of the county where the robber chief resided, had him seized within a short time, and sent to Perth, where the court was then held. He was instantly tried and condemned; a linen shirt was thrown over him, upon which was painted a rude representation of his

* MS. Chronicon ab anno 1390 ad annum 1402. Cartulary of Moray, p. 220.

crime; and, after being paraded in this ignominious dress through the streets of the town, he was dragged at a horse's tail, and hanged on a gallows.* Such examples, there can be little doubt, had an excellent effect upon the fierce classes, for a warning to whom they were intended, and caused them to associate a degree of terror with the name of the king; which accounts, in some measure, for the promptitude of their obedience when he arrived among them in person.

The other story to which I have alluded is almost equally characteristic. A noble of high rank, and nearly related to the king, having quarrelled with another baron in presence of the monarch and his court, so far forgot himself, that he struck his adversary on the face. James instantly had him seized, and ordered him to stretch out his hand upon the council table; he then unsheathed the short cutlass which he carried at his girdle, gave it to the baron who received the blow, and commanded him to strike off the hand which had insulted his honour, and was forfeited to the laws, threatening him with death if he refused. There is little doubt, from what we know of the character of this prince, that he was in earnest; but a thrill of horror ran through the court, his prelates and council reminded him of the duty of forgiveness, and the queen, who was present, fell at his feet, implored pardon for the guilty, and at last obtained a remission of the sentence. The offender, however, was instantly banished from court.†

One of the most remarkable features in the government of this prince, was the frequent recurrence of his parliaments. From the period of his return from England till his death, his reign embraced only thirteen

---

* Fordun a Goodal, vol. ii. p. 510.
† Fordun a Hearne, vol. iv. pp. 1334, 1335.

years; and, in that time, the great council of the nation was thirteen times assembled. His object was evidently to render the higher nobles more dependent upon the crown, to break down that dangerous spirit of pride and individual consequence which confined them to their separate principalities, and taught them, for year after year, to tyrannise over their unhappy vassals, without the dread of a superior, or the restraint even of an equal, to accustom them to the spectacle of the laws, proceeding not from their individual caprice or authority, but from the collective wisdom of the three Estates, sanctioned by the consent, and carried into execution by the power, of the crown acting through its ministers.

In a parliament, of which the principal provisions have been already noticed, it had been made incumbent upon all earls, barons, and freeholders, to attend the meeting of the Estates in person; and the practice of sending procurators or attorneys in their place, which, there seems reason to believe, had become not infrequent, was strictly forbidden, unless due cause of absence be proved. In two subsequent meetings of the great council of the nation, the first of which appears to have been held at Perth on the thirtieth of September, 1426, and the second on the first of July, 1427, some important enactments occur, which evince the unwearied attention of the king to the manufactures, the commerce, the agriculture of his dominions, and to the speedy and impartial administration of justice to all classes of his subjects.* It is evident, from the tenor of a series of regulations concerning the deacons of the trades, or crafts, that the government of James, probably from its extreme firmness and severity, had already become un-

---

* Acts of the Parliament of Scotland, vol. ii. pp. 13, 14.

popular. It was first commanded, that the deacons of the crafts should confine themselves strictly and simply to their duties, of ascertaining, by an inspection every fifteen days, whether the workmen be sufficiently expert in their business, but it was added that they should have no authority to alter the laws of the craft, or to punish those who have offended against them; and in the parliament of 1427, it was declared, that the provisions regarding the appointment of deacons of the crafts within the royal burghs having been found productive of grievous injury to the realm, were henceforth annulled; that no deacon be permitted after this to be elected, whilst those already chosen to fill this office were prohibited from exercising their functions, or holding their usual meetings, which had led to conspiracies.* It is possible, however, that these conspiracies may have been combinations amongst the various workmen, on subjects connected with their trade, rather than any serious plots against government.

To the aldermen and council of the different towns was committed the charge of fixing the prices of the various kinds of work, which they were to regulate by an examination of the value of the raw material, and an estimate of the labour of the workman; whilst the same judges were to fix the wages given to wrights, masons, and such other handicraftsmen, who contributed their skill and labour, but did not furnish the materials. Every farmer and husbandman who possessed a plough and eight oxen, was commanded to sow annually, a firlot of wheat, half a firlot of pease, and forty beans, under a penalty of ten shillings, to be paid to the baron of the land for each infringement of the law; whilst the baron himself, if he either neglected to

* Acts of the Parliament of Scotland, vol. ii. pp. 13, 14.

sow the same quantity within his own demesnes, or omitted to exact the penalty from an offending tenant, was made liable in a fine of forty shillings for every offence, to be paid to the king. The small quantity of beans here mentioned, renders it probable that this is the era of their earliest introduction into Scotland.*

It would appear, that although the castles of the lowland barons, during the regencies of the two Albanys, had been maintained by their proprietors in sufficient strength; the houses of defence, and the various fortalices of the country, beyond that lofty range of hills, known anciently by the name of the Mounth, had gradually fallen into decay, a state of things proceeding, without doubt, from the lawless state of these districts, divided amongst a few petty tyrants, and the extreme insecurity of life and property to any inferior barons who dared to settle within them. To remedy this evil, it was determined by the parliament, that every lord who had lands beyond the Mounth, upon which, in "auld tymes," there were castles, fortalices, or manor places, should be compelled to rebuild or repair them, and either himself to reside therein, or to procure a friend to take his place. The object of the statute is described to be the gracious government of the lands by good polity, and the happy effects which must result from the produce of the soil being consumed upon the lands themselves where it was grown; an error, perhaps, in civil policy, but which evinced, even in its aberration, an anxiety to discover the causes of national prosperity, which is remarkable for so remote a period.†

The extreme jealousy with which the transportation of money, or bullion, out of the realm, had always been regarded, was carried to an extraordinary height in the

* Acts of the Parliament of Scotland, vol. ii. p. 13. † Ibid.

parliament of the first of July, 1427; for we find an enactment, entitled, " Anent the finance of clerks, by which all such learned persons proposing to go beyond seas, were strictly enjoined either to make change of their money, which they had allotted for the expenses of their travel, with the money changers within the realm, or at least with the merchants of the country." The same act was made imperative upon all lay travellers; and both clerks and laymen were commanded not to leave the country before they had duly informed the king's chancellor of the exchange which they had transacted, and of the object of their journey.

Some of the most important regulations in this parliament of July 1427 regarded the administration of civil and criminal justice, a subject upon which the king appears to have laboured with an enthusiasm and assiduity which evinces how deeply he felt the disorders of this part of the government. It was first declared, that all persons who should be elected judges, in this or any succeeding parliament, for the determination of causes or disputes, should be obliged to take an oath that they will decide the questions brought before them to the best of their knowledge, and without fraud or favour. In the settlement of disputes by arbitration, it was enacted, that for the future, where the arbiters consist of clerks, a churchman, having the casting vote, was to be chosen by the bishop of the diocese, with advice of his chapter; where the case to be determined had arisen without burgh, between the vassals of a baron or others, the oversman having the casting vote was to be chosen by the sheriff, with advice of the lord of the barony; and if the plea took place between citizens within burgh, the provost and his council were to select the oversman, it being specially provided, that for the future all arbitrations were to be determined, not by an even but an uneven number of arbiters.* With regard to the case of Scottish merchants dying abroad in Zealand, Flanders, or other parts of the continent, if it be certain that they were not resident in these parts, but had merely visited them for the purposes of trade, all causes or disputes regarding their succession, or their other transactions, were declared cognizable by the ordinary judge, within whose jurisdictions their testaments were confirmed; even although it was proved that part of the property of the deceased trader was at that time in England, or in parts beyond seas.

In a general council held at Perth on the first of March, 1427, a change was introduced relative to the attendance of the smaller barons and free tenants in parliament, which, as introducing the principle of representation, is worthy of particular attention. It was determined by the king, with consent of his council general, that the small barons and free tenants needed not come hereafter to parliaments nor general councils, provided that from each sheriffdom there be sent two or more *wise men*, to be chosen at the head court of each sheriffdom, in proportion to its size. An exception, however, was introduced with regard to the sheriffdoms of Clackmannan and Kinross, which were directed to return each a single representative. It was next declared, that by these commissaries in a body there should be elected an expert man, to be called the Common Speaker of the Parliament, whose duty it should be to bring forward all cases of importance involving the rights or privileges of the commons; and that such commissaries should have full powers intrusted to them by the rest of the smaller barons and free tenants, to

* Acts of the Parliament of Scotland, vol. ii. p. 14.

discuss and finally to determine what subjects or cases it might be proper to bring before the council or parliament. It was finally ordained, that the expenses of the commissaries and of the speaker should be paid by their electors who owed suit and presence in the parliament or council, but that this new regulation should have no interference with the bishops, abbots, priors, dukes, earls, lords of parliament, and bannerets, whom the king declared he would continue to summon by his special precept.* It is probable that in this famous law, James had in view the parliamentary regulations which were introduced into England as early as the reign of Henry the Third, relative to the elections of knights of the shire, and which he had an opportunity of observing in full force, under the fourth and fifth Henries, during his long residence in England.† As far as we can judge from the concise, but clear, expressions of the Act itself, it is evident that it contained the rude draught or first embryo of a Lower House, in the shape of a committee or assembly of the commissaries of the shires, who deliberated by themselves on the proper points to be brought before the higher court of parliament by their speaker.

It is worthy of remark, that an institution which was destined afterwards to become the most valuable and inalienable right of a free subject,—that of appearing by his representatives in the great council of the nation,—arose, in the first instance, from an attempt to avoid or to elude it. To come to parliament, was considered by the smaller barons who held of the crown *in capite*, an intolerable and expensive grievance; and

---

* Acts of the Parliament of Scotland, vol. ii. pp. 15, 16, cap. 2.
† Rapin's Acta Regia, vol. i. p. 41. Statutes of the Realm, vol. ii. pp. 156, 170, 235.

the act of James was nothing else than a permission of absence to this numerous body on condition of their electing a substitute, and each paying a proportion of his expenses.

In the same parliament, other acts were passed, strikingly illustrative of the condition of the country. Every baron, within his barony, was directed, at the proper season, to search for and slay the wolves' whelps, and to pay two shillings a-head for them to any man who brought them: the tenants were commanded to assist the barons on all occasions when a wolf-hunt was held, under the penalty of "a wedder" for non-appearance; and such hunts were to take place four times in the year: no cruves, or machines for catching fish, were to be placed in waters where the tide ebbed and flowed, for three years to come: where the merchants trading to the continent could not procure Scottish ships, they were permitted to freight their cargoes in foreign vessels: no lepers were to dwell anywhere but in their own hospitals, at the gate of the town, or other places without the bounds of the burgh; strict inquiries were directed to be made by the officials of the bishops, in their visitations, with regard to all persons, whether lay or secular, who might be smitten with this loathsome disease, so that they should be denounced, and compelled to obey the statute; and no lepers were to be allowed to enter any burgh, except thrice in the week,—on Mondays, Wednesdays, and Fridays, between the hours of ten and two, for the purpose of purchasing their food; if, however, a fair or market happened to be held on any of these days, they were to come in the morning, and not to mix indiscriminately with the multitude.

If any clerk, whether secular or religious, were desirous of passing beyond seas, it was made incumbent on him first to come to his ordinary to show good cause for his expedition, and to make faith that he should not be guilty of any kind of simony or "*barratrie*,"—a word meaning the purchasing of benefices by money. All such defaulters or "barratoures," were to be convicted, under the statute already made against those who carried money out of the realm; and not only who were convicted of this crime in time to come, but all now without the realm, being guilty of it, were made liable to the penalties of the statute, and none permitted either to send them money, or to give them assistance, to whatever rank or dignity in the church they may have attained.* It was enacted, that no man should dare to interpret the statutes contrary to their real meaning, as understood by those who framed them; and that the litigants in any plea, should attend at court simply accompanied by their councillors and "forespeakers," and such sober retinue as befitted their estate, and not with a multitude of armed followers on foot or horseback.

In the same general council some strict regulations occur regarding the prices charged by various craftsmen, such as masons, smiths, tailors, weavers, and the like, who had been in the practice of insisting upon a higher price for their labour than they were by law entitled to. Wardens of each craft were directed to be yearly elected in every burgh, who, with the advice of other discreet and unsuspected men, were to examine and estimate the materials and workmanship of every trade, and fix upon it a certain price, not to be exceeded by the artificer, under the forfeiture of the article thus overcharged. In lands without the burgh the

---

* Acts of the Parliament of Scotland, vol. ii. p. 16. Skene, De Verborum Significatione, voce Barratrie.

duty of the warden was to be performed by the baron, and the sheriff to see that he duly performs it. The council concluded by an act, imposing a penalty of forty shillings upon all persons who should slay partridges, plovers, black cocks, grey hens, muir cocks, by any kind of instrument or contrivance between, "lentryn and August."

It may be remarked, that the meeting of the three Estates in which these various enactments were passed, is not denominated a parliament, but a General Council, a term possibly implying a higher degree of solemnity, and conferring perhaps upon the statutes passed in it a more unchallengeable authority than the word parliament. It is difficult, however, to understand the precise distinction, or to discover wherein this superior sanctity consists; for, in looking to its internal constitution, we find that the members who composed the general council were exactly the same as those who sat in the parliament; the bishops, abbots, priors, earls, barons, and free tenants who held of the king *in capite*, and certain burgesses from every burgh in the kingdom, "some of whom were absent upon a legitimate excuse, and others contumaciously, who, on this account, were found liable in a fine of ten pounds."* Within four months after the meeting of this last General Council, the king convoked another solemn assembly of the same description at Perth, on the twelfth of July, 1428, in which it was determined that all successors of prelates, and all the heirs of earls, barons, and free tenants of the crown, should be bound before they were permitted to enter into possession of their temporalities or their estates, to take the same oath of allegiance to the queen, which they had sworn

* Acts of the Parliament of Scotland, vol. ii. p. 15.

to the sovereign, a regulation by which the king, in the event of his death, prepared his subjects to regard the queen as regent, and endeavoured to guard against those convulsions which were too likely to arise during a minority.*

It is time, however, to return from this history of our early legislation to the course of our narrative. Although gradually gaining ground, France was still grievously oppressed by the united attacks of England and Burgundy; and Charles the Seventh, esteeming it of consequence to secure the friendship and assistance of Scotland, followed up the betrothment between James's only daughter and the Dauphin by a contract of marriage, for which purpose the Archbishop of Rheims, and Stuart lord of Darnley and count of Dreux, again visited Scotland. Instead of a dower, which Scotland was at that time little able to offer, James was requested to send to France six thousand soldiers; and the royal bride was, in return, to be provided in an income as ample as any hitherto settled upon the Queens of France. In addition to this, the county of Xaintonge and the lordship of Rochfort were to be made over to the Scottish King; all former alliances were to be renewed and ratified by the mutual oaths of the two monarchs; and the French monarch engaged to send transports for the passage of the Scottish soldiers to France.

The extraordinary rise and splendid military successes of the Maid of Orleans, which occurred in the year immediately following this embassy, rendered it unnecessary for the French King to insist upon this article in the treaty; but the jealousy and apprehensions of England were roused by the prospect of so

* Acts of the Parliament of Scotland, vol. ii. pp. 16, 17.

intimate an alliance, and the Cardinal Beaufort, the uncle of James's queen, who, at this time, was one of the leading directors in the government of England, made proposals for an interview upon the marches, between the Scottish monarch and himself, for the purpose of consulting upon some affairs intimately connected with the mutual weal and honour of the two realms. James, however, seems to have considered it beneath the dignity of an independent sovereign to leave his kingdom and engage in a personal conference with a subject, and the meeting never took place.* The two countries, however, fortunately continued on amicable terms with each other, and time was given to the Scottish monarch to pursue his schemes of improvement, and to evince his continued zeal for everything which affected the happiness of his subjects and the internal prosperity of his kingdom.

It appears, that at this period the poor tenants and labourers of the soil had been reduced to grievous distress by being dispossessed of their farms, and turned out of their cottages, whenever their landlord chose to grant a lease of the estate, or dispose of it to a new proprietor; and such was then the enslaved condition of the lower classes in Scotland, that the king, who was bound to respect the laws which affected the rights of the feudal lords, could not, of his own authority, ameliorate the condition of the labourers. He made it a request, however, to the prelates and barons of his realm, in a parliament held at Perth on the twenty-sixth of April, 1429, that they would not summarily and suddenly remove the husbandmen from any lands of which they had granted new leases; for the space of a year after such transaction, unless where the baron to whom

---

* Rymer, vol. x. p. 410. Rotuli Scotiæ, vol. ii. p. 264.

the estate belonged proposed to occupy the lands himself, and keep them for his own private use; a benevolent enactment, which perhaps may be regarded as the first step towards that important privilege, which was twenty years afterwards conceded to the great body of the farmers and labourers, and which is known in Scottish law under the name of the real right of tack.*

A sumptuary law was passed at the same time, by which it was ordered that no person under the rank of knight, or having less than two hundred marks of yearly income, should wear clothes made of silk, adorned with the richer kinds of furs, or embroidered with gold or pearls. The eldest sons or heirs of all knights were permitted to dress as sumptuously as their fathers; and the aldermen, bailies, and council of the towns, to wear furred gowns; whilst all others were enjoined to equip themselves in such grave and honest apparel as befitted their station, that is to say, in "serpis, beltis, uches, and chenzies." In these regulations, the apparel of the women was not forgotten. The increasing wealth and luxury of the commercial classes had introduced a corresponding, and, as it was then esteemed, an unseemly magnificence in the habiliments of the rich burghers' wives, who imitated, and in all probability exaggerated, the dresses of the ladies of the court. It was commanded that neither commoners' wives nor their servants should wear long trains, rich hoods or ruffs, purfled sleeves, or costly "curches" of lawn; and that all gentlemen's wives should take care that their array did not exceed the personal estate of their husband.†

* Acts of the Parliament of Scotland, vol. ii. pp. 17, 35.
† Ibid. 17, 18.

All persons who were possessed of property affording a yearly rent of twenty pounds, or of moveable goods to the value of a hundred pounds, were to be well horsed, and armed "from head to heel," as became their rank as gentlemen; whilst others of inferior wealth, extending only to ten pounds in rent, or fifty pounds in goods, were bound to provide themselves with a gorget, rerebrace, vambrace, breastplate, greaves, and legsplints, and with gloves of plate, or iron gauntlets. The arms of the lower classes were also minutely detailed. Every yeoman, whose property amounted to twenty pounds in goods, was commanded to arm himself with a good doublet of fence, or a habergeon, an iron hat, or knapscull, a bow and sheaf of arrows, a sword, buckler, and dagger. The second rank of yeomen, who possessed only ten pounds in property, were to provide for themselves a bow and sheaf of arrows, a sword, buckler, and dagger; whilst the lowest class of all, who had no skill in archery, were to have a good "*suir*" hat, a doublet of fence, with sword and buckler, an axe also, or at least a staff pointed with iron. Every citizen, or burgess, possessing fifty pounds in property, was commanded to arm himself in the same fashion as a gentleman; and the burgess yeoman of inferior rank, possessing property to the extent of twenty pounds, to provide a doublet and habergeon, with a sword and buckler, a bow and sheaf of arrows, and a knife or dagger. It was finally made imperative on the barons within their barony, and the bailies within burgh, to carry these enactments into immediate execution, under certain penalties or fines, which, in the event of failure, were to be levied by the sheriff of the county.*

* Acts of the Parliament of Scotland, vol. ii. p. 18.

In the late rebellion of the Lord of the Isles, the want of a fleet had been severely felt, and these statutes regarding the land force of the country, were followed by other regulations of equal importance, concerning the establishment of a navy—a subject which we have seen occupying the last exertions of Bruce.

All barons and lords possessing estates within six miles of the sea, in the western and northern portions of the kingdom, and opposite the isles, were commanded to contribute to the building and equipment of galleys for the public service, in the proportion of one oar to every four marks worth of land,* and to have such vessels ready to put to sea within a year. From this obligation, all such barons as held their lands by the service of finding vessels, were of course excepted, they being still bound to furnish them according to the terms of their charter. In the event of any merchant-ships having been wrecked upon the coast, the confiscation of their cargoes to the king, or their preservation for their owners, was made dependant upon the law respecting wrecks in the country to which such vessels belonged; it being just that they should receive from foreign governments the same protection which it was the practice of their government to extend to foreign vessels. It was enacted in the same parliament, that all advocates, or forespeakers, who were employed in pleading causes in any temporal court, and also the parties litigant, if they happened to be present, should swear, before they be heard, that the cause which they were about to plead was just and true, according to their belief; or, in the simple words of the act itself,

---

* Acts of the Parliament of Scotland, vol. ii. p. 19. What is here the precise value of an oar, cannot be discovered from any expression in the act.

"that they trow the cause is gude and lele that they shall plead."

In the same year, to the great joy of the monarch and the kingdom, his queen was delivered of twin sons, whose baptism was celebrated with much solemnity, one of them being named Alexander, probably after Alexander the Third, whose memory was still dear to the people, and the other James. At the font the king created both these infants knights, and conferred the same honour on the youthful heirs of the Earl of Douglas, the Chancellor, Lord Crichton, Lord Borthwick, Logan of Restalrig, and others of his nobility.* The first of these boys died very young, but the second, James, was destined to succeed his father in the throne.

The truce with England was now on the point of expiring, and the king, who was anxious to concentrate his whole efforts upon the pacification of the northern parts of his dominions, and whose unremitted attention was required at home to carry his new laws into execution, felt equally disposed with Henry the Sixth, to negotiate for a renewal of the armistice, and to discuss the possibility of concluding a permanent peace. For this purpose, a meeting took place between commissioners from both nations, who concluded a truce for five years, from the first of April, 1431, in the provisions of which, an anxious desire was manifested on both sides to adopt every possible expedient for restraining the intolerable lawlessness of the Border warfare. In the same truce, various rude accomodations to each other's commerce were agreed upon by the governments of the sister kingdoms; it was forbid to seize merchants, pilgrims, and fishers of either

---

* Fordun a Goodal, vol. ii. p. 490.

country, when driven into strange ports by stress of weather; shipwrecked men were to be allowed to pass to their own homes; in cases of piracy, not only the principal aggressors, but all who had encouraged the adventure or received the plunder, were to be liable in compensation, and amenable to punishment; and it was lastly agreed, that no aggressions by the subjects of either kingdom, should occasion a breach of the truce.*

Having concluded this measure, James found himself at leisure to take into consideration the condition of the highlands, which, notwithstanding the severity of the examples already made, called loudly for his interference. Donald Balloch, a near relation of the Lord of the Isles, enraged at what he deemed the pusillanimous submission of his kinsman, having collected a fleet and an army in the Hebrides, ran his galleys into the neck of sea which divides Morven from the little island of Lismore, and, disembarking at Lochaber, broke down upon that district with all the ferocity of northern warfare, cutting to pieces a superior force commanded by Alexander earl of Mar, and Alan Stewart earl of Caithness, whom James had stationed there for the protection of the highlands. The conflict took place at Inverlochy; and such was the fury of the attack, that the superior discipline and armour of the lowland knights was unavailing against the broadswords and battle-axes of the islesmen. The Earl of Caithness, with sixteen of his personal retinue, and many other barons and knights, were left dead on the field; while Mar, with great difficulty, succeeded in rescuing the remains of the royal army. From

* Rymer Fœdera, vol. x. p. 482. M'Pherson's Annals of Commerce, vol. i. p. 646.

the result of this battle, as well as the severe loss experienced at Harlaw, it was evident that the islesmen and the ketherans were every day becoming more formidable enemies, and that their arms and their discipline must have been of late years essentially improved. Donald Balloch, however, notwithstanding the dispersion of the royal army, appears to have considered it hazardous to attempt to follow up his success; and having ravaged Lochaber, and carried off as much plunder as he could collect, re-embarked in his galleys, and retreated first to the isles, and afterwards to Ireland.*

About the same time, in the wild and remote country of Caithness, a desperate conflict took place between Angus Dow Mackay and Angus Murray, two leaders of opposite septs or clans, which, from some domestic quarrel, had arrayed themselves in mortal opposition. They met in a strath or valley upon the water of Naver; when such was the ferocity and exterminating spirit with which the battle was contested, that out of twelve hundred only nine are said to have remained alive;† an event which, considering the infinite mischiefs lately occasioned by their lawless and undisciplined manners, was perhaps considered a subject rather of congratulation than of regret to the kingdom.

These excesses, however, for the time, had the effect of throwing the whole of the northern parts of the country into a state of tumult and rebellion; and the king, having collected an army, summoned his feudal barons to attend him, and determined to proceed against his enemies in person. With some of the

---

* Fordun a Hearne, vol. iv. p. 1289. Extracta ex Chronicis Scotiæ, p. 277.

† Fordun a Goodal, vol. ii. p. 491.

most powerful of the nobility, this northern expedition seems to have been unpopular; and the potent Earl of Douglas, with Lord Kennedy, both of them nephews to James, were committed to ward in the castles of Lochleven and Stirling, probably from some disgust expressed at the royal commands.* The rendezvous was appointed at Perth, where, previous to his northern expedition, a parliament was held on the fifteenth of October; and to defray the expenses of the undertaking, a land-tax, or "*zelde*," was raised upon the whole lands in the kingdom, ecclesiastical as well as temporal. Its amount was declared to be ten pennies in every pound from those lands where, upon a former occasion, the tax of two pennies had been levied, and twelve pennies in the pound out of all lands which had been excepted from the payment of this smaller contribution. At the same time, the king directed his justices to take proper measures for the punishment of those vassals who had disobeyed his summons, and absented themselves from the host; and, with the intention of passing into the Western Isles, and inflicting exemplary vengeance against the pirate chiefs who had joined Donald Balloch, he proceeded to Dunstaffinch castle. Here he found himself in a short time surrounded by crowds of suppliant island lords, who, dreading the determined character of James, were eager to make their submission, and to throw the whole blame of the rebellion upon Balloch, whose power they dared not resist. By their means three hundred of the most noted thieves and robbers were seized and led to immediate execution; and soon after Donald Balloch was himself betrayed by one of the petty kings of Ireland, who, having entered into a

* Fordun a Hearne, vol. iv. p. 1288.

secret treaty with James, cut off his head, and sent it to the king.*

It was at this period that the pestilence again broke out in Scotland; but the visitation, although sufficiently dreadful, appears to have assumed a less fatal character than that which in 1348 carried off almost a third part of the population of the kingdom. The winter had been unusually severe and stormy, and the cold so intense, that not only the domestic cattle, but the hardier beasts of the chase, almost entirely perished. It is difficult, in the meagre annals of contemporary historians, to detect anything like the distinguishing symptoms of this awful scourge. In contradistinction to the pestilences which, in 1348, 1361, and 1378, had committed such fatal ravages, Bower denominates this the "pestilentia volatilis;"† and we know that, having first appeared at Edinburgh in the month of February 1430, it continued throughout the year 1432, at which time it was prevalent in Haddington;‡ while in the year immediately preceding, (1431,) during the parliament which was held at Perth in October, the volatile character of the disease seems to be pointed out by the provision, that the collectors of the land-tax should be obliged to arrange their accounts on the Feast of the Purification of the Virgin, next to come, "at Perth, provided the pestilence be not there, and if it is there, at Saint Andrews."§ The inclemency of the season, the poverty of the lower classes, and the dreadful rav-

* Acts of the Parliament of Scotland, vol. ii. p. 20. Buchanan, book x. chap. xxxiii. xxxvi. It is singular that James's expedition against his northern rebels in 1431 is not mentioned either by Fordun, or Bower in his Continuation; yet that such an expedition took place the Acts of the Parliament held at Perth, fifteenth of October, 1431, afford undoubted evidence.
† Fordun a Goodal, vol. ii. pp. 347, 365, 391, 490.
‡ Extracta ex Chronicis Scotiæ, p. 277.
§ Acts of Parliament, vol. ii. p. 20.

ages occasioned by private war, and by the ferocity of the northern clans, must have greatly increased the distresses occasioned by such a calamity; and it appears from the accounts of our contemporary chroniclers, that during the height of the ravages which the pestilence occasioned, the popular mind, under the influence of terror and ignorance, became agitated with frightful stories, and wild and romantic superstitions. A total eclipse of the sun, which occurred on the seventeenth of June, 1432, increased these terrors, the obscuration beginning at three in the afternoon, and for half an hour causing a darkness as deep as midnight. It was long remembered in Scotland by the name of the Black Hour.*

The continuance of the successes of the French, and the repeated defeats which the English had experienced, now rendered it of importance to the government of Henry the Sixth to make a serious effort for the establishment of a lasting peace with Scotland; and for this purpose Lord Scrope proceeded as envoy to the court of James, with proposals so decidedly advantageous, that it is difficult to account for their rejection. The English king, he declared, was ready to purchase so desirable a blessing as a peace by the delivery of Roxburgh and Berwick into the hands of the Scots, and the restitution of all that had anciently belonged to their kingdom. Anxious to obtain the advice of his parliament upon so momentous an offer, James appointed a general council of the whole states of the realm to be held at Perth in October,† in which he laid before them the proposals of England.

The whole body of the temporal barons agreed in the

* Fordun a Hearne, vol. iv. p. 1307.
† Ibid. vol. iv. p. 1308. I do not find in Rymer's Fœdera, in the Acts of the Parliament, or in the Rotuli Scotiæ, any deed throwing light upon this transaction.

expediency of entering upon an immediate negotiation, preparatory to a treaty of peace, and the majority of the prelates and higher churchmen concurred in this proposal; but amongst the minor clergy there existed a party attached to the interests of France, which was headed by the Abbots of Scone and Inchcolm. They warmly contended, that considering the engagements with that country, and the treaty of marriage and alliance which the king had lately ratified, it was impossible to accept the proposals of England, consistently with his honour, and the regard due to a solemn agreement, which had been examined by the University of Paris, and had received the ratification of the pope. These arguments were seconded by the Abbot of Melrose, and with much violence opposed by Lawrence of Lindores, who, as the great inquisitor of all heretical opinions, imagined that he detected, in the propositions of his brethren of the church, some tenets which were not strictly orthodox. This led to a warm reply, and the debate, instead of a temperate discussion of the political question which had been submitted to the parliament, degenerated into a theological controversy of useless length and bitterness, which unfortunately led, in the first instance, to a delay of the principal business, and ultimately to a rejection of all proposals of peace.*

The succeeding year was barbarously signalized by the trial and condemnation of Paul Crawar, a Bohemian, who was burnt for heresy at St Andrews on the twenty-third of July. He had been sent by the citizens of Prague, who had adopted the tenets of Wickliff, to open an intercourse with their brethren in Scotland. Of these earnest inquirers after truth, there appears to have been a small sect, who, undaunted by the dread-

* Fordun a Hearne, vol. iv. pp. 1309, 1310.

ful fate of Resby, continued secretly to examine the alleged errors of the Catholic church, and to disseminate what they contended were principles more orthodox and scriptural. Crawar was a physician, and came into Scotland with letters which spoke highly of his eminence in his art; but he seized every opportunity of inculcating principles contrary to the established doctrines of the church, and the Inquisitor, Lawrence of Lindores, arraigned him before his court, and entered into a laboured confutation of his opinions. He found him, however, not only a courageous, but, according to the admission of his enemies, a singularly acute opponent. In theological controversy, in an acquaintance with the sacred Scriptures, and in the power of prompt and apposite quotation, the Bohemian physician was unrivalled; but it was soon discovered that he had adopted all the opinions of the disciples of Wickliff, and of the heretics of Prague, and that his profession of a physician was merely a cloak to conceal his real character as a zealous reformer.

That he had made many converts, there can be no doubt, from the expressions used by Bower; and the laboured exposition and denunciation of his errors, which is given by the historian, contains evidence that his opinions were on some points those of Wickliff, which had been propagated twenty-six years before by Resby. He and his followers taught, that the Bible ought to be freely communicated to the people; that, in a temporal kingdom, the spiritual power should be subservient to the civil; that magistrates had a right to arraign, on trial, and to punish delinquent ecclesiastics and prelates; that purgatory was a fable; the efficacy of pilgrimages an imposition; the power of the "keys," the doctrine of transubstantiation and the ceremonies of absolution, a delusion and invention of man. The historian adds, that this sect denied the resurrection of the dead, recommended a community of goods, and that their lives were gross and licentious.* In the celebration of the Lord's Supper, they departed entirely from the solemnities which distinguished this rite in the usage of the Catholic church. They used no splendid vestments, attended to no canonical hours or set form of words, but began the service at once by the Lord's Prayer; after which, they read the history of the institution of the Supper as contained in the New Testament, and then proceeded to distribute the elements, using common bread and a common drinking cup or goblet.†

These practices and principles, in some of which we can recognise not merely a dawning, but nearly a full development of the tenets of Luther, excited a deep alarm amongst the clergy, who found a warm supporter in the king. James had been brought up in a cruel and selfish school; for both Henry the Fourth and his son were determined persecutors, and the price which they did not scruple to pay for the money and the influence of the clergy, was the groans and tortures of those who sealed their confession with their blood. A familiarity with religious persecution, and an early habit of confounding it with a zeal for the truth, became thus familiar to the mind of the youthful king; and the temptations to favour and encourage his clergy, as a check and counterpoise to the power of his nobles, was not easily resisted. When, accordingly, Lawrence of Lindores, the Inquisitor of heresy, became ambitious to signalise the same controversial powers against Crawar, which he had already exerted in the confutation of Resby, he

* Fordun a Goodal, vol. ii. pp. 495, 496. † Ibid, vol. ii. p. 495.

found no difficulties thrown in his way. The Bohemian reformer was seized, arraigned, confuted, and condemned; and as he boldly refused to renounce his opinions, he was led to the stake, and gave up his life for the principles he had disseminated, with the utmost cheerfulness and resolution.* The great Council of Basle, which was held at this time, had taken special cognizance of the errors of Wickliff; and as the Bishops of Glasgow and Moray, with the Abbot of Arbroath, and many of the Scottish nobles, attended at this solemn assembly of the church, it is probable that their increased devotion to the Catholic faith, and anxiety for the extermination of heretical opinions in their own country, proceeded from their late intercourse with this great theological convocation.†

In the midst of his labours for the pacification of his northern dominions, and his anxiety for the suppression of heresy, the king never forgot his great plan for the diminution of the exorbitant power of the nobles; and with this view he now disclosed a design of a bold character, but which, however expedient, was scarcely reconcileable to the principles of justice. The strong castle of Dunbar, and the extensive estate, or rather principality, of the Earl of March, since the days of David the First, had been a perpetual thorn in the side of the Scottish government; its situation having enabled each successive earl to hold in his hands a power far too great for any subject. It was a common saying, that March held the keys of the kingdom at his girdle. The possession of the various castles which commanded the passes, permitted him to admit an enemy at pleasure into the heart of the country, and

* Fordun a Goodal, vol. ii. pp. 442, 495.
† Rotuli Scotiæ, vol. ii. pp. 276, 284.

almost rendered the prosperity of the nation dependent upon the fidelity of a single baron. These circumstances, accordingly, had produced the effects which might have been anticipated; and the Earls of March had shown themselves for many generations the most ambitious and the most intriguing of the whole race of Scottish nobles; as pre-eminent in their power as they were precarious in their loyalty.

The conduct of the father of the present earl had been productive of infinite distress and misery to Scotland. Disgusted at the affront offered to his daughter, by the Duke of Rothesay's breach of his betrothed promise, and by his subsequent marriage with the house of Douglas, he had fled to England in 1401, and for eight years had acted the part of an able and unrelenting renegade. He had ravaged Scotland in company with Hotspur; he had been the great cause of the disastrous defeat at Homildon; his military talents were still more decidedly displayed upon the side of Henry the Fourth at Shrewsbury; and his son, the earl, against whom James now resolved to direct his vengeance, had defeated the Scots at West Nesbit. After the accession of Albany to the kingdom, the elder March, in 1408, returned to his native country; and having been restored to his estates, which had been forfeited to the crown in consequence of his rebellion, he continued in the quiet possession of them till his death, which happened in 1420.

He was succeeded by his son, George earl of March, a baron, who, with the single exception of having fought against the Scots at Nesbit, does not appear to have inherited any part of his father's versatility; and who, although arrested by James at the time when Duke Murdoch was imprisoned, shared that fate in common with many others of the nobility, who seem to have purchased their peace with the king by sitting upon the jury which condemned his unfortunate cousin. It was a remarkable feature, however, in the character of this monarch, that he retained his purposes with a steadiness and patience, that gave little alarm, while it enabled him quietly to watch his opportunity: that he was calculating upon the removal of obstacles, and smoothing the road for the execution of his designs, when no one suspected that such designs existed. In the parliament held at Perth, on the fifteenth of October, 1431, it had been declared by the three Estates,* that the governor of the realm, during the period of his government, had no power to alienate any lands, which, by the decease of a bastard, might have fallen to the crown; and that, on this ground, the donation of the lands of Yetholm, which had been made by Albany, when governor, to Adam Ker, was of none effect, although it had been completed by feudal investiture. It is very probable that, at this or a subsequent period, other enactments may have been passed relative to the power possessed by the king to resume such estates as, having once been forfeited for treason, had been restored by the governor. No record of such, however, remains; and we only know that James, having felt his way, and being probably sure of his own strength, determined on the resumption of the immense estates of March into the hands of the crown.

A parliament was accordingly assembled at Perth, on the tenth of January, 1434, and its first proceeding was to select a committee of nine persons, including three of the clergy, three of the barons, and three of the burgesses, to determine all causes which might be brought before them. The Abbots of Scone and of St

* Acts of the Parliament of Scotland, vol. ii. p. 20.

Colm,* the Provost of the collegiate church of Methven, Sir Robert Stewart of Lorn, Sir Thomas Somerville of Somerville, and Sir Walter Haliburton of Dirleton, along with John Spens of Perth, Thomas Chambers of Aberdeen, and James Parkle of Linlithgow, were the judges chosen upon this occasion; but whether the important cause relating to the earldom of March came before them, or was pleaded in presence of the whole body of the parliament, is not easily ascertained. It is certain that the question regarding the forfeiture of the property, and its reversion to the crown, in consequence of the treason of the late Earl of March, was discussed with all due solemnity by the advocates or prolocutors of the king, and of the earl then in possession; after which, this baron and his counsel being ordered to retire, the judges considered the reasons which had been urged on both sides, and made up their opinion upon the case. March and his prolocutors were then re-admitted, and the doomster declared it to be the decision of the parliament, that, in consequence of the forfeiture of Lord George of Dunbar, formerly Earl of March, all title of property to the lands of the earldom of March and lordship of Dunbar, with whatever other lands the same baron held of the crown, belonged of right to the king, and might immediately be insisted on.†

Against this measure, which in a moment reduced one of the most powerful subjects in the realm to the condition of a landless dependant upon the charity of the crown, it does not appear that the earl or his friends dared to offer any remonstrance or resistance. They probably knew it would be ineffectual, and might bring

---

* Walter Bower, the excellent Continuator of Fordun.
† Acts of the Parliament of Scotland, vol. ii. p. 23.

upon them still more fatal consequences; and James proceeded to complete his plan for the security of the kingdom, by taking possession of the forfeited estate, and delivering the keeping of the castle of Dunbar, which he had seized in the preceding year, to Sir Walter Haliburton of Dirleton. He then, to soften in some degree the severity of his conduct, conferred upon March the title of Earl of Buchan, and assigned to him, out of the revenues of that northern principality, an annual pension of four hundred marks. That noble person, however, full of resentment for the cruelty with which he had been treated, disdained to assume a title which he regarded as only a mark of his degradation; and almost immediately after the judgment, bidding adieu to his country, in company with his eldest son, retired to England.* Although this extraordinary proceeding appears not to have occasioned any open symptoms of dissatisfaction at the moment, it is impossible to conceive that it should not have roused the jealousy and alarmed the minds of the great body of the feudal nobility. It cannot, perhaps, be pronounced strictly unjust; yet there was a harshness, it may almost be said, a tyranny in the manner in which such princely estates were torn from the family, after they had been possessed for twenty-six years, without challenge or remonstrance.

During the long usurpation of Albany, many of the nobles had either acquired, or been permitted to retain their lands, upon tenures in every respect as unsound as that by which March possessed his earldom, and none knew whether they might not be the next victims. A dark suspicion that the life of the king was incompatible with their security and independence, began

* Rotuli Scotiæ, vol. ii. p. 293.

secretly to infuse itself into their minds; and from a proceeding which took place before the dissolution of the parliament, the monarch himself appears to have been aware of the probability of conspiracy, and to have contemplated the possibility of his being suddenly cut off in the midst of his schemes for the consolidation of his power. He did not allow them to separate and return to their homes, before the whole lords of parliament, temporal and spiritual, as well as the commissaries of the burghs, had promised to give their bonds of adherence and fidelity to their sovereign lady the queen.*

About the same time, the king acquired a great accession of property and power by the death of Alexander Stewart, the famous Earl of Mar, and a natural son of the Earl of Buchan, James's uncle. The estates of this wealthy and potent person, who, from a rude and ferocious highland freebooter, had become one of the ablest captains, and most experienced statesmen, in the nation,† reverted upon his death to the crown, upon the ground of his bastardy. The humiliation of the hated race of Albany was now complete. Murdoch and his sons, with the Earl of Lennox, had perished on the scaffold, and their whole estates had reverted to the crown; although the Earl of Buchan, who was slain at Verneuil, had left an only daughter, to whom the title belonged, by a stretch of power, bordering upon injustice, the title had been bestowed upon the disinherited March, and now the immense estates of the Earl of Mar, the natural son of Buchan, reverted to the crown. The power of the king became thus every

---

* Acts of the Parliament of Scotland, vol. ii. p. 23. The expression is, " dare literas suas retenenciæ et fidelitatis Domine nostre Regine."
† Fordun a Goodal, vol. ii. p. 500.

day more formidable; but it was built upon the oppression of his feudal nobility, a set of men with whom it was considered a meanness to forget an injury, and whose revenge was generally deep and terrible—and so the result showed.

Entirely occupied with a vain and unsuccessful effort to retain their conquests in France, the English government evinced every anxiety to preserve inviolate the truce with Scotland; but the spirit of Border hostility could not be long restrained, and Sir Robert Ogle, from some cause which is not easily discoverable, broke across the marches, at the head of a strong body of knights and men-at-arms. He was met, however, and totally routed, near Piperden, by the Earl of Angus, Hepburn of Hailes, and Sir Alexander Ramsay of Dalhousie, he himself being taken captive, forty slain, and nearly the whole of his party made prisoners.* James violently remonstrated against this unprovoked infraction of the truce, and, in his letters to the English regency, insisted upon immediate redress; but his complaints were overlooked or rejected, and the king was not of a temper to bear such an affront with tameness, or to forget it when an opportunity for retaliation occurred.

These indignant feelings were increased by an occurrence which followed soon after the conflict at Piperden. The Dauphin of France, who had been betrothed to Margaret, the daughter of the Scottish king, had now attained his thirteenth year, and the princess herself was ten years old: it was accordingly resolved to complete the marriage; and with this view, two French envoys having arrived in Scotland, the youthful bride was sent to the court of the king of France, accompanied by a splendid train of the nobility. The fleet

* Fordun a Goodal, vol. ii. p. 501.

which carried her to her future kingdom, where her lot was singularly wretched, was commanded by the Earl of Orkney, William Sinclair. The Bishop of Brechin, Sir Walter Ogilvy the treasurer, Sir Herbert Harris, Sir John Maxwell of Calderwood, Sir John Campbell of Loudon, Sir John Wishart, and many other barons, attended in her suite. They were waited on by a hundred and forty youthful squires, and a guard of a thousand men-at-arms; and the fleet consisted of three large ships, and six barges.*

In defiance of the truce which then subsisted between the two kingdoms, the English government determined, if possible, to intercept the princess upon her passage to France, and for this purpose fitted out a large fleet, which anchored off the coast of Bretagne, in order to watch the motions of the Scots. It was impossible that so flagrant an insult should fail to rouse the indignation of the Scottish king. It convinced him how little was to be trusted to the honour of a government which disregarded a solemn truce the moment a favourable opportunity for conquest, or annoyance, presented itself, whilst it reminded him of the treachery by which he had himself been seized, and brought all the bitterness of his long captivity before him. The project, however, was unsuccessful. The English were drawn away from their watch by the appearance of a company of Flemish merchantmen, laden with wine from Rochelle, which they pursued and captured; but the triumph was of short duration; for almost immediately after a Spanish fleet appeared in sight, and an engagement took place, in which the English were beaten, their Flemish prizes wrested from their hands, and they themselves compelled to take to flight. In the

* Fordun a Goodal, vol. ii. p. 485.

midst of these transactions, the little Scottish squadron, with the Dauphiness and her suite, safely entered the port of Rochelle, and disembarked at Neville Priory, where she was received by the Archbishop of Rheims and the Bishop of Poictiers and Xaintonge. The marriage was afterwards celebrated at Tours, with much magnificence, in presence of the King and Queen of France, the Queen of Sicily, and the nobility of both kingdoms.* By the common practice of most feudal states, an expensive ceremony of this kind was considered a proper occasion for the imposition of a general tax throughout the kingdom; but James refused to oppress the great body of his subjects by any measure of this nature, and contented himself with those gifts or largesses which the prelates and the chief nobility of the court were wont to contribute upon such joyful occurrences.†

The late infraction of the truce by Ogle, and the insidious attempt upon the part of the English government to intercept the Dauphiness, his daughter, had inflamed the resentment of the Scottish king, and rendered him not averse to the renewal of the war. It is probable, however, that there were other causes for this sudden resolution; and these are perhaps to be sought in the irritated feelings with which a portion of the nobility began to regard the government of James. To find excitement and employment for such dangerous spirits, the monarch assembled the whole force of his dominions; and with an army, formidable indeed in numbers, but weakened by intrigues and discontent amongst the principal leaders, he commenced the siege of Roxburgh.‡

* Fordun a Goodal. vol. ii. pp. 485, 501. † Ibid.
‡ Ibid. p. 502. The king was engaged in the siege of Roxburgh, 10th August, 1436. Rotuli Scotiæ, vol. ii. p. 295.

The subsequent course of events is involved in much obscurity, which the few original documents that remain do not in any satisfactory manner remove. After having spent fifteen days in the siege, during which time the warlike engines for the attack were broken and rendered useless, and the quarrels, arrows, and missiles, entirely exhausted, the castle was on the eve of being surrendered, when the queen suddenly arrived in the camp, and James, apparently in consequence of the secret information which she communicated, abruptly put a period to the siege, disbanded his army, and with a haste which implied some weighty cause of alarm, returned ingloriously into the interior of his dominions. For such an abrupt step no certain cause can be assigned, but such, beyond question, was the fact; and it naturally leads to the conjecture, that James was suddenly informed of some treacherous designs against him, and suspected that the conspirators lurked within his own kingdom.*

This precipitate dismissal of his forces took place in August, and two months afterwards the king held a General Council at Edinburgh, on the twenty-second of October, 1436, in whose proceedings we can discern nothing intimating any continued suspicion of a conspiracy. Some commercial regulations were passed, which, under the mistaken idea that they were encouragements, proved, in reality, restrictions upon commerce. Exporters of wool were in future to give security to bring home and deliver to the master of the mint three ounces of bullion for every sack of wool, nine

---

* Bower (Fordun a Goodal, vol. ii. p. 502) says nothing of the arrival of the queen at Roxburgh; but the ancient MS., entitled Extracta ex Chronicis Scotiæ, p. 279, expressly states the fact:—" Per quindecim dies obsidioni vacabant, et nihil laudis actum est veniens regina abduxit regem; reliqui sunt secuti et sic cessavit."

ounces for a last of hides, and three ounces for such quantity of other goods as paid freight, equal to an ancient measure called a *serplaith*; whilst, in addition to the impolicy of restricting the merchants from importing such goods as they esteemed most likely to increase their profits, the delivery of the silver was regulated by weight or measure, and not by value. Other unwise restrictions were imposed. No English cloth was permitted to be purchased by the Scottish merchants, nor were English traders allowed to carry any articles of Scottish trade or manufacture out of the kingdom, unless such were specified particularly in their letters of safe conduct.*

Yet, in the midst of these parliamentary proceedings, more dark designs were in agitation amongst the nobility; and the seeds of discontent and rebellion, which the king imagined had been entirely eradicated after the retreat from Roxburgh, were secretly expanding themselves into a conspiracy, of which the history and ramifications are as obscure as the result was deplorable. Its chief actors, however, and the temper and objects by which they were regulated, may be ascertained on authentic evidence. The chief promoters of the plot were Sir Robert Graham, brother of Sir Patrick Graham of Kincardine; Walter Stewart earl of Athole, a son of Robert the Second; and his grandson Sir Robert Stewart, who filled the office of chamberlain to the king, by whom he was much caressed and favoured. Graham's disposition was one which, even in a civilized age, would have made him a dangerous enemy; but in those feudal times, when revenge was a virtue, and forgiveness a weakness, it became,

* Acts of the Parliament of Scotland, vol. ii. pp. 23, 24. M'Pherson's Annals of Commerce, vol. i. p. 650.

under such nurture, peculiarly dark and ferocious. Unshaken courage, and a contempt of pain and danger, a persuasive power of bending others to his purposes, a dissimulation which enabled him to conceal his private ambition under a zeal for the public good, and a cruelty which knew neither hesitation nor remorse, were the moral elements which formed the character of this daring conspirator.

Upon the return of the king from his detention in England, and at the time that he inflicted his summary vengeance upon the house of Albany, Sir Robert Graham had been imprisoned, along with the other adherents of that powerful family; but it seems probable that he obtained his liberty, and for a while became reconciled to the government. Another transaction, however, was at hand, which, it is said, rekindled his feelings into a determined purpose of revenge. This was the seizure or resumption of the earldom of Strathern by the king. David earl of Strathern, the brother of the Earl of Athole, was the eldest son of Robert the Second, by his second wife Euphemia Ross. He left an only daughter, who married Patrick Graham, son of Sir Patrick Graham of Kincardine, and, in right of his wife, Earl of Strathern, to whose children, as the transmission of these feudal dignities through females was the acknowledged law of Scotland, the title and estates undoubtedly belonged. James, however, fixed his eyes upon this powerful earldom. He contended that it was limited to heirs-male; that upon the death of David earl of Strathern it ought to have reverted to the crown; and that Albany the governor had no power to permit Patrick Graham or his son to assume so extensive a fief, which he resumed as his own. Although, however, he dispossessed

Malise Graham, the son of the Earl of Strathern, of his lands and dignity, James appears to have been anxious to remove the appearance of injustice from such conduct, and to conciliate the disinherited family. For this purpose he conferred the liferent of the earldom of Strathern upon Athole, and he created the new earldom of Menteith in favour of Malise Graham.*

This attempt at conciliation, however, did not succeed; and indeed, notwithstanding the disguise which the king threw over it, it is easy to see that his conduct must have appeared both selfish and tyrannical. It was selfish, because, from the extreme age of Athole, James looked to the almost immediate possession of the rich earldom which he had torn from the Grahams; and tyrannical, because there appears no ground for the assertion that it was a male fief. Malise Graham was now a youth, and absent in England; but his uncle, Sir Robert Graham, remonstrated, as the natural guardian of his rights; and finding it in vain to sue for redress, he determined upon revenge. It was no difficult matter for a spirit like his to work upon the jealousies and discontented feelings of the nobles; and there were yet remaining many friends of Albany, who remembered the dreadful fate of that unhappy house, and who considered themselves bound by those strict ties of feudal vassalage then esteemed sacred, to revenge it the moment an opportunity presented itself.

Amongst these persons, Graham, who himself felt the influence of such feelings in the strongest possible manner, found many ready associates; but although the body of the higher nobility were sufficiently eager to enter into his designs for the abridgment of the

* Hailes, Sutherland Case, chap. v. p. 57

royal prerogative, and the resumption of the power which they had lost, they appear at first to have shrunk from anything beyond this.* It was determined, meanwhile, that Graham, who was an eloquent speaker, should detail their grievances in parliament, and that his remonstrance should be seconded by the rest of the nobles. The natural audacity of his character, however, made him exceed his commission. He spoke with open detestation of the tyrannical conduct of the government; pointed out in glowing language the ruin of the noblest families in the state; and concluded by an appeal to the barons who surrounded him, beseeching them to save the authority of the laws, were it even at the risk of laying a temporary restraint upon the person of the sovereign. The temerity of this speech confounded the barons who had promised to support him: they trembled and hesitated; whilst James, starting from his throne, commanded them instantly to arrest the traitor, and was promptly obeyed. Graham meanwhile loudly expressed the bitterest contempt for the pusillanimity of his associates; but he was hurried to prison, soon after banished from court, and his estates confiscated to the crown.†

James, if not already sensible of the dangerous character of Graham, must have now been fully aware of it; and how he should have suffered so bold and able a rebel to escape, is difficult to understand. It is evident, I think, that the connexion between Graham, the Earl of Athole, and Sir Robert Stewart, had not at this time proceeded to the formation of those atrocious designs which they afterwards carried into exe-

* Contemporary Account of "The dethe of the King of Scotis," first printed by Pinkerton, Hist. vol. i. p. 462.
† Ibid. p. 464.

cution, for we cannot doubt that the king must have examined the whole affair with the utmost anxiety; and his banishment of Graham only, may convince us that, in this instance, he did not suspect him of plotting with others of his nobility.

Enraged at the ruin of his fortunes, this audacious man retreated to the highlands, and within their gloomy recesses meditated a desperate revenge. But the mode in which he proceeded had something great about it, and showed that he was no hired or common assassin. He sent a letter to James, in which he renounced his allegiance; he defied him, as a tyrant who had ruined his family, and left him houseless and landless; and he warned him, that wherever he could find opportunity, he would slay him as his mortal enemy. These threats, coming from a vagabond traitor, James despised; but he made proclamation for his apprehension, and fixed a large sum of gold on his head.*

In the meantime parliament met, and Graham, although immured in his highland retreats, found means to communicate with the discontented nobles, and to induce the Earl of Athole, and his grandson Sir Robert Stewart, to enter fully into his schemes for the destruction of the king. He represented to this baron, who, though now aged, inherited the proud ambition of his family, that Robert the Third was born out of wedlock, and that the crown belonged to him, as the lawful son of the second marriage of Robert the Second, or, if he chose to decline it, to Stewart, his grandson. The single life of a tyrant, who had destroyed his house, and whose power was every day becoming more formidable, was, he contended, all that

* Contemporary Account.

stood between him and the throne, for James's son was yet a boy in his sixth year, and might be easily disposed of; and such was the unpopularity of the government, that the whole body of the nobility would readily welcome a change. It is said, also, that Graham worked upon Athole's ambition by the predictions of a highland seer, who had prophesied that this earl should be crowned in that same year; a story much in the superstitious character of the times, and not unlikely to be true, as the conspiracy was undoubtedly brought to its height within the highlands. If Graham was thus able to seduce the age and experience of Athole, it is not surprising that the prospect of a crown easily captivated the youthful ambition of Sir Robert Stewart, his grandson; and as he was chamberlain to the king, enjoyed his most intimate confidence, and was constantly employed in offices about his person, his accession to the plot may be regarded as the principal cause of its success. Graham's inferior assistants were principally some obscure dependants on the house of Albany, Christopher and Thomas Chambers,* with Sir John Hall and his brother; but his influence in the highlands had collected a body of three hundred ketherans, without whose co-operation it is not probable that he could have effected his purpose.

All things were now nearly ready, whilst the king, naturally of a fearless and confident temper, and occupied with his schemes for the amelioration of the commerce of the kingdom, and the better execution of the laws, appeared to have forgotten the insolence of Graham, and to have been persuaded that the discontents

---

* Contemporary Account, p. 466. In the Rotuli Scotiæ, vol. ii. p. 159, we find John del Chambre in the employment of Albany in 1401.

amongst his nobility had passed away. Christmas approaching, it was determined that the court should keep the festival at Perth, in the monastery of the Dominicans, or Black Friars, a noble edifice, which gave ample room for the accommodation of the royal retinue. This resolution gave an unlooked-for facility to the traitors, for it brought their victim to the borders of the highlands. It was accordingly resolved by Graham, that the murder should be committed at this holy season; and, after his preparations had been made, he waited patiently for the arrival of the king.

It was impossible, however, that a plot which embraced so many agents should be kept completely secret; and a highland woman, who in those days of superstition laid claim to prophetic skill, becoming acquainted with the design, resolved to betray it to the king. Accordingly, as the monarch and his nobles were on their road to cross the Firth of Forth, then called the Scottish sea, she presented herself before the royal cavalcade, and addressing James, solemnly warned him, "that if he crossed that water he should never return again alive."* He was struck with her wild appearance, and the earnestness of her manner, stopt for a moment, and commanded a knight who rode beside him to inquire what she meant. Whether from stupidity or treachery is not certain, the commission was hurriedly executed, and she had only time to say that her information came from one Hubert; when the same knight observing, that she was either mad or intoxicated, the king gave orders to proceed, and, having crossed the Firth, rode on to Perth. James, as was expected, took up his residence in the Dominican monastery, and the court was unusually

* Contemporary Account. Pinkerton, vol. i. p. 465.

brilliant and joyous. Day after day passed in every species of feudal delight and revelry; and the conspirators had matured their plan, and fixed the very hour for the murder, whilst the unhappy prince dreamt of nothing but pleasure.

It was on the night between the twentieth and the twenty-first of February that Graham resolved to carry his purpose into effect. After dark, he had procured Sir Robert Stewart, whose office of chamberlain facilitated his treachery, and rendered him above all suspicion, to place wooden boards across the moat which surrounded the monastery, over which the conspirators might pass without disturbing the warder, and to destroy the locks and remove the bolts of the doors by which the royal bedchamber communicated with the outer room, and this apartment with the passage. On this fatal evening the revels of the court were kept up to a late hour. The common sports and diversions of the time, the game of tables, the reading romances, the harp and the song, occupied the night; and the prince himself appears to have been in unusually gay and cheerful spirits. He even jested about a prophecy which had declared that a king should that year be slain; and when engaged in playing at chess with a young knight, whom in his sport he was accustomed to call the King of Love, warned him to look well to his safety, as they were the only two kings in the land.* In the midst of this playful conversation, Christopher Chambers, one of the conspirators, being seized with remorse, repeatedly approached the royal presence, intending to warn James of his danger; but either his heart failed him, or he was prevented by the crowd of knights and ladies who filled the pre-

* Contemporary Account, p. 466.

sence chamber, and he renounced his purpose. It was now long past midnight, and the traitors, Athole and Stewart, who knew by this time that Graham and the other conspirators must be near at hand, heard James express his wishes for the conclusion of the revels with secret satisfaction; when, at this moment, a last effort was made to save the unhappy prince, which had almost succeeded. The faithful highland woman who had followed the court to Perth, again presented herself at the door of the chamber, and so earnestly implored to see the king, that the usher informed him of her wishes. It was a moment on which his fate seemed to hang, but his evil genius presided; he bade her call again and tell her errand on the morrow, and she left the monastery, after solemnly observing that they would never meet again.*

Soon after this James called for the parting cup, and the company dispersed. The Earl of Athole, and Sir Robert Stewart the chamberlain, were the last to leave the apartment; and the king, who was now partly undressed, stood in his night-gown before the fire talking gaily with the queen and her ladies of the bedchamber, when he was alarmed by a confused clang of arms, and a glare of torches in the outer court. A suspicion of treason, and a dread that it was the traitor Graham, instantly darted into his mind, and the queen and the women flew to secure the door of the apartment, but to their dismay found the locks destroyed and the bolts removed. James thus became certain that his destruction was resolved on; but his presence of mind did not forsake him, and commanding the women to obstruct all entrance as long as they were able, he

---

* Contemporary Account, p. 467. "The said woman of Yreland that cleped herself a dyvenouresse."

rushed to the windows, but found them so firmly secured by iron bars, that all escape was impossible. The steps of armed men now came nearer and nearer, and in utter despair he seized the tongs of the fireplace in the apartment, and by main force wrenching up one of the boards of the floor, let himself down into a small vault situated below; he then replaced the board, and thus completely concealed himself from observation. From this incommodious retreat there was a communication with the outer court by means of a drain or square hole used for cleansing the apartment, and of width enough to have permitted the king to escape; but it had unfortunately been built up only three days before this by James's own direction, as the tennis court was near it, and the balls had frequently run in and been lost in the aperture.* Meanwhile, Graham and his accomplices rushed towards the king's bedchamber, and having slain Walter Straiton, a page, whom they met in the passage, began to force open the door amidst the shrieks of the queen and the women, who feebly attempted to barricade it. One of the ladies, named Catherine Douglas, with heroic resolution thrust her arm into the staple from which the bolt had been treacherously removed; but it was instantly snapt and broken by the brutal violence of the conspirators, who, with furious looks, and naked weapons stained with blood, burst into the chamber, and in their first attack had the cowardice to wound some of the queen's women, as they fled screaming into the corners of the apartment. The queen alone did not move, but, wrought up to a pitch of horror and frenzy which paralyzed every member, stood rooted to the floor, her hair hanging loosely around her shoulders,

* Contemporary Account, p. 468.

and with nothing on but her kirtle and mantle.* Yet in this helpless state one of the villains, in the most brutal manner, attacked and wounded her, and she would assuredly have been slain had the deed not been prevented by a son of Graham's, who peremptorily commanded him to leave the women and join the search for the king, whom the conspirators now perceived had escaped them. Every part of the chamber was now diligently examined, every place of probable concealment opened up without success; and after a tedious search, they dispersed through the outer rooms and passages, and from thence extended their scrutiny to the remoter parts of the building.

A considerable time had now elapsed since the first alarm, and although Graham had secured the gates and occupied the outer courts of the monastery by his highlanders, yet the citizens, and the nobles who were quartered in the town, already heard the noise of the tumult, and were hastening to the spot. It seemed exceedingly likely, therefore, that the king would still be saved, for his place of concealment had totally escaped the attention of the conspirators, and every moment brought his rescue nearer. But he was ruined by his own impatience. Hearing no stir, and imagining that they who sought his life had left the place not to return, he called to the women to bring the sheets from the bed, and draw him up again into the apartment; but in their attempt to effect this, Elizabeth Douglas, one of the queen's women, fell down. The noise recalled the conspirators, and at this moment Thomas Chambers, one of Graham's accomplices, who knew the monastery well, suddenly remembered the small closet beneath the bed-chamber, and conceiving, if James

* Contemporary Account, p. 468.

had not escaped, that he must be there concealed, quickly returned to the apartment. In a moment he discovered the spot where the floor was broken, raised up the plank, and looking in, by the light of his torch perceived the king, and the unfortunate lady who had fallen into the vault; upon which he shouted to his fellows, with savage merriment to come back, for the bride was found for whom they had sought and carolled all night.* The dreadful scene was now soon completed; yet James, strong in his agony, although almost naked, and without a weapon, made a desperate defence. He seized Sir John Hall, who had leapt down, by the throat, and with main strength threw him under his feet; another of the murderers, Hall's brother, who next descended, met with the same fate; and such was the convulsive violence with which they had been handled, that at their execution, a month after, the marks of the king's grasp were seen upon their persons. But the villains being armed with large knives, James's hands and arms were dreadfully lacerated in the struggle. Sir Robert Graham now entered the chamber, and springing down with his drawn sword, threw himself upon his victim, who earnestly implored his mercy, and begged his life, should it be at the price of half his kingdom. "Thou cruel tyrant," said Graham, "never hadst thou compassion upon thine own noble kindred, therefore expect none now." —"At least," said James, "let me have a confessor for the good of my soul."—"None," cried Graham, "none shalt thou have but this sword!" upon which he wounded him mortally in the body, and the unhappy prince instantly fell down, and, bleeding and exhausted,

---

* Contemporary Account, p. 469. "Saying to his felows, Sirs, the spows is foundon, wherfor we ben comne, and al this nycht haf carold here."

continued faintly to implore his life. The scene was so piteous, that it is said at this moment to have shook the nerves, and moved the compassion, of the ruffian himself, who was about to come up, leaving the king still breathing, when his companions above threatened him with instant death if he did not finish the work. He then obeyed, and, assisted by the two Halls, completed the murder by repeated wounds.*

In this atrocious manner was James the First cut off in the prime of life, and whilst pursuing his schemes for the consolidation of his own power, and the establishment of the government upon a just and equitable basis, with a vigour and impetuosity which proved his ruin. The shocking deed being thus consummated, the traitors anxiously sought for the queen, but by this time she had escaped; and, warned by the increasing tumult in the town, and the alarm in the court, they fled in great haste from the monastery, and were descried crossing the outer moat, and making off in the direction of the Highlands. Sir David Dunbar, brother to the Earl of March, overtook and slew one of their number, after being himself grievously wounded;† but he who fell was of inferior note, and the principal conspirators made good their retreat to the highlands.

On entering the chamber where the murder had been committed, a miserable spectacle presented itself, —the king's naked body bathed in blood, and pierced with sixteen wounds. The lamentable sight, by the pity and execration which it universally inspired, stimulated the activity of pursuit, and whetted the appetite for revenge; and the queen, disdaining to

* Contemporary Account, p. 470.
† Ibid. p. 471. Fordun a Goodal, vol. ii. p. 503.

abandon herself to the helplessness of womanly grief, used such unwearied efforts to trace and apprehend the murderers, that in less than a month they were all taken and executed. Little, however, is known as to the exact mode of their apprehension. The principal conspirator, Graham, and some of his accomplices, appear to have escaped into the wilds of Mar; but they were traced to their concealments, and seized by two highland chieftains, John Stewart Gorm, and Robert Duncanson, the ancestor of the ancient family of Robertson of Strowan.*

The shocking scenes of torture which preceded their death must not be detailed, and are, it is hoped, chiefly to be ascribed to the ferocity of the times. It must be remembered that at this period the common death of every traitor was accomplished by torture; and in the present instance, the atrocity of the murder was thought to call for a refinement and complication in the punishment. Sir Robert Stewart and Thomas Chambers were first taken and brought to Edinburgh, where, after a full confession of their guilt, which unfortunately does not remain, they were beheaded on a high scaffold raised in the market-place, and their heads fixed upon the gates of Perth. Athole, who had been seized by the Earl of Angus, was the next sufferer. After being exhibited to the populace, tied to a pillar in the city, and crowned with a paper diadem, upon which was thrice written the name of traitor, his head was struck off, adorned with an iron crown, and fixed upon the top of a spear. He denied to the last that he was a party

* Chamberl. Accounts, sub anno 1438. "Et per solucionem factam Johanni Stewart Gorme pro arrestacione Roberti Grahaam traditoris, et suorum complicum, ut patet per literas regis moderni, de precept. sub signeto, et dicti Johannis Stewart de recept. concess. super compotum 56 lib. 13 s. 4 d. Computum Dni Ade fanconar Camerarii Comitatus de Mar." See Illustrations, H.

to the conspiracy, although he pleaded guilty to the knowledge and concealment of it, affirming, that he exerted every effort to dissuade his grandson against such atrocious designs, and believed that he had succeeded. As he was an old man, on the verge of seventy, his fate was not beheld without pity.

Very different were the feelings excited by the execution of the arch-traitor Graham, whose courage and characteristic audacity supported him to the last. He pleaded to his judges, that having renounced his allegiance under his hand and seal, and publicly challenged and arraigned the king as his mortal enemy, he was no longer his subject, but his feudal equal, and that it was lawful for him to slay him wherever they met, without being amenable to any court whatever; seeing, said he, he did no wrong nor sin, but only slew God's creature his enemy.* He knew well, he said, that his death was resolved on, but that the time would come when they would gratefully pray for the soul of him who had delivered them from a merciless tyrant, whose avarice was so unbounded, that it ruined friends as well as enemies, and preyed alike on the poor and the rich. The firmness with which he endured his complicated sufferings, was equal to the boldness of his defence. Nailed alive and naked to a tree, dragged through the city, followed by the executioners, who tore him with pincers, whilst his son was tortured and beheaded before his face, he bore all with amazing fortitude; and when his sufferings became utterly insupportable, warned his tormentors, that if his anguish should drive him to blasphemy, the guilt would rest on their heads who had thus destroyed his soul.† Graham was at last be-

* Contemporary Account, p. 473. † Ibid. p. 474.

headed: and this dreadful scene of feudal vengeance, which it is impossible to read in the original account without sentiments of the utmost loathing and horror, concluded with the execution of Thomas Hall, one who had apparently belonged to the household of the Duke of Albany, and who to the last vindicated the share he had taken in the king's death.

There was nothing little in the character of James the First: his virtues and his faults were alike on a great scale; and his reign, although it embraced only a period of thirteen years, reckoning from his return to his assassination, stands forward brightly and prominently in the history of the country. Perhaps the most important changes which he introduced, were the publication of the acts of parliament in the spoken language of the land; the introduction of the principle of representation by the election of the commissaries for shires; the institution of the court entitled the "Session;" and the regularity with which he assembled the parliament. Before his time it had been the practice for the laws, the resolutions, and the judgments of the parliament to be embodied in the Latin language; a custom which evidently was calculated to retard improvement, and perpetuate the dominion of barbarism and feudal oppression. Before his time the great body of the judges, to whom the administration of the laws was intrusted, the barons within their regalities, the bailies, the sheriffs, mayors, sergeants, and other inferior officers, were incapable of reading or understanding the statutes; and the importance of the change from this state of darkness and uncertainty, to that which presented them with the law speaking in their own tongue, cannot be too highly estimated. It is of itself enough to stamp originality upon the character of the king, and to cause us to regard his reign as an era in the legislative history of the country.

Nor was the frequency in the assembling his parliaments of less consequence. Of these convocations of the legislature, no less than thirteen occurred during his brief reign; a striking contrast to their infrequency under the government of his predecessors. His great principle seems to have been, to govern the country through the medium of his parliament; to introduce into this august assembly a complete representation of the body of the smaller landed proprietors, and of the commercial classes; and to insist on the frequent attendance of the great temporal and spiritual lords, not, as they were formerly wont, in the character of rivals of the sovereign, surrounded by a little court, and backed by numerous bands of armed vassals, but in their accredited station, as forming the principal and essential portion of the council of the nation, bound to obey their summons to parliament upon the same principle which obliged them to give suit and service in the feudal court of their liege lord the king.

Another striking feature in James's reign, was his institution of the " Session," his constant anxiety for the administration of justice amongst the middle ranks and the commons, and the frequent and anxious legislative enactments for the severe and speedy punishment of offenders. His determination, that "he would make the bracken-bush keep the cow,"—that proverb already alluded to, and still gratefully remembered in Scotland,*—was carried into execution by an indefatigable activity, and a firmness so inexorable as sometimes to assume the appearance of cruelty; but in estimating his true character upon this point, it is

* Fordun a Goodal, vol. ii. p. 511.

necessary to keep clearly before our eyes the circumstances in which he found the country, and the dreadful misrule and oppression to which the weaker individuals in the state were subjected from the tyranny of the higher orders. It is impossible, however, to deny that the king was sometimes cruel and unjust; and that when Graham accused him of tyranny and oppression, he had perhaps more to say in his vindication than many of our historians are willing to admit. The explanation, and, in some little measure, the excuse for this, is to be found in the natural feelings of determined and undisguised hostility with which he undoubtedly regarded the family of Albany, and their remotest connexions. James considered the government of the father and the son in its true light—as one long usurpation; for although the first few years of Albany's administration as governor had been sanctioned by royal approval and the voice of the parliament, yet it is not to be forgotten, that the detention of the youthful king in England extended through the sickening period of nineteen years, during the greater part of which time the return of this prince to his throne and to his people was thwarted, as we have seen, by every possible intrigue upon the part of Albany. This base conduct was viewed by James with more unforgiving resentment from its being crowned with success; for the aged usurper by a quiet death escaped the meditated vengeance, and transmitted the supreme authority in the state to his son, ransomed from captivity for this very end, whilst his lawful prince beheld himself still detained in England. When he did return, therefore, it was not to be wondered at that his resentment was wrought to a high pitch; and deep and bloody as was the retribution which he exacted, it was neither unnatural, nor, according to the feelings of those times, wholly unjustifiable.

But making every allowance for the extraordinary wrongs he had suffered, the determination which he appears to have formed, of considering every single act of Albany's administration, however just it may have been in itself, as liable to be challenged and cut down, necessarily led, when attempted to be acted upon, to a stretch of power which bordered upon tyranny. The dilapidation, indeed, of the crown lands, and the plunder of the royal revenues which had taken place under the government of Albany and his son, afforded James a sufficient ground for resuming a great part of what had originally belonged to him; but as far as we are able to trace his schemes for the re-establishment of the royal authority, and the diminution of the overgrown power of the feudal aristocracy, there does appear about them a stern rigour, and a love of power, little removed from absolute oppression. It is not, therefore, a subject of wonder, that this spirit, which was solely directed against his nobles, incurred their bitterest hatred, and ultimately led to his ruin.

If we except his misguided desire to distinguish himself as a persecutor of the Wickliffites, James's love for the church, as the best instrument he could employ in disseminating the blessings of education, and of general improvement throughout the country, was a wise and politic passion. He found his clergy a superior and enlightened class of men, and he employed their power, their wealth, and their abilities, as a counterpoise to his nobility: yet he was not, like David the First, a munificent founder of new religious houses; indeed, his income was so limited as to make this impossible. His efforts were directed to the preservation of the discipline and learning of the church; to the revival of the custom of holding general councils or chapters, which had been discontinued during his detention in England, but of which three appear to have been assembled during his brief reign; to a personal inspection of the various monasteries and religious establishments during his progresses through the kingdom, and an affectionate reproval, if he found they had degenerated from the strictness of their rule or the sanctity of their deportment.*

It is well known that the personal accomplishments of this prince were of a high character. After his return, indeed, his incessant occupation in the cares of government left him little leisure for the cultivation of literature or of the fine arts; but his long detention in England gave him ample opportunities of mental cultivation, of which he appears to have anxiously availed himself. He was a reformer of the language and of the poetry of his country; he sang beautifully, and not only accompanied himself upon the harp and the organ, but composed various airs and pieces of sacred music, in which there was to be recognised the same original and inventive genius which distinguished this remarkable man in everything to which he applied his mind.†

In his person, James was of the middle size, of a make rather powerful and athletic than elegant, and which fitted him to excel in all martial feats and exercises. Of these he was extremely fond; and we have the testimony of a contemporary, that in drawing the bow, in the use of the lance, in horsemanship, wrest-

---

* Innes, MS. Chronology, quoted by Chalmers in his Poetic Remains of the Scottish kings, pp. 8, 16. Fordun a Goodal, vol. ii. p. 508.
† Fordun a Goodal, vol. ii. p. 504.

ling and running, in throwing the hammer, and "putting the stane," few of his courtiers could compete with him. His great strength, indeed, was shown in the dreadful and almost successful resistance which he made to his murderers. He died in the forty-fourth year of his age, and was buried in the church of the Carthusians at Perth, which he had himself founded. He left by his Queen Joanna, an only son, James, his successor, then a boy in his seventh year, and five daughters. To two of these, Margaret, who became Queen of France, and Eleanor, who married Sigismund duke of Austria, their father transmitted his love of literature.*

James's remaining daughters were Isabella, married to Francis duke of Bretagne; Mary, who took to her husband the Count de Boncquan, son to the Lord of Campvere; and lastly, Jane, wedded to the Earl of Angus, and subsequently to the Earl of Morton.

* The story of the Dauphiness and Alain Chartier is well known. Finding this famous poet asleep in the saloon of the palace, she stooped down and kissed him—observing to her ladies, who were somewhat astonished at the proceeding, that she did not kiss the man, but the mouth which had uttered so many fine things: a singular, and, as they perhaps thought, too minute a distinction. Menagiana, vol. ii. p. 130.

Eleanor, although equally fond of literature, confined herself to a more decorous mode of exhibiting her predilection, by translating the romance of Ponthus et Sidoyne into German, for the amusement of her husband.

END OF THE REIGN OF JAMES THE FIRST.

HISTORICAL REMARKS

ON THE

DEATH OF RICHARD THE SECOND.

HISTORICAL REMARKS

ON THE

DEATH OF RICHARD THE SECOND.

It is generally known, that much obscurity hangs over the common stories relative to the death of Richard the Second, and that Henry the Fourth was greatly annoyed by reports of the captive king having escaped to Scotland; reports which he, of course, invariably treated as false, and which all our modern historians, both of England and of Scotland, have been disposed to consider fabulous: some contenting themselves with a brief notice, that an impostor appeared under the name of Richard the Second, and others passing over the circumstance altogether.

In investigating this obscure part of our history, it was lately my fortune to discover some very interesting evidence, which induced me to believe that there was much more truth in these reports than I was at first disposed to admit. This led to an examination of the whole proofs relative to Richard's disappearance and alleged death in England; and the result was, a strong conviction that the king actually did make his escape from Pontefract castle; that he succeeded in conveying himself to Scotland, where he was discovered, detained, and supported, by Robert the Third and the Duke of Albany; and that he actually died in that country, long after his reputed murder in England. I am well aware that this is a startling proposition, too broadly in the face of long-established opinion to be admitted upon any evidence inferior almost to demonstration. It is quite possible, also, that there may exist, in the manuscript treasures of the public libraries of England or of France, absolute proof that Richard was murdered, or that he died in prison ; and one great object of these observations will be attained, if they have the effect of directing the attention of the learned to the farther investigation of a subject still very obscure. In the meantime, I trust I shall succeed in showing, that my hypothesis, as to Richard's escape, for it pretends to no higher name, is supported by a body of direct as well as of negative evidence, superior to that which could be adduced upon many other historical facts, the truth of which has not be questioned by the most fastidious and sceptical writers.

It is stated by Bower, or Bow-maker, the continuator of Fordun, and one of the most ancient and authentic of our early historians, that Richard the Second found means to escape from Pontefract castle ; that he succeeded in conveying himself to the Scottish isles; and, travelling in disguise through those remote parts, was accidentally recognised and discovered, when sitting in the kitchen of Donald lord of the Isles, by a jester who had been educated at the court of the king. The same historian proceeds to say, that Donald of the Isles sent him, under the charge of Lord Montgomery, to Robert the Third, with whom, as long as the Scottish monarch lived, he was supported as became his rank; and that, after the death of this king, the royal fugitive was delivered to the Duke of Albany, then governor of Scotland, by whom he was honourably treated; and he concludes this remarkable sentence, which I have given nearly in his own words, by affirming, that Richard at length died in the castle of Stirling, and was buried in the church of the preaching friars, on the north side of the altar.*

In another part of his history, the same writer, in describing the devastations committed by Richard in his expedition into Scotland, alludes in equally positive terms, and almost in the same words, to his subsequent escape into that country, and his being discovered by Donald of the Isles;† and again, in the passage in which he mentions the death of Robert the Third, the same historian remarks, that about this time many persons fled out of England from the face of Henry the Fourth, and came to King Richard in Scotland; amongst whom were Henry Percy the elder, with his grandson, Henry Percy the younger, who had come a little before this, and being of the same age with James the First, had been brought up with him

---

* Fordun a Goodal, vol. ii. p. 427. "Isto modo rex Ricardus fuit regno privatus et perpetuis carceribus, cito deficiendus deputatus ; sed subtiliter abinde ereptus, et ad insulas Scotiæ transvectus, et in coquina Dovenaldi domini Insularum, a quodam fatuo qui in curia Regis Ricardi dum floreret, educatus fuerat cognitus et repertus, et a dicto domino Insularum ad Regem Scotiæ Robertum Tertium per Dominum de Monte-Gomorry transmissus, cum quo dum Rex Scotiæ vixerat reverenter, ut decuit, procuratus, et post mortem regis Duci Albaniæ gubernatori Scotiæ presentatus ; cum quo regifice quoad statum honoratus, tandem in castro de Strivelyn mortuus, et in ecclesia fratrum ejusdem ad aquilonare altaris cornu ejusdem tumulatus."— "Hic Ricardus fuit filius Edwardi principis Walliæ, filii Eduardi Windesor, qui rexit annis viginti duobus ; mortuus sine liberis."

† Fordun a Goodal, vol. ii. 402. "Unde ad id deventum est, ut ipse idem Rex Ricardus II., qui olim in florenti majestate sua, stipatus, turmis militum, et multitudine clientum, Salomoni magno in expensis æquiparabatur, tandem carceres evadens, insulas Scotiæ petens, cognitus est a quodam fatuo, qui in sua curia ante hoc educatus fuerat, et inventus in culina, tanquam vilis elixa, Dovenaldi domini Insularum."

in the castle of St Andrews. At the same time, he continues, there came also the Lord Bardolph, two Welsh prelates, the Bishops of St Asaph and of Bangor, the Abbot of Welbeck, and other honourable persons; but, he adds, King Richard would in nowise be persuaded, either by the governor, or by any other persons, to have a private interview with the Earl of Northumberland.* Lastly, under the events of the year 1419, the historian has this brief entry: "In this year died Richard king of England, on the Feast of St Luke, in the castle of Stirling."† These passages are sufficiently direct and positive: and in estimating the weight to which they are entitled, it must be remembered that Bower states them upon his own knowledge; that he was a contemporary engaged in the collection of materials for his history at the period in question; and that, from his rank in the church, from his employment in responsible offices of state, and his connexion with those best able to give him information upon this subject, his evidence is of an unexceptionable kind. It is indeed true, that in the remote annals of the country, he may be convicted of error; but with regard to events falling within the range of his own personal observation, Bower is entitled to high credit; and he assuredly does not throw out the slightest suspicion as to the identity of the king.

But the credit due to this passage is much strength-

* Fordun a Goodal, vol. ii. p. 441. "His diebus fugerunt multi de Anglia a facie regis Henrici IV., et in Scotiam ad regem Ricardum venerunt. Venit enim Henricus Percy, senior, cum nepote suo Henrico juniore qui paulo ante venerat et cum principe nostro Jacobo I. coævus in Castro Sancti Andreæ extiterat. Venitque tunc temporis, dominus de Bardolf, cum diversis honestis personis, et duo Episcopi Wallenses, viz. Dominus Griffinus Episcopus Bangorenus et alius episcopus, viz. Assavensis et Abbas de Welbeck. Quo in tempore rex Angliæ Ricardus non potuit induci, neque per gubernatorem nec alios quoscunque ad habendum familiare colloquium cum Comite Northumbriæ."

† Fordun a Goodal, vol. ii. p. 459.

ened by the circumstance, that he is corroborated in the greater part, if not in the whole of his story, by another valuable original writer, Andrew Winton, whose testimony cannot be regarded as borrowed from Bower, as we know that his Chronicle was completed before the history of Bower was begun.* It is stated by this historian, in a passage of singular simplicity, of the contents of which I now give a literal transcript, " that after Richard's deposition by King Henry the Fourth, he was confined in the Tower of London; they then (says he) brought him to Pontefract, where he was delivered to two gentlemen of rank and reputation, named Swinburn and Waterton, who felt compassion for him, and spread a report of the king's death; after which there arose a rumour that King Richard was still alive." Winton then proceeds to say, " that he will tell how this report arose, as he heard, although he possesses no information as to the manner in which the king effected his escape from Pontefract : But," says he, " at this time a poor traveller appeared in the *Oute Isles* of Scotland; and it happened that he was met by a lady of the family of Bisset, a daughter of an Irish lord, who was wedded to the brother of the Lord of the Isles. She had before seen the king in Ireland, and she immediately declared to her husband, that this traveller was King Richard;

---

* Winton, by Macpherson, preface, p. 22. " It was at his request (Sir John of the Wemyss) that he undertook his Chronicle, 1 Prolog. 54, which was finished between the third of September, 1420, and the return of King James from England in 1424, as appears by Robert duke of Albany being mentioned as dead, and the prayer for the prosperity of his children, ix. xxvi. 51."— " Bower was born in 1385. In 1403, when eighteen years old, he put on the habit ; he afterwards completed his theological studies at Paris ; and having returned to Scotland, was elected Abbot of Inchcolm in 1418. After this, he was employed in various offices of trust under the government; and at length, in 1441, began his continuation of Fordun, whose Collectanea he had in his possession."—Goodal's Preface to Fordun, p. 3.

upon which he called him, and inquired whether this was true; but he denied it, and would not allow that it was so. However," continues Winton, "they sent this person to the Lord Montgomery in haste, and afterwards he was kept by Robert king of Scotland; then he was held for some time by the Lord of Cumbernauld; and lastly delivered to the Duke of Albany, who kept him for a long time after this." The historian then concludes his notice of this mysterious person by the following observation:—" Whether he had been the king or not, there were few who knew for certain. He was little inclined to devotion, and seldom showed a desire to hear mass; from the manner in which he conducted himself, it seemed likely that he was half mad or wild."* Such is almost a literal translation of Winton's testimony, who was Prior of

* After describing Richard's deposition, Winton thus proceeds—vol. ii. pp. 387, 388, 389:—

"Wythoutyn dout the court wes hard
Wyth this forsaid King Richard,
For in the Toure of Londone syne
Haldyne he wes a quhile in pyne:
And eftyre that on purpos set
Thai brocht hym north on til Powmfret;
Thare wes he delyverit then
Tyl twa wele trowit famous men,
Swynburn and Wattyrton,
Men of gud reputacioune;
Thare he bade, and wes hard stade,
Gret pité of hym thir gud men had,
The word in Yngland thai gert spred
That this Richard king wes dede,
Bot eftyr that thare ras tithand,
That this King Richard wes livand.
And quhon that rais, I will tel here
As I hard thare-of the manere.
Bot I can nocht tell the case
Off Poumfret as he chapit wase.
" Bot in the Owt-llys of Scotland than
Thare wes traveland a pure man,
A Lordis douchtyr of Ireland
Of the Bissetis, thare dwelland
Wes weddit wyth a Gentylman,
The Lord of the Ilys bruthir than,

Lochleven at the time of Richard's appearance, and must have had the best opportunities of informing himself of the truth of the story. He cautiously, indeed, declines giving us his own opinion upon the subject, contenting himself with declaring, that few knew for certain whether this mysterious person was the king; but this, I think, may be accounted for, from his high admiration of Albany, and his evident desire not to reveal anything which might throw a stain upon his government, or that of his son, Duke Murdoch.

We know, from his own words, that Winton regarded Henry the Fourth as an unprincipled usurper, who had unjustly dethroned the rightful king;[*] and to have admitted that Albany detained Richard in an honourable captivity, whilst he recognised the title of Henry to the throne, would have little corresponded

> In Ireland before quhen scho had bene,
> And the King Richard thare had sene,
> Quhen in the Islis scho saw this man,
> Scho let that scho weil kend hym than,
> Til hir Maistere sone scho past
> And tauld thare til hym als-sa fast,
> That he wes that King of Yngland
> That scho be-fore saw in Ireland,
> Quhen he wes therein before
> As scho drew than to memore;
> Quhen til hir Mastere this scho had tauld,
> That man rycht sone he tyl hym cald.
> And askit hym, gyf it wes swa.
> That he denyit; and said nocht, Ya.
> Syn to the Lord of Montgwmery
> That ilke man wes send in hy;
> That ilke man syne eftyr that
> Robert oure King of Scotland gat,
> The Lord als of Cumbirnald
> That man had a quhile to hald.
> The Duke of Albany syne hym gat,
> And held hym lang tyme eftyr that:
> Quhethir he had bene king, or nane,
> Thare wes bot few, that wyst certane.
> Of devotioune nane he wes
> And seildyn will had to here Mes,
> As he bare hym, like wes he
> Oft half wod or wyld to be."

[*] Winton, vol. ii. p. 386.

with the high character which he has elsewhere given of him. This disposition of the historian is strikingly illustrated by the manner in which he passes over the murder of the Duke of Rothesay. It is now established by undoubted evidence, that the prince was murdered by Albany and Douglas; yet Winton omits the dreadful event, and gives us only a brief notice of his death.* And I may observe, that in his account of the deposition of Henry, and the subsequent escape of Richard into Scotland, he has introduced a remark which is evidently intended as an apology to the reader for the concealment of part of the truth. "Although," says he, "everything which you write should be true, yet in all circumstances to tell the whole truth, is neither needful nor speedful."†

Yet although the cautious Prior of Lochleven did not choose to commit himself by telling the whole truth, he states two remarkable circumstances which do not appear elsewhere. The first of these is the denial, by the person in question, that he was the king, when he was discovered by Donald of the Isles: a very extraordinary step certainly to be taken by an impostor, but a natural one to be adopted by the fugitive king himself, for at this time Donald of the Isles was in strict alliance with Henry the Fourth.‡ The second is the new fact, that Richard was delivered at Pontefract to two trust-worthy and well-known gentlemen, Swinburn and Waterton. Such strict secrecy was observed by Henry as to the mode in which the dethroned monarch

* Winton's Chronicle, vol. ii. p. 397.
† Id. vol. ii. pp. 383, 384.
"And in al thing full suth to say
Is noucht neidful na speidful ay.
Bot quhat at suld writyn be
Suld be al suth of honestè."
‡ Rotuli Scotiæ, vol. ii. pp. 155, 156.

was conveyed to Pontefract, and the persons to whose custody he was intrusted, that neither in the state papers of the time, nor in the contemporary English historians, is there any particular information upon the subject. But it is certain, that Sir Thomas Swinburn and Sir Robert Waterton were two knights in the confidence and employment of Henry, and that Waterton, in particular, was steward of the honour of Pontefract;* a circumstance which tends strongly to corroborate the account of Winton, and to show that, although he did not think it prudent to tell the whole truth, he yet possessed sources of authentic information. There is no mention of Winton in Bower's additions to Fordun; a strong proof, I think, that this last author had never seen his Chronicle, so that we are entitled to consider these two passages as proceeding from two witnesses, who, being unconnected with each other, yet concur in the same story. Nor is it difficult to account for the more particular and positive account of Bower, if we recollect that this author composed his history under the reign of James the Second; twenty years after Winton had completed his Chronicle, when all were at liberty to speak freely of the actions and character of Albany, and time had been given to this writer to investigate and discover the truth.

* Whitaker's Loidis and Elmete, p. 269. Waterton was Master of the Horse to Henry the Fourth, who employed him in a foreign mission to the Duke of Gueldres. Cottonian Catalogue, p. 245. No. 88, also p. 244. In May 7, 1404, Sir Thomas Swinborne was sent on a mission to the magistrates of Bruges. Ibid. p. 244. See also Fordun a Goodal, vol. ii. p. 428. I have much pleasure in acknowledging the polite and friendly attention of Sir John Swinburn, Bart. of Capheaton, to my inquiries upon this subject. From his information I am enabled to state, that although in his own family there is no evidence, either written or traditionary, on the subject of Richard the Second, yet in the family of the present Mr Waterton of Walton Hall, the descendant of Sir Robert Waterton, Master of the Horse to Henry the Fourth, there is a long-established tradition, that his ancestor had the charge of Richard the Second in Pontefract castle.

In an ancient manuscript in the Advocates' Library, which I conjecture to have been written posterior to the time of Fordun, and prior to the date of Bower's continuation, I have found three passages which corroborate the accounts of this author and of Winton in a striking manner. The manuscript is entitled, Extracta ex Chronicis Scotiæ, and at folio 254 has the following passage:—" Henry Percy earl of Northumberland, with his nephew Henry the younger, and many others of the prelates and nobles of England, who fled from the face of Henry the Fourth, came into Scotland to King Richard, at this time an exile, but well treated by the governor."* In another part of the same manuscript, the account given of the death of Richard, by Bower, is thus briefly but positively confirmed, with the valuable addition of the monkish or leonine epitaph inscribed above his tomb : " Richard the Second king of England, died in the castle of Stirling, in the aforesaid year, and was buried on the Feast of St Lucie the Virgin, on the north side of the high altar of the Preaching Friars;" above whose royal image there painted, it is thus written :

> " Angliæ Ricardus jacet hic rex ipse sepultus.
> Loncaste quem Dux dejecit arte, mota prodicione
> Prodicione potens, sceptro potitur iniquo.
> Supplicium luit hunc ipsius omne genus.
> Ricardum inferis hunc Scotia sustulit annis
> Qui caustro Striveling vite peregit iter
> Anno milleno quaterceno quoque deno
> Et nono Christi regis finis fuit iste."†

The church of the Dominican friars at Stirling has

---

* " Percy Henricus Comes Northumbriæ cum nepote suo Henrico minore et multi alii nobiles Angliæ ac prælati fugientes a facie Henrici quarti Regis Angliæ Scotiam venerunt ad regem Ricardum exulem, per gubernatorem bene tractati."—Extracta ex Chronicis Scotiæ, folio 254.   MS. Adv. Lib.

† Extracta ex Chronicis Scotiæ, fol. 263, dorso.

ON THE DEATH OF RICHARD II.

long since been destroyed, and other buildings erected on its site. It existed, however, in the time of Boece, who mentions the inscription over Richard's tomb as being visible in his day.* Such being the clear and positive statements of these respectable contemporary writers; whilst, as I shall afterwards show, the accounts of the reputed death of the king by the English historians were extremely vague and contradictory, and the reports of his escape frequent, I certainly did not feel disposed to follow Buchanan, and the whole body of English and Scottish historians who succeeded him, in treating the story as fabulous, or in considering the person whom Bower so positively asserts to have been the king, as an impostor.

Having proceeded thus far in these researches, I began the examination of that part of the Chamberlain Accounts, which forms the continuation of those valuable unpublished records, of which I have already given a description, in the appendix to the second volume of this history. It contains the accounts of the great chamberlains and other ministers of the crown during the government of the Duke of Albany; and in examining them with that deep interest which such authentic documents demanded, I came upon the following extraordinary passages, which I shall translate literally from the Latin. The first occurs at the end of the accounts for the year 1408, and is as follows: "Be it remembered also, that the said lord governor, down to the present time, has neither demanded nor received any allowance for the sums expended in the support of Richard king of England, and the messengers of France and of Wales, at different times coming into the country, upon whom he has defrayed much,

* Boece, Hist. p. 339.

as is well known."*   Again, at the conclusion of Accounts for the year 1414, the following passage is to be found: " Be it remembered also, that our lord the duke, governor of the kingdom, has not received any allowance or credit for the expenses of King Richard incurred from the period of the death of his brother our lord the king of good memory, last deceased."†
The same memorandum, in precisely the same words, is inserted at the termination of the Chamberlain Accounts for the year 1415;‡ and lastly, at the conclusion of the year, 1417, there is this passage: "Be it remembered, that the lord governor has not received any allowance for the expenses and burdens which he sustained for the custody of King Richard of England from the time of the death of the late king his brother of good memory, being a period of eleven years, which expenses the lords auditors of accounts estimate at the least to have amounted annually to the sum of a hundred marks, which for the past years makes in all £733, 6s. 8d."§

The discovery of these remarkable passages in records of unquestionable authenticity, was very satisfactory. I considered them as affording a proof, nearly as con-

---

* " Et memorandum quod dictus Dominus Gubernator regni non peciit neque recepit ad presens aliquam allocationem pro expensis suis factis super Ricardum regem Angliæ ; Nuncios Franciæ vel Walliæ diversis vicibus infra regnum venient: circa quos multa exposuit, ut est notum." Rotuli Compotorum, voL iii. p. 18.

† "Et memorandum quod dominus dux gubernator regni non recepit allocationem aliquam pro expensis regis Ricardi, a tempore obitus bone memorie Domini regis fratris sui ultimo, defuncti."   Rotuli Compotorum vol. iii. p. 69.

‡ Id. voL iii. p. 78.

§ " Et memorandum quod dominus gubernator non recepit allocacionem pro expensis et oneribus quas sustinuit pro custodia regis Ricardi Anglie, a tempore obitus bone memorie quondam domini regis fratris sui, jam per undecim annos. Quas expensas annuatim dni auditores compotorum estimant ad minus fuisse in quolibet, anno centum marcas. Quæ summa se extendit pro annis præteritis ad vii° xxxiii lib. vi sh. viii d. quæ summa debetur domino duci." Id. p. 95.

vincing as the nature of the subject admitted, that the story given by Bower and by Winton was substantially true; as establishing upon direct evidence, which hitherto I can see no cause to suspect, the fact so positively asserted during the reign of Henry the Fourth and Henry the Fifth, that Richard the Second had escaped into Scotland, and lived there for many years after his reputed death in England. That an impostor should, as we learn from Winton, deny that he was the king, or that, in the face of this denial, a poor maniac should be supported at great expense, and detained for more than eleven years at the Scottish court, seems to me so extravagant a supposition, that I do not envy the task of any one who undertakes to support it. It was due, however, to the respectable historians who had adopted the common opinion regarding the death of Richard in 1399, that the evidence upon which they proceeded should be diligently weighed and examined. This I have done, with an earnest desire to arrive at the truth in this mysterious story; and the result has been, the discovery of a body of negative evidence, superior, I think, to that which could be brought in support of most historical facts.

And here I may first remark, that there is no certain proof furnished by contemporary English writers, that Richard the Second either died or was murdered in Pontefract castle; the accounts of the best historians being not only vague and inconsistent with each other, but many of them such as can easily be proved to be false by unexceptionable evidence. So much, indeed, is this the case, that some ingenious English authors have of late years attempted to clear up the mass of obscurity and contradiction which hangs over the fate of Richard, and after having done all which could be accomplished by erudition and acuteness, have been compelled to leave the question, as to the manner of his death, in nearly the same uncertainty in which they found it.*

Walsingham, a contemporary historian of good authority, although attached to the house of Lancaster, affirms, that, according to common report, "*ut fertur*," he died by a voluntary refusal of food, on the fourteenth of February, 1399. " Richard," says he, " the former king of England, when he had heard of these disasters, became disturbed in his mind, and, as is reported, put an end to his life by voluntary abstinence, breathing his last at Pontefract castle on St Valentine's day."† Thomas of Otterburn, however, who was also a contemporary, gives a story considerably different: for he informs us that the king, although he at first determined to starve himself to death, afterwards repented, and wished to take food, but that in consequence of his abstinence, the orifice of the stomach was shut, so that he could not eat, and died of weakness. "When Richard," he observes, " the late King of England, who was then a prisoner in Pontefract castle, had learnt the misfortune of his brother John of Holland, and the rest of his friends, he fell into such profound grief, that he took the resolution of starving himself, and, as it is reported, he so long abstained from food, that the orifice of his stomach was closed; so that when he was afterwards persuaded by his keepers to satisfy the craving of nature, by attempting to take nourishment, he found himself unable to

---

* See the learned dissertations of Mr Webb and Mr Amyot, in the twentieth volume of the Archæologia.

† Walsingham, p. 363. "Ricardus quondam rex Angliæ cum audisset hæc infortunia, mente consternatus, semetipsum extinxit inedia voluntaria, ut fertur, clausitque diem extremum apud castrum de Pontefracto die Sancti Valentini.

eat, and his constitution sinking under it, he expired in the same place on St Valentine's day."*

In direct opposition to this story of death by voluntary abstinence, (a mode of extinction which is pronounced by an excellent historian to be inconsistent with the previous character of the king,)† a completely different tale is given by the author of a French manuscript work, in the royal library at Paris, who seems to be the first to whom we owe the introduction of Sir Piers Exton, and his band of eight assassins, who murdered Richard with their halberts and battle-axes. This account has been repeated by Fabyan and Hall in their Chronicles, by Hayward in his Life of Richard, and, in consequence of its adoption by Shakspeare, has become, and will probably continue, the general belief of Europe. For a complete exposure of the falsehood of this tale of assassination, I shall content myself with a simple reference to Mr Amyot's paper on the death of Richard the Second, which is printed in the Archæologia.‡

There is lastly a class of contemporary authorities which ascribe the death of the king neither to voluntary abstinence, nor to the halbert of Sir Piers Exton —but to starvation by his keepers. The manuscript Chronicle of Kenilworth uses expressions which amount to this:—" Fame et siti, ut putatur, dolenter consummatus." A Chronicle, in the Harleian collection, the work of Peter de Ickham, is more positive: " A cibo

---

* Otterburn, pp. 228, 229. "Ricardus quondam rex Angliæ in castro de Pontefracto existens custoditus, cum audisset infortunium fratris sui Joannis Holland, et ceterorum, in tantam devenit tristitiam, quod semet inedia voluit peremisse, et tantum dicitur abstinuise, quod clauso orificio stomachi, cum ex post, consilio custodum, voluisset naturæ satisfecisse comedendo, præcluso omni appetitu comedere non valeret, unde factum est, ut natura debelitata, defecerit, et die Sancti Valentini, diem clausit supremum ibidem."

† Turner, Hist. of England, vol. ii. p. 352.

‡ Archæologia, vol. xx. pp. 427, 428.

et potu per iv. aut v. dies restrictus, fame et inedia expiravit." Hardyng, the chronicler, who was a contemporary, and lived in the service and enjoyed the confidence of Hotspur and his father, repeats the same story.* Whilst we thus see that the accounts of so many writers who lived at the time are completely at variance; one saying that he starved himself, another that he repented, and wished to eat, but found it too late, and died; a third, that it took all the efforts of Exton and his accomplices, by repeated blows, to fell him to the ground; and the last class of writers, that his death was occasioned by his keepers depriving him of all nourishment, the proper inference to be drawn from such discrepancies in the various accounts amounts simply to this—that about this time the king disappeared, and no one knew what became of him.

It may be said, however, that all contemporary writers agree that the king did die, although they differ as to the manner of his death; yet even this is not the case: on the contrary, the belief that he had escaped, and was alive, seems to have been entertained in England by many, and those the persons most likely to have access to the best information, almost immediately after his being committed to Pontefract, and apparently before there was time to have any communication with Scotland. This can be very convincingly shown.

Some time after Richard had been conveyed with great secrecy to his prison in Pontefract castle, and previous to his reported death, a conspiracy was formed against Henry the Fourth by the Earls of Kent, Salisbury, and Huntingdon.† These noblemen, along

---

* Cron. Harl. MS. 4323, p. 68. Archæologia, vol. xx. p. 282.
† Walsingham, pp. 362, 363.

with the Bishop of Carlisle and the Abbot of Westminster, were the chief actors in the plot; but they had drawn into it many persons of inferior rank, and, amongst the rest, Maudelain, a priest, who had been a favourite of the king, and who resembled him so completely in face and person, that it is said the likeness might have deceived any one.* Their design was to murder Henry at a tournament which they were to hold at Windsor, and to restore King Richard. After everything, however, as they supposed, had been admirably organized, the plot was betrayed to Henry by one of their own number; and on arriving at Windsor, they found that their intended victim had fled to London. They now changed their purpose, and marched to Sunning, near Reading, where Richard's youthful queen resided, who had not at this time completed her ninth year. Here, according to the accounts of Walsingham and Otterburn, the Earl of Kent, addressing the attendants and friends of the queen, informed them that Henry of Lancaster had fled to the Tower of London, and that they were now on their road to meet King Richard, their lawful prince, who had escaped from prison, and was then at the bridge of Radcote with a hundred thousand men.† The last part of the assertion was undoubtedly false; the first clause of the sentence contains the first assertion of Richard's escape which I have met with; and I may remark, that with the exception of the two dignified ecclesiastics, none of the conspirators,

* Metrical History of Deposition of Richard the Second, Archæologia, vol. xx. p. 213.
† The expressions of Walsingham, p. 363, are slightly different from those of Otterburn. Walsingham's words are, "Quia jam evasit de carcere et jacet ad Pontem-fractum cum centum millibus defensorum." Those of Otterburn are, "Qui jam evasit carcere et jacet ad pontem de Radcote cum 100,000 hominum defensionis," pp. 225, 226.

whose testimony could have thrown light upon the subject, were suffered to live. The Earls of Surrey and of Salisbury were taken and executed at Cirencester; the Lords Lumley and Despencer shared the same fate at Bristol; the Earl of Huntingdon was seized near London, and beheaded at Pleshy; two priests, one of them Maudelain, whose extraordinary likeness to the king has been already noticed, with another named Ferriby, were executed at London; Sir Bernard Brocas and Sir John Shelly shared their fate; and others, whose names Walsingham has not preserved, suffered at Oxford.* Rapin has asserted, that both the ecclesiastics who were involved in the plot, the Abbot of Westminster and the Bishop of Carlisle, died almost immediately, the abbot of a stroke of apoplexy, and the bishop of absolute terror;† but this is an error. The Bishop of Carlisle, who was tried and pardoned, undoubtedly lived till 1409. And although the Abbot of Westminster appears to have died of apoplexy, neither the cause nor the time of his death agree with the story in Rapin.‡ It is quite clear, however, that previous to Richard's reported death, it was asserted that he had escaped from Pontefract castle.

A contemporary French manuscript, being a Metrical History of the Deposition of Richard the Second, which has been translated and published by Mr Webb in the Archæologia, whilst it confirms the story of Richard's alleged escape, adds, that to induce the people to believe it, they brought Maudelain the priest with them, and dressed him up to personate the king. The passage,

* Metrical Hist. of Deposition of Richard the Second, p. 215. Archæologia, vol. xx.
† Rapin, vol. i. p. 490. Fol. ed. London, 1732.
‡ Godwin, p. 767.

which is as follows, is amusing and curious:—"They," says this author, speaking of the conspirators, "had many archers with them. They said that good King Richard had left his prison, and was there with them. And to make this the more credible, they had brought a chaplain, who so exactly resembled good King Richard in face and person, in form and in speech, that every one who saw him certified and declared that he was the old king. He was called Maudelain. Many a time have I seen him in Ireland, riding through the country with King Richard his master. I have not for a long time seen a fairer priest. They armed the aforesaid as king, and set a very rich crown upon his helm, that it might be believed of a truth that the king was out of prison."* I have given this passage from the metrical history, because I wish the reader to be possessed of all the contemporary evidence which may assist him in the discovery of the truth; whilst I acknowledge at the same time, that the additional circumstance as to the personification of Richard by Maudelain the priest, seems at first to militate against the accuracy of the story as to Richard's escape. It ought to be remembered, however, that Walsingham says nothing of this personification; and his evidence, which is that of a contemporary in England, ought to outweigh the testimony of the French Chronicle, which in this part is avowedly hearsay. Neither does Otterburn mention this circumstance, although it was too remarkable to be omitted if it really occurred.

* Archæologia, vol. xx. pp. 213, 214. Translation of a French Metrical History of the Deposition of Richard the Second, with prefatory observations, notes, and an appendix, by the Rev. John Webb. Mr Webb's notes are learned and interesting, and have furnished me with som evaluable corroborations of the truth of my theory as to Richard's fate. In the above passage, Mr Webb translates "le roy ancien" "the old king:" "the former king" would express the meaning more correctly.

There is, however, another manuscript in the library of the King of France, entitled, " Relation de la prise de Richard Seconde, par Berry Roy d'Armes," which in some measure enables us to reconcile this discrepancy. According to the account which it contains, it was resolved at the meeting of the conspirators, which was held in the house of the Abbot of Westminster, that " Maudelain was to ride with them, to represent King Richard;" but this plan was not afterwards carried into execution. It appears from the same manuscript, that Henry himself, when marching against the conspirators, believed the story of Richard's escape. This, I think, is evident from the following passage: " Next morning Henry set out to meet his enemies, with only fifty lances and six thousand archers; and drawing up his men without the city, waited three hours for his reinforcements. Here he was reproached by the Earl of Warwick for his lenity, which had brought him into this danger; but he vindicated himself for his past conduct, adding, ' that if he should meet Richard now, one of them should die.'"* I do not see how Henry could have expressed himself in this way to the Earl of Warwick, unless he then believed that Richard had really escaped, and was about to meet him in the field.

It was almost immediately after the suppression of this conspiracy, and the execution of its authors, that Richard was reported to have died in Pontefract castle; and we now come to the consideration of an extraordinary part of the story, in the exposition of the dead body by Henry, for the purpose of proving to the

* Archæologia, vol. xx. pp. 218, 219. From this curious manuscript, which belonged to the celebrated Baluze, large extracts were made by Mr Allen, Master of Dulwich College, a gentleman of deep research in English history, and communicated to Mr Webb, from whose notes I have taken them.

people that it was the very body of their late king. Of this ceremony Otterburn gives the following account: " His body was carried and exposed in the principal places intervening betwixt Pontefract and London; that part, at least, of the person was shown, by which he could be recognised, I mean the face, which was exposed from the lower part of the forehead to the throat. Having reached London, it was conveyed to the church of St Paul's, where the king, along with some of his nobles, and the citizens of London, attended the funeral, both on the first and the second day; after the conclusion of the mass, the body was carried back to Langley, in order to be there interred amongst the preaching friars; which interment accordingly took place, being conducted without any pomp, by the Bishop of Chester, and the Abbots of St Albans and of Waltham." * The manner in which this funeral procession to St Paul's was conducted, is minutely described in the following passage, extracted by Mr Allen from the manuscript in the royal library at Paris, already quoted : " In the year 1399–1400, on the twelfth day of March, was brought to the church of St Paul of London, in the state of a gentleman, the body of the noble king Richard. And true it is, that it was in a carriage which was covered with a black cloth,† having four banners thereupon, whereof two were the arms of St George, and the other two the arms of St Edward; to wit, Azure, over all a cross Or; and there

---

* Otterburn, p. 229.

† " There is a curious representation of this chariot in the fine illuminated Froissart in the British Museum, from whence it appears, that the carriage was drawn by two horses, one placed before the other, as the five horses were placed in the French carriage of Henry VII., as described by Hall, vol. iii. p. 800."—Gough's Sepulchral Monuments, vol. iii. p. 166.

There is in the same MS. a portrait of Richard the Second when going to arrest the Duke of Gloucester at Pleshy.—Archæologia, vol. vi. p. 315.

were a hundred men all clad in black; and each bore a torch. And the Londoners had thirty torches and thirty men, who were all clad in white, and they went to meet the noble King Richard; and he was brought to St Paul's, the head church of London. There he was two days above ground, to show him to those of the said city, that they might believe for certain that he was dead; for they required no other thing."*

This ceremony took place on the twelfth of March, 1399, nearly a month after the king's reputed death on the fourteenth of February; and it would appear, from the expressions which are employed, that the citizens of London believed that Richard had escaped, and was alive, and that the exposure of the body was resorted to by Henry, as the most probable means of putting down this dangerous report. The question now immediately arises, if Richard was alive, according to the theory which I entertain, in what manner are we to account for this ceremony at St Paul's, and for the body lying in state at the different churches between Pontefract and London? My answer is, that the whole was a deception, ingeniously got up for the purpose of blinding the people, but when narrowly examined, betraying the imposition in a very palpable manner. It is accordingly positively asserted by the contemporary author of the French metrical history of Richard's deposition, that the body thus exposed in London was not that of the king, but of Maudelain the priest. I give the passage in Mr Webb's translation: "Then was the king so vexed at heart by this evil news, that he neither ate nor drank from that hour: and thus, as they say, it came to pass that he died. But, indeed, I do not believe it; for some de-

* French Metrical History.—Archæologia, vol. xx. p. 221.

clare for certain that he is still alive and well, shut up in their prison;—which is a great error in them; although they caused a dead man to be openly carried through the city of London, in such pomp and ceremony as becometh a deceased king, saying that it was the body of the deceased King Richard. Duke Henry there made a show of mourning, holding the pall after him, followed by all those of his blood in fair array, without regarding him, or the evils that they had done unto him. * * Thus, as you shall hear, did they carry the dead body to St Paul's, in London, honourably and as of right appertaineth to a king. But I certainly do not believe that it was the old king; but I think it was Maudelain, his chaplain, who, in face, size, height, and make, so exactly resembled him, that every one firmly thought it was good King Richard. And if it were he, morn and night I heartily make my prayer to the merciful and holy God, that he will take his soul to heaven."*

A late author, Mr Amyot, in an ingenious paper in the Archæologia, considers that the circumstance of Maudelain having been beheaded, rendered such deception impossible. To the support of my ideas as to Richard's escape, it is of little consequence whether Maudelain's remains were employed, or some other mode of deception was resorted to—all that I contend for is, that the body thus carried in a litter, or car, to St Paul's, was not that of the king. Now, the more narrowly we examine the circumstances attending this exposition of the body at St Paul's, the more completely shall we be convinced, I think, that the French historian is correct, and that it was not the true Richard. Of the king's person a minute description

* French Metrical Hist. pp. 219, 220, 221

has been left us by the monk of Evesham. "He was of the common or middle size, with yellow hair, his face fair, round, and feminine, rather round than long, and sometimes flushed and red."*

Keeping in mind this description of the person of the real Richard, and comparing it with the manner in which Henry conducted the exhibition at St Paul's, a strong suspicion arises that he was not in possession of the actual body of the king. Why was his head entirely concealed, and the face only shown from the lower part of the forehead to the throat? Richard's yellow hair was the very mark which would have enabled the people to identify their late monarch; and so far from being concealed, we should have been led to expect that it would have been studiously displayed. Had the king, indeed, died by the murderous strokes of Exton and his accomplices, inflicted on the head, there might have been good cause for concealing the gashes; but it will be recollected this cannot be pleaded, as this story is now given up on all hands as a fable.

There is another circumstance, which in my mind corroborates this suspicion of deception: Henry's wish was to do public honour to the body of the late king. He attended, we see, the service for the dead, and held the pall of the funeral car; but no interment followed, the body was not permitted to be buried in London at all; although there was then a tomb ready, which Richard, previous to his deposition, had prepared for himself in Westminster Abbey, and to which Henry the Fifth afterwards removed the reputed remains of the king.† It was conveyed, apparently, in the same

* Vita Ricardi II. p. 169.
† Richard the Second's Will is to be found published amongst the Royal and Noble Wills, p. 191. The king there directs his body to be buried in "Ecclesia Sancti Petri Westmonasterii—in monumento quod ad nostrum et

car in which it lay in state, to Langley, in Hertfordshire, and there interred with great secrecy, and without any funeral pomp. " When the funeral service," says Walsingham, " was concluded in the church of St Paul, the king and the citizens of London being present, the body was immediately carried back to Langley, to be interred in the church of the Preaching Friars; the last offices being performed by the Bishop of Chester, the Abbots of St Albans and of Waltham, without the presence of the nobles, and unattended by any concourse of the people, nor was there any one who, after their labours, would invite them to dinner."* It must be evident to every one, that as Henry's avowed object was to convince the English people that Richard their late king was dead and buried, the greater concourse of people who attended his funeral, and the more public that ceremony was made, the more likely was he to attain his desire. In this light, then, the sudden removal from London, the secret burial at Langley, "*sine pompa, sine magnatum præsentia, sine populari turba,*" are circumstances which, I own, create in my mind a strong impression that Henry was not in possession of the real body of the king; that either the head of Maudelain the priest, or some other specious contrivance, was employed to deceive the people, and that the king did not think it prudent to permit a public funeral; because, however easy it may have been to impose upon the spectators, so long as they were merely permitted to see the funeral car in which the body lay covered up with black cloth, and having nothing but the face exposed, the process of removing

inclitæ recordacionis Annæ dudum Reginæ Angliæ consortis nostræ, cujus animæ prospicietur altissimus erigi fecimus memoriam." A description and engraving of this monument is to be seen in Gough's Sepulchral Monuments.
* Walsingham, p. 363. Otterburn, p. 229.

from the litter, arraying it for the grave, and placing it in the coffin, might have led to a discovery of the deception which had been practised. It is clear, that the evidence of a single person who had known the king, had he been permitted to uncover the head and face, and to examine the person, would have been itself worth the testimony of thousands who gazed for a moment on the funeral car, and passed on; and it is for this reason that I set little value on the account of Froissart, (whose history of the transactions connected with Richard's deposition is full of error,)* when he asserts that the body was seen by twenty thousand persons, or of Hardyng, who relates that he himself saw the "corse in herse rial;" and that the report was, he had been "forhungred" or starved, "and lapte in lede."

Another proof of the conviction of the country, that this exhibition of the body of Richard was a deception upon the part of Henry, is to be found in the reports of his escape which not long afterwards arose in England, and the perpetual conspiracies in which men of rank and consequence freely hazarded, and in many cases lost their lives, which were invariably accompanied with the assertion that Richard was alive in Scotland. It is a remarkable circumstance, that these reports and conspiracies continued from the alleged year of his death, through the whole period occupied by the reigns of Henry the Fourth and Henry the Fifth. The year 1402 absolutely teemed with reports that Richard was alive, as appears from Walsingham. A priest of Ware was one of the first victims of Henry's resentment. He had, it seems, encouraged his brethren, by affirm-

---

* Webb's Translation of the Metrical Hist. of the Deposition of Richard the Second, p. 7. Archæologia, vol. xx.

ing that Richard was alive, and would shortly come forward to claim his rights; in consequence of which he was drawn and quartered. Not long after, eight Franciscan friars were hanged at London, for having asserted that Richard was alive, one of whom, a doctor of divinity, named Frisby, owing to the boldness and obstinacy with which he maintained his loyalty, was executed in the habit of his order. About the same time, Walter de Baldock prior of Launde in Leicestershire, was hanged because he had published the same story. Sir Roger de Clarendon, a natural son of the Black Prince, and one of the gentlemen of the bedchamber to Richard the Second, along with his armour-bearer and page, were condemned and executed for the same offence.* In these cases there appears to have been no regularly formed conspiracy, as in the instances to be afterwards mentioned. The Franciscan friars, it is well known, were in the habit of travelling through various countries, and were in constant intercourse with Scotland, where they had many convents.† They had probably seen the king, or become possessed of certain evidence that he was alive, and they told the story on their return.

Of these reports, however, we have the best evidence in a paper issued by Henry himself, and preserved in the Fœdera Angliæ.‡ It is a pardon under the privy seal to John Bernard of Offely; and from it we learn some interesting particulars of the state of public belief as to the escape and existence of Richard. Bernard, it seems, had met with one William Balshalf of Lancashire, who, on being asked what news he had to

* Walsingham, p. 365. Otterburn, p. 234. Nichol's Leicestershire, vol. iii. pp. 260, 305.
† Quetif et Echard, Scriptores Ordinis Prædicatorum, pp. 10, 11.
‡ Rymer, Fœdera, vol. viii. p. 262. A.D. 1402, 1st June.

tell, answered, "That King Richard, who had been deposed, was alive and well in Scotland, and would come into England upon the Feast of St John the Baptist next to come, if not before it." Balshalf added, "That Serle, who was then with King Richard, had arranged everything for his array and entrance into England, and that they would have timely warning of it; whilst he reported that Henry the Fourth, in fear of such an event, had collected great sums of money from his lieges with the intention of evacuating the kingdom, repairing to Brittany, and marrying the duchess of that country. Bernard then asked Balshalf what was best to be done,—who bade him raise certain men, and take his way to meet King Richard; upon which he went to John Whyte and William Threshire of Offely, to whom he told the whole story, and who immediately consented to accompany him to Athereston, near the Abbey of Merivale, there to await the king's arrival, and give him their support." This conversation Bernard revealed to Henry, and having offered to prove it on the body of Balshalf, who denied it, the king appointed a day for the trial by battle, which accordingly took place, and Balshalf was vanquished. The consequence was a free pardon to Bernard, which is dated on the first of June, 1402, and in which the above circumstances are distinctly stated. The person of the name of Serle here mentioned, as being with Richard in Scotland, was undoubtedly William Serle, gentleman of the bedchamber to Richard the Second, and one of the executors of his will.* He was infamous as one of the murderers of the Duke of Gloucester, and was soon after engaged in a second plot to restore the king. These transactions took place in 1402, and

* Richard's Will, in Nichols, p. 200. It is dated 16th April, 1399

sufficiently prove the little credit given by the people of England to the story of the king's death, and the funeral service which was enacted at Westminster.

Next year, in 1403, occurred the celebrated rebellion of the Percies, which ended in the battle of Shrewsbury, and the death of Hotspur. Previous to the battle, the Earl of Worcester and Henry Percy drew up a manifesto, which was delivered to King Henry upon the field by two squires of Percy, in which Henry was charged with having caused Richard to perish by hunger, thirst, and cold, after fifteen days and nights of sufferings unheard of among Christians. Yet, however broad and bold this accusation of murder, the principal persons who made it, and the only ones who survived its publication, afterwards altered their opinions, and employed very different expressions. This manifesto was drawn up in the name of the old Earl of Northumberland, although he had not then joined the army which fought at Shrewsbury, and it was sanctioned and approved by Richard Scrope archbishop of York. It commences, " Nos Henricus Percy, comes Northumbrie, constabularius Angliæ;" and Hardyng the chronicler, who was then with Hotspur and Worcester in the field, as he himself informs us, adds, "that their quarrel was be goode advyse and counseill of Maister Richard Scrope archebishope of Yorke." Now, it will immediately be seen, that two years after this, in 1405, Scrope and the Earl engaged in a second conspiracy against Henry; and in the articles which they then published, the positive statement in the manifesto as to Richard's death, is materially changed.* I may

* We owe the publication of this curious and interesting manifesto to Sir Henry Ellis. Archæologia, vol. xvi. p. 141. "Tu ipsum dominum nostrum regem et tuum, proditorie in castro tuo de Pountefreite, sine consensu suo, seu judicio dominorum regni, per quindecim dies et tot noctes, quod horrendum

here again use the words of Mr Amyot, in his paper on the death of Richard the Second. " On turning," says he, " from this letter of defiance in 1403, to the long and elaborate manifesto of Archbishop Scrope and the Yorkshire insurgents in 1405, we shall find a considerable diminution in the force of the charge, not indeed that one single day is abated out of the fifteen allotted to the starvation, but the whole story is qualified by the diluting words, '*ut vulgariter dicitur*.' So that in two years, the tale, which had before been roundly asserted as a fact, must have sunk into a mere rumour."* The accusation of the Percies, therefore, which is the only broad and unqualified charge brought against Henry by contemporaries, is not entitled to belief, as having been virtually abandoned by the very persons to whom it owes its origin.

This conspiracy of Hotspur having been put down in 1403, in 1404 Henry was again made miserable by new reports proceeding from Scotland regarding the escape of Richard, and his being alive in that country. These rumours, we learn from Otterburn, not only prevailed amongst the populace, but were common even in the household of the king.† Serle, one of the gentlemen of Richard's bedchamber, who, as we have already seen, had repaired to Scotland, returned from that country, with positive assertions that he had been with Richard, from whom he brought letters and communications, addressed under his privy seal to his friends in England.‡ Maud, the old Countess of

est inter Christianos audiri, fame, scitu, et frigore interfici fecisti, et murdro periri, unde perjuratus es, et falsus."
  * Archæologia, vol. xx. p. 436.
  † Otterburn, p. 249. " Quo mortuo cessavit in regno de vita Regis Ric: confabulatio quæ prius viguit non solum in vulgari populo sed etiam in ipsa dominis regis domo."
  ‡ Walsingham, p. 370.

Oxford, a lady far advanced in life, and little likely to engage, upon slight information, in any plot, "caused it to be reported," say Walsingham, "throughout Essex, by her domestics, that King Richard was alive, and would soon come back to recover and assert his former rank. She caused also little stags of silver and gold to be fabricated, presents which the king was wont to confer upon his most favourite knights and friends; so that, by distributing these in place of the king, she might the more easily entice the most powerful men in that district to accede to her wishes. In this way," continues Walsingham, "she compelled many to believe that the king was alive; and the report was daily brought from Scotland, that he had there procured an asylum, and only waited for a convenient time, when, with the strong assistance of the French and the Scots, he might recover the kingdom."* Walsingham then goes on to observe, that the plot of the countess was not only favoured by the deception of Serle, but that she had brought over to her belief several abbots of that country, who were tried and committed to prison; and that, in particular, a clerk, who had asserted that he had lately talked with the king, describing minutely his dress, and the place of the meeting, was rewarded by being drawn and hanged.†

It is stated by Dr Lingard, in his account of this conspiracy,‡ on the authority of Rymer's Fœdera, and the Rolls of Parliament, that Serle being disappointed of finding his master alive, prevailed upon a person named Warde to personate the king; and that many were thus deceived. Although, however, this personification by Warde is distinctly asserted in Henry's proclamation, it is remarkable that it is not only

* Walsingham, p. 370. † Ibid. pp. 370, 371. ‡ Vol. iv. p. 398.

omitted by Walsingham, but is inconsistent with his story; and the total silence of this historian, as also that of Otterburn, (both of them contemporaries,) induces me to believe, that the story of Thomas Warde personating King Richard, was one of those forgeries which Henry, as I shall afterwards show, did not scruple to commit when they could serve his purposes. What became afterwards of Warde cannot be discovered; but Serle was entrapped, and taken by Lord Clifford, and, according to Walsingham, confessed that the person whom he had seen in Scotland was indeed very like the king, but not the king himself, although, to serve his own ends, he had persuaded many, both in England and in Scotland, that it was Richard.* It would be absurd, however, to give much weight to this confession, made by a convicted murderer, and spoken under the strongest motives to conciliate the mind of the king, and obtain mercy for himself. To obtain this, the likeliest method was to represent the whole story regarding Richard as a falsehood. It may be remarked, also, that in Otterburn there is not a word of Serle's confession, although his seizure, and subsequent execution, are particularly mentioned.†

The conduct of the king immediately after this is well worthy of remark; as we may discern in it, I think, a striking proof of his own convictions upon this mysterious subject. He issued instructions to certain commissioners, which contain conditions to be insisted on as the basis of a treaty with Scotland;‡ and in these there is no article regarding the delivery of this pretended king, although his proclamation, as far back as the fifth June, 1402, § shows that he was

---

* Walsingham, p. 371.   † Otterburn, p. 249.
‡ Rymer, Fœdera, vol. viii. p. 384.   § Ibid. vol. viii. p. 261.

quite aware of his existence, and his constant intercourse with that country must have rendered him perfectly familiar with all the circumstances attending it. Is it possible to believe that Henry, if he was convinced that an impostor was harboured at the court of the Scottish king, whose existence there had been the cause of perpetual disquiet and rebellion in his kingdom, would not have insisted that he should be delivered up, as Henry the Seventh stipulated in the case of Perkin Warbeck? But Warbeck was an impostor, and the seventh Henry never ceased to adopt every expedient of getting him into his hands; whilst Henry the Fourth, at the very moment that he has put down a conspiracy, which derived its strength from the existence of this mysterious person in Scotland, so far from stipulating as to his delivery, does not think it prudent to mention his name. This difference in the conduct of the two monarchs, both of them distinguished for prudence and sagacity, goes far, I think, to decide the question; for, under the supposition that he who was kept in Scotland was the true Richard, it became as much an object in Henry the Fourth to induce the Scots to keep him where he was, as in Henry the Seventh to get Perkin into his hands; and a wary silence was the line of policy which it was most natural to adopt.

There is a remarkable passage in Walsingham, regarding an occurrence which took place in this same year, 1404, which proves that, in France, although Henry at first succeeded in persuading Charles the Sixth that his son-in-law Richard was dead, the deception was discovered, and, in 1404, the French considered the king to be alive. "The French," says this writer, "at the same time came to the Isle of Wight with a large fleet, and sent some of their men ashore, who demanded supplies from the islanders in the name of King Richard and Queen Isabella; but they were met by the answer that Richard was dead."*

An additional proof of the general belief in France of Richard's escape and safety, is to be found in a ballad composed by Creton, the author of the Metrical History of the Deposition of Richard the Second, which has been already quoted. We see, from the passage giving a description of the exposition of the body at St Paul's, that this author inclined to believe the whole a deception, and gave credit to the report, even then prevalent, that the king was alive. In 1405, however, he no longer entertains any doubt upon the subject, but addresses an epistle in prose to the king himself, expressing his joy at his escape, and his astonishment that he should have been able to survive the wretched condition to which he had been traitorously reduced. I am sorry that the learned author, from whose notes I take this illustration, enables me only to give the commencement of the epistle, and the first stanza of the ballad; but even these, though short, are quite decisive. His epistle is thus inscribed: "Ainsi come vraye amour requiert a tres noble prince et vraye Catholique Richart d'Engleterre, je, Creton ton liege serviteur te renvoye ceste Epistre." The first stanza of the ballad is equally conclusive.

> "O vous, Seignors de sang royal de France,
> Mettez la main aux armes vistement,
> Et vous avez certaine cognoissance
> Du roy qui tant a souffert de tourment

* Walsingham, p. 370. "Gallici," says this writer, "circa tempus illud venerunt ante Vectam insulam cum magna classe, miseruntque de suis quosdam qui peterent nomine regis Richardi et Isabellæ reginæ tributum, vel speciale subsidium ab insulanis. Qui responderunt regem Richardum fuisse defunctum."

Par faulx Anglois, qui traiteusement
Lui ont tollu la domination;
Et puis de mort fait condempnation.
Mais Dieu, qui est le vray juge es saintz cieulx,
Lui a sauvé la vie. Main et tart
Chascun le dit par tut, jeunes et vieulx.
C'est d'Albion le noble Roy Richart."*

Not long after the plot of Serle had been discovered and put down in 1404, there arose, in 1405, the conspiracy of the Earl of Northumberland and Archbishop Scrope, to which I have already alluded. In their manifesto, published before the battle of Shrewsbury, they had accused Henry in unqualified terms of the murder, whereas now, in the "Articles of Richard Scrope against Henry the Fourth,"† the addition of the words "*ut vulgariter dicitur*," shows, as I have already observed, that the strong convictions of Henry's guilt had sunk by this time into vague rumour; but the Parliamentary Rolls,‡ which give a minute and interesting account of the conspiracy, furnish us with a still stronger proof of Northumberland's suspicion of Richard's being alive, and prove, by the best of all evidence, his own words, that one principal object of the conspirators was to restore him, if this was found to be true.

It appears from these authentic documents, that in the month of May, 1405, the Earl of Northumberland seized and imprisoned Sir Robert Waterton, "esquire to our lord the king," keeping him in strict confinement in the castles of Warkworth, Alnwick, Berwick, and elsewhere. The reader will recollect, that according to the evidence of Winton, Richard was delivered

---
* Metrical History of the Deposition of Richard the Second, with notes by Mr Webb. Archæologia, vol. xx. p. 189.
† Wharton's Anglia Sacra, p. 362, pars. ii.
‡ Rolls of Parliament, vol. iii. p. 605.

to two gentlemen of the name of Waterton and Swinburn, who spread a report of his escape; and it is not improbable that the object of Northumberland, in the seizure of Waterton, was to arrive at the real truth regarding this story of his escape, to ascertain whether it was a mere fable, and whether the king actually had died in Pontefract castle, or might still be alive in Scotland, as had been confidently reported. It is of consequence, then, to observe Northumberland's conduct and expressions regarding Richard, after having had Waterton in his hands; and of both we have authentic evidence in the Parliamentary Rolls. He, and the rest of the conspirators, the Archbishop of York, Sir Thomas Mowbray, Sir John Fauconberg, Lord Hastings, and their accomplices, sent three commissioners, named Lasingsby, Boynton, and Burton, into Scotland, to enter into a treaty with Robert the Third, who died soon after, and at the same time to communicate with certain French ambassadors, who, it appears, were at that time in Scotland; and the avowed object of this alliance is expressly declared by Northumberland in his letter to the Duke of Orleans. It is as follows—"Most high and mighty prince, I recommend myself to your lordship; and be pleased to know, that I have made known by my servants, to Monsieur Jehan Chavbreliack, Mr John Andrew, and John Ardinguill, called Reyner, now in Scotland, and ambassadors of a high and excellent prince, the King of France, your lord and brother, my present intention and wish, which I have written to the king your brother. It is this, that with the assistance of God, with your aid, and that of my allies, I have embraced a firm purpose and intention to sustain the just quarrel of my sovereign lord King Richard, if he is alive, and if he is dead, to avenge his death; and, moreover, to sustain the right and quarrel which my redoubted lady, the Queen of England, your niece, may have to the kingdom of England, and for this purpose I have declared war against Henry of Lancaster, at present Regent of England." This letter, which will be found at length in the note below,* is written from Berwick, and although the precise date is not given, it appears, by comparison with other deeds connected with the same conspiracy preserved in the Fœdera and the Rotuli Scotiæ, to have been written about the tenth of June. The Parliamentary Rolls go on to state, that in this same month of June, Northumberland and his accomplices seized Berwick, and traitorously gave it up to the Scots, the enemies of the king, to be pillaged and burnt.

It is of importance to attend to the state of parties in Scotland at this time. The persons in that country with whom Northumberland confederated to sustain

---

* Rolls of Parliament, vol. iii. p. 605. "Tres haut et tres puissant prince, jeo me recomance a vostre seigneurie ; a laquelle plese asavoir que jay notifie par mes gentz, a Monʳ. Johan Chavbreliak, Meistre Johan Andrew, et Johan Ardinguill dit Reyner, ambassatours de tres haut et tres excellent prince le Roy de France, vostre sieur et frere, esteantz en Escoce, mon entencion et voluntée, laquell je escriptz au roy vostre dit sieur et frere ; laquelle est, que a l'aide de Dieu, de le vostre et des plusours mes allies, j'ay entencion et ferme purpos de sustener le droit querelle de mon soverein sieur le Roy Richard, s'il est vif, et si mort est, de venger sa mort, et aussi de sustener la droit querele que ma tres redoubte dame le Royne d'Engleterre, vostre niece, poit avoir reasonablement au Roiaeme d'Engleterre, et pur ceo ay moeve guerre a Henry de Lancastre, a present regent d'Angleterre ; et car jeo foy que vouz ames et sustenuz ceste querelle, et autres contre le dit Henry jeo vous prie et require, que en ceo vous moi voilles aider et soccorer, et ausi moi aider eius le tres haut et tres excellent prince le Roy de France, vostre dit sieur et frere, que les choses desquelles jeo lui escriptz, et dont vous enformeront au plain les ditz ambassatours, preignent bone et brief conclusion, quar en vite, en tout ceo que jeo vous pourra servier a sustener de par decea les ditz querelles encontre le dit Henry, jeo le ferra voluntiers de tout mon poair. Et vous plese de croiere les ditz ambassatours de ceo qu'ils vous dirront de par moy ; le Saint Esprit tres haut et tres puissant prince vous ait en sa garde. Escript à Berwyck, &c.

"A tres haut et tres puissant prince le Duc d'Orleans, Count de Valois et de Blois, et Beaumond et Sieur de Courcy." No date is given but it immediately succeeds June 11, 1405.

the quarrel of King Richard, were the loyal faction opposed to Albany, and friends to Prince James, whom that crafty and ambitious statesman now wished to supplant. Albany himself was at this moment in strict alliance with Henry the Fourth, as is shown by a manuscript letter preserved in the British Museum, dated from Falkland on the second of June, and by a mission of Rothesay herald, to the same monarch, on the tenth of July.* Wardlaw bishop of St Andrews, Sinclair earl of Orkney, and Sir David Fleming of Cumbernauld, to whose care, it will be recollected, Winton informs us Richard of England had been committed, opposed themselves to Albany, and having determined, for the sake of safety, to send Prince James to France, entered, as we see, into a strict alliance with the Earl of Northumberland, in his conspiracy for overturning the government of Henry the Fourth.

The events which followed immediately after this greatly favoured the usurpation of Albany. Prince James was taken on his passage to France, probably in consequence of a concerted plan between Albany and Henry. David Fleming, according to Bower,† was attacked and slain on his return from accompanying James to the ship, by the Douglases, then in alliance with Albany; and the old king, Robert the Third, died, leaving the government to the uncontrolled management of his ambitious brother, whilst his son, now king,

* Pinkerton, Hist. vol. i. p. 82. In the Cottonian Catalogue, p. 498, No. 114, I find a letter from Robert duke of Albany to Henry the Fourth thanking him for his good treatment of Murdoch his son, and the favourable audiences given to Rothesay his herald, dated Falkland, June 4, 1405.

† If we believe Walsingham, pp. 374, 375, however the chronology is different. Fleming was not slain till some months afterwards, and lived to receive Northumberland and Bardolph on their flight from Berwick; after which he discovered to them a plot of Albany's for their being delivered up to Henry, and, by his advice they fled into Wales, in revenge for which, Fleming was slain by the party of Albany.‡

‡ Ypodigma Neustria, p. 566.

was a prisoner in the Tower. Meanwhile, Sinclair the Earl of Orkney joined Northumberland at Berwick;* but the rebellion of that potent baron and his accomplices having entirely failed, he and the Lord Bardolph fled into Scotland, from which, after a short while, discovering an intention upon the part of Albany to deliver them into the hands of Henry, they escaped into Wales. We know, from the Chamberlain Accounts, that immediately after the death of Robert the Third, Albany obtained possession of the person of Richard. In this way, by a singular combination of events, while the Scottish governor held in his hands the person who, of all others, was most formidable to Henry, this monarch became possessed of James the First of Scotland, the person of all others to be most dreaded by the governor. The result was, that Albany and Henry, both skilful politicians, in their secret negotiations could play off their two royal prisoners against each other; Albany consenting to detain Richard so long as Henry agreed to keep hold of James. The consequence of this policy was just what might have been expected. Richard died in Scotland, and James, so long as Albany lived, never returned to his throne or to his kingdom; although, during the fifteen years of Albany's usurpation, he had a strong party in his favour, and many attempts were made to procure his restoration. It seems to me, therefore, that this circumstance of Albany having Richard in his hands, furnishes us with a satisfactory explanation of two points, which have hitherto appeared inexplicable. I mean, the success with which the governor for fifteen

* John, son of Henry, says, in a letter to his father, Vesp. F. vii. f. 95, No. 2, that Orkney had joined Northumberland and Bardolph at Berwick. The letter is dated 9th June, in all appearance 1405, says Pinkerton, vol. i. p. 82. The circumstances mentioned prove that it was, without doubt, in 1405.

years defeated every negotiation for the return of James, and the unmitigable severity and rage which this monarch, on his return, and throughout his reign, evinced towards every member of the family of Albany.

Even after this grievous disaster of Northumberland in 1405, the reports regarding Richard being still alive revived, and broke out in the capital; and Percy, the indefatigable enemy of Henry, along with Lord Bardolph, made a last attempt to overturn his government. "At this time," says Walsingham, speaking of the year 1407, "placards were fixed up in many places in London, which declared that King Richard was alive, and that he would soon come to claim his kingdom with glory and magnificence; but not long thereafter, the foolish inventor of so daring a contrivance was taken and punished, which allayed the joy that many had experienced in consequence of this falsehood."* Who the person was whom Walsingham here designates as the inventor of these falsehoods, does not appear from any part of his own history, or from any of the public papers in the Fœdera or the Parliamentary Rolls; but we may connect these reports, on good grounds I think, with Percy and Lord Bardolph, who, in 1408, proceeded from Scotland into Yorkshire, and after an ineffectual attempt to create a general insurrection in that country, were entirely defeated, Northumberland being slain, and Bardolph dying soon after of his wounds. The reader will recollect, perhaps, a passage already quoted from Bower,† in which this historian states, that amongst other honourable persons who fled with Northumberland and Lord Bardolph into Scotland, was the Bishop of Bangor; and I may mention

* Walsingham, p. 376.
‡ Fordun a Goodal, vol. ii. p. 441.

it as a striking confirmation of the accuracy of this account, that the Bishop of Bangor, according to Walsingham, was taken in the battle along with Percy, and that, as the historian argues, he deserved to have his life spared because he was unarmed. His fellow priest, the Abbot of Hayles, who was likewise in the field, and had changed the cassock for the steel coat, was hanged.* When Bower is thus found correct in one important particular, I know not why we are entitled to distrust him in that other limb of the same sentence, which mentions the existence of Richard in Scotland.

It was originally my intention to have entered into an examination of the diplomatic correspondence which took place subsequent to this period between Albany the governor of Scotland, and Henry the Fourth and Fifth; in which, I think, it would not be difficult to point out some transactions, creating a presumption that Albany was in possession of the true King Richard. The limits, however, within which I must confine these observations, will not permit me to accomplish this; and any intelligent reader who will take the trouble to study this correspondence as it is given in the Rotuli Scotiæ, will not find it difficult to discover and arrange the proofs for himself. I must be permitted, therefore, to step at once from this conspiracy of Northumberland, which took place in 1408, to the year 1415, when Henry the Fifth was preparing for his invasion of France. At this moment, when the king saw himself at the head of a noble army, and when everything was ready for the embarkation of the troops, a conspiracy of a confused and obscure nature was discovered, which, like every other conspiracy against the govern-

* Walsingham, p. 377.

ment of Henry the Fourth and Henry the Fifth, involved a supposition that Richard the Second might still be alive. The principal actors in this plot were Richard earl of Cambridge, brother to the Duke of York, and cousin to the king, Henry lord Scroop of Marsham, and Sir Thomas Grey of Heton in Northumberland; and the only account which we can obtain of it, is to be found in a confession of the Earl of Cambridge, preserved in the Fœdera Angliæ, and in the detail of the trial given in the Rolls of Parliament, both papers evidently fabricated under the eye of Henry the Fifth, and bearing upon them marks of forgery and contradiction.

According to these documents, the object of the conspirators was to carry Edmund the Earl of March into Wales, and there proclaim him king, as being the lawful heir to the crown, in place of Henry of Lancaster, who was stigmatized as a usurper. This, however, was only to be done, provided (to use the original words of the confession of the Earl of Cambridge) "yonder manis persone, wych they callen Kyng Richard, had nauth bene alyve, as Y wot wel that he wys not alyve."* The absurdity and inconsistency of this must be at once apparent. In the event of Richard being dead, the Earl of March was without doubt the next heir to the crown, and had been declared so by Richard himself; and the avowed object of the conspirators being to place this prince upon the throne, why they should delay to do this, till they ascertain whether the person *calling himself King Richard is alive*, is not very easily seen, especially as they declare, in the same breath, that they are well aware this person is not *alive*. Yet this may be almost pronounced con-

* Fœdera, vol. ix. p. 300.

sistency, when compared with the contradiction which follows: for we find it stated, in almost the next sentence, by the Earl of Cambridge, that he was in the knowledge of a plan entered into by Umfraville and Wederyngton, for the purpose of bringing in this very " persone wych they name Kyng Richard," and Henry Percy, out of Scotland, with a power of Scots, with whose assistance they hoped to be able to give battle to the king, for which treasonable intention the earl submits himself wholly to the king's grace. It is difficult to know what to make of this tissue of inconsistency. The Earl of March is to be proclaimed king, provided it be discovered that the impostor who calls himself Richard is not alive, it being well known that he is dead, and although dead, ready, it would seem, to march out of Scotland with Umfraville and Wederyngton, and give battle to Henry.*

The account of the same conspiracy given in the Parliamentary Rolls is equally contradictory, and in its conclusion still more absurd. It declares, that the object of the conspirators was to proclaim the Earl of March king, "in the event that Richard the Second king of England was actually dead;" and it adds, that the Earl of Cambridge and Sir Thomas Grey had knowledge of a design to bring Thomas of Trumpyngton, an idiot, from Scotland, to counterfeit the person of King Richard, who, with the assistance of Henry Percy and some others, was to give battle to Henry.† It was already remarked, in the account of the conspiracy of the old Countess of Oxford, in 1404, that the assertion then made by Henry the Fourth, in a proclamation in Rymer, that Thomas Warde of

* Fœdera, vol. ix. p. 300.
† Parliamentary Rolls, vol. iv. p. 65.

Trumpyngton "pretended that he was King Richard," was one of those forgeries which this monarch did not scruple to commit to serve his political purposes; none of the contemporary historians giving the least hint of the appearance of an impostor at this time, and Serle, in his confession, not having a word upon the subject. Besides, we hear nothing of Warde till 1404; and we know, from Henry's own proclamation, that Richard the Second was stated to be alive in Scotland as early as June 1402;* whilst, in 1404, when Warde is first mentioned, he comes before us as having personated the king in England, or rather, as then in the act of personating the king in England. Here, too, by Henry the Fourth's description of him in 1404, he is an Englishman, and in his sound senses; how then, in 1415, does he come to be a Scotsman, and an idiot? The truth seems to be, that Henry the Fifth, in manufacturing these confessions of the Earl of Cambridge, having found it stated by his father that Thomas Warde of Trumpyngton, in 1404, pretended to be King Richard, and that "there was an idiot in Scotland who personated the king," joined the two descriptions into one portentous person, Thomas of Trumpyngton, a Scottish idiot, who was to enact Richard the Second, and, at the head of an army, to give battle to the hero of Agincourt. Most of my readers, I doubt not, will agree with me in thinking, that, instead of an idiot, this gentleman from Trumpyngton must have been a person of superior powers.

It is impossible, in short, to believe for a moment that the accounts in the Parliamentary Rolls and in Rymer give us the truth, yet Cambridge, Scroop, and Grey were executed; and the summary manner in

* Rymer, vol. viii. p. 261.

which their trial was conducted, is as extraordinary as the accusation. A commission was issued to John, Earl Marshal, and eight others, empowering any two of them, William Lasingsby, or Edward Hull, being one of the number, to sit as judges for the inquiry of all treasons carried on within the county by the oaths of a Hampshire jury. Twelve persons, whose names Carte observes were never heard of before, having been impannelled, the three persons accused were found guilty on the single testimony of the constable of Southampton castle, who swore, that having spoke to each of them alone upon the subject, they had confessed their guilt, and thrown themselves on the king's mercy. Sir Thomas Grey was condemned upon this evidence, of which, says Carte, it will not be easy to produce a precedent in any former reign; but the Earl of Cambridge and Lord Scroop pleaded their peerage, and Henry issued a new commission to the Duke of Clarence, who summoned a jury of peers. This, however, was a mere farce; for the commission having had the records and process of the former jury read before them, without giving the parties accused an opportunity of pleading their defence, or even of appearing before their judges, condemned them to death, the sentence being carried into instant execution.

It is obvious, from the haste, the studied concealment of the evidence, the injustice and the extraordinary severity of the sentence, that the crime of Cambridge, Scroop, and Grey, was one of a deep dye; and, even in the garbled and contradictory accounts given in the Parliamentary Rolls, we may discern, I think, that their real crime was not the design of setting up March as king, but their having entered into a correspondence with Scotland for the restoration of Richard the

Second. That the story regarding March was disbelieved, is indeed shown by Henry himself, who instantly pardoned him, and permitted him to sit as one of the jury who tried Scroop and Cambridge; but that Cambridge, Scroop, and Grey, were in possession of some important secret, and were thought guilty of some dark treason which made it dangerous for them to live, is quite apparent.*

It seems to me that this dark story may be thus explained: Scroop and Cambridge, along with Percy, Umfraville, and Wederyngton, had entered into a correspondence with the Scottish faction who were opposed to Albany, the object of which was to restore Richard, and to obtain the return of James, Albany himself being then engaged in an amicable treaty with Henry, with the double object of obtaining the release of his son Murdoch, who was a prisoner in England, and of detaining James the First in captivity. At this moment the conspiracy of Cambridge was discovered; and Henry, in order to obtain full information for the conviction of the principals, pardoned Percy, and the two accomplices Umfraville and Wederyngton, and obtained from them a disclosure of the plot. He then agreed with Albany to exchange Murdoch for Percy; but we learn, from the MS. instructions regarding this exchange, which are quoted by Pinkerton,† that a secret clause was added, which declared,

---

* We have seen, that Henry directs that one of the two justices who are to sit on the trial, shall be either Edward Hull or William Lasingsby; and it may perhaps be recollected, that William Lasingsby, Esq., was himself engaged with Northumberland in 1405, in the conspiracy for the restoration of Richard, being one of the commissioners sent into Scotland to treat with Robert the Third and the French ambassadors. It is probable, therefore, that he knew well whether Richard of Scotland was, or was not, the true Richard; and his being selected as one of the judges makes it still more probable, that the real crime of the conspirators was a project for the restoration of the king.

† Vol. i. p. 97.

that the exchange was only to take place, provided "Percy consent to fulfil what Robert Umfraville and John Witherington have promised Henry in his name." Percy's promise to Henry was, as I conjecture, to reveal the particulars of the plot, and renounce all intercourse with Richard.

This conspiracy was discovered and put down in 1416, and the campaign which followed was distinguished by the battle of Agincourt, in which, amongst other French nobles, the Duke of Orleans was taken prisoner, and became a fellow captive with James the First. In July, 1417, Henry the Fifth again embarked for Normandy; but when engaged in preparations for his second campaign, he detected a new plot, the object of which was to bring in the "*Mamuet*" of Scotland, to use the emphatic expression which he himself employs. I need scarcely remark, that the meaning of the old English word Mamuet, or Mammet, is a puppet, a figure dressed up for the purpose of deception; in other words, an impostor. The following curious letter, which informs us of this conspiracy, was published by Hearne, in his Appendix to the Life of Henry the Fifth, by Titus Livius of Forojulii. " Furthermore I wole that ye commend with my brother, with the Chancellor, with my cousin of Northumberland, and my cousin of Westmoreland, and that ye set a good ordinance for my north marches; and specially for the Duke of Orleans, and for all the remanent of my prisoners of France, and also for the King of Scotland. For as I am secretly informed by a man of right notable estate in this lond, that there hath bene a man of the Duke of Orleans in Scotland, and accorded with the Duke of Albany, that this next summer he shall bring in the Mamuet of Scotland, to stir what he may; and also, that there should be foundin wayes to the having away especially of the Duke of Orleans, and also of the king, as well as of the remanent of my forsaid prisoners, that God do defend. Wherefore I wole that the Duke of Orleance be kept still within the castle of Pomfret, without going to Robertis place, or any other disport. For it is better he lack his disport, than we were disteyned of all the remanent."* With regard to Albany's accession to this plot, it is probable that Henry was misinformed; and that the party which accorded with Orleans, was the faction opposed to the governor, and desirous of the restoration of James. The letter is valuable in another way, as it neither pronounces the Mamuet to be an idiot, nor identifies him with Thomas of Trumpyngton.

There is yet, however, another witness to Richard's being alive in 1417, whose testimony is entitled to the greatest credit, not only from the character of the individual himself, but from the peculiar circumstances under which his evidence was given: I mean Lord Cobham, the famous supporter of the Wickliffites, or Lollards, who was burnt for heresy on the twenty-fifth of December, 1417. When this unfortunate nobleman was seized, and brought before his judges to stand his trial, he declined the authority of the court; and being asked his reason, answered, that he could acknowledge no judge amongst *them, so long as his liege lord King Richard was alive in Scotland.* The passage

* Titi Livii Forojul. Vita Henrici V. p. 99. This letter, also, is the first in that very interesting publication of Original Letters, which we owe to Sir Henry Ellis. Neither this writer, however, nor Hearne, have added any note upon the expression, the *Mamuet* of Scotland, which must be obscure to an ordinary reader. The letter itself, and the proof it contains in support of this theory of Richard's escape, was pointed out to me by my valued and learned friend, Adam Urquhart, Esq.

in Walsingham is perfectly clear and decisive: " Qui confestim cum summa superbia et abusione respondit, se non habere judicem inter eos, vivente ligio Domino suo, in regno Scotiæ, rege Richardo; quo responso accepto, quia non opus erat testibus, sine mora jussus est trahi et suspendi super furcas atque comburi, pendens in eisdem."* Lord Cobham, therefore, at the trying moment when he was about to answer to a capital charge, and when he knew that the unwelcome truth which he told was of itself enough to decide his sentence, declares that Richard the Second, his lawful prince, is then alive in Scotland. It is necessary for a moment to attend to the life and character of this witness, in order fully to appreciate the weight due to his testimony. It is not too much to say, that, in point of truth and integrity, he had borne the highest character during his whole life; and it is impossible to imagine for an instant, that he would have stated anything as a fact which he did not solemnly believe to be true. What, then, is the fair inference to be drawn from the dying declaration of such a witness? He had sat in parliament, and had been in high employments under Richard the Second, Henry the Fourth, and Henry the Fifth. He was Sheriff of Herefordshire in the eighth year of Henry the Fourth; and as a peer, had summons to parliament among the barons in the eleventh, twelfth, and thirteenth of that king's reign, and in the first of Henry the Fifth. He was, therefore, in high confidence and employment, and could not have been ignorant of the measures adopted by Henry the Fourth to persuade the people of England that Richard was dead. He sat in the parliament of 1399, which deposed him; there is every

* Walsingham, p. 591.

reason to believe he was one of the peers summoned in council on the ninth of February, 1399–1400, only four days previous to Richard's reputed death; and that he sat in the succeeding parliament, which met on the twenty-first of January, 1401. The exhibition of the body at St Paul's, where all the nobility and the barons attended; the private burial at Langley, and the proclamations of Henry, declaring that Richard was dead and buried, must have been perfectly well known to him; and yet in the face of all this, he declares in his dying words, pronounced in 1417, that Richard the Second, his liege lord, is then alive in Scotland. We have, therefore, the testimony of Lord Cobham, that the reputed death of Richard in Pontefract castle, the masses performed over the dead body at St Paul's, and its burial at Langley, were all impudent fabrications. It is, I think, impossible to conceive evidence more clear in its enunciation, more solemn, considering the time when it was spoken, and, for the same reason, more perfectly unsuspicious.

I know not that I can better conclude these remarks upon this mysterious subject, than by this testimony of Lord Cobham, in support of the hypothesis which I have ventured to maintain. Other arguments and illustrations certainly might be added, but my limits allow me only to hint at them. It might be shown, for instance, that not long after Sir David Fleming had obtained possession of the person of Richard, Henry the Fourth engaged in a secret correspondence with this baron, and granted him a passport to have a personal interview; it might be shown, also, that in 1404, Robert the Third, in his reply to a letter of Henry the Fourth, referred the English king to David Fleming for some particular information; that Henry was about the same time carrying on a private negotiation with Lord Montgomery, to whom the reader will recollect Richard had been delivered; whilst there is evidence, that with the lord of the isles, and with the chaplain of that pirate prince in whose dominions Richard was first discovered, the King of England had private meetings, which appear to have produced a perceptible change in the policy of Henry's government towards Scotland. I had intended, also, to point out the gross forgeries of which Henry had condescended to be guilty, in his public account of the deposition of Richard, in order to show the very slender credit which is due to his assertions regarding the death and burial of this prince; but I must content myself with once more referring to Mr Webb's Notes on the Metrical History of the Deposition of Richard, from which I have derived equal instruction and amusement.

In conclusion, I may observe, that whatever side of the question my readers may be inclined to adopt, an extraordinary fact, or rather series of facts, is established, which have hitherto been overlooked by preceding historians. If disposed to embrace the opinion which I have formed after a careful, and, I trust, impartial examination of the evidence, the circumstance of Richard's escape, and subsequent death in Scotland, is a new and interesting event in the history of both countries. If, on the other hand, they are inclined still to believe the ordinary accounts of the death of this monarch in 1399, it must be admitted, for it is proved by good evidence, that a mysterious person appeared suddenly in the dominions of Donald of the Isles; that he was challenged by one who knew Richard, as being the king in disguise; that he denied it steadily, and yet was kept in Scotland in an honourable captivity for eighteen years, at great expense; that it was believed in England by those best calculated to have accurate information on the subject, that he was the true King Richard; and that, although his being detained and recognised in Scotland was the cause of repeated conspiracies for his restoration, which shook the government both of Henry the Fourth and Henry the Fifth, neither of these monarchs ever attempted to get this impostor into their hands, or to expose the cheat by insisting upon his being delivered up, in those various negotiations as to peace or truce which took place between the two kingdoms. This last hypothesis presents to me difficulties which appear at present insurmountable; and I believe, therefore, that the chapel at Stirling contained the ashes of the true Richard.

I entertain too much respect, however, for the opinion of the many learned writers who have preceded me, and for the public judgment which has sanctioned an opposite belief for more than four hundred years, to venture, without farther discussion, to transplant this romantic sequel to the story of Richard the Second into the sacred field of history. And it is for this reason that, whilst I have acknowledged the royal title in the Appendix, I have expressed myself more cautiously and hypothetically in the body of the work.[*]

---

[*] The critical reader is referred to an able answer to these " Remarks," by Mr Amyot, in the twenty-third vol. of the " Archæologia," p. 277; to some additional observations by the same gentleman, Archæologia, vol. xxv. p. 394; to a critical "Note," by Sir James Macintosh, added to the first volume of his " History of England;" to a " Dissertation on the Manner and Period of the Death of Richard the Second," by Lord Dover; to observations on the same historical problem, by Mr Riddell, in a volume of Legal and Antiquarian Tracts, published at Edinburgh in 1835; and to some remarks on the same point by Sir Harris Nicolas in the Preface to the first volume of his valuable work, the " Proceedings and Ordinances of the Privy Council of England," Preface, p. 29 to 32.

NOTES AND ILLUSTRATIONS.

NOTES AND ILLUSTRATIONS.

LETTER A, p. 2.

It is not conceivable, says Mr Thomson, from whom I have procured some information on this obscure subject, that this claim of the Earl of Douglas could have any other basis than a revival of the right of the Baliol family, whose titles appear to have devolved at this period on the Earl of Douglas. John Baliol, it is well known, left a son, Edward, whom we have seen crowned King of Scotland in 1332, who afterwards died in obscurity, and without children. (History, vol. ii. pp. 16, 90.) The right of the Baliol family upon this reverted to the descendants of Alexander de Baliol of Kavers, brother of King John Baliol;* and we find that, in the reign of David the Second, the representative of this Alexander de Baliol was Isobel de Baliol, Comitissa de Mar, who married Donald, twelfth Earl of Mar. This lady, it appears, by a deed in the Rotuli Scotiæ, vol. i. p. 708, married, secondly, William de Careswell, who during the minority of her son, Thomas, thirteenth Earl of Mar, Lord of Garryach and Cavers, obtained from Edward the Third "the custody of all the lands which belonged to Isabella the late Countess of Mar, his consort." Thomas earl of Mar died without issue, but he left a sister, Margaret, who succeeded her brother, and became Countess of Mar in her own right. She married for her first husband William earl of Douglas, who in her right, became Earl of Mar; and, as possessing through her the right of the house of Baliol, upon this ground laid claim to the crown. Winton, vol. ii. p. 304, does not mention the ground upon which the Earl of Douglas disputed the throne with Robert the Second. But the ancient manuscript, entitled "Extracta ex Chronicis Scotiæ, fol.

* Dugdale's Baronage, vol. i. p. 525.

225, is more explicit. Its words are, "Dowglace Willmus Comes manu valida militari, coram eis comparuit allegans jus corone et successionis in regnum ad se ex parte Cuminensium et Balliorum pertinere." And this is corroborated by Bower, Fordun a Goodal, vol. ii. p. 382. Douglas's right through his wife we have just explained; and I may refer to a paper on the ancient lordship of Galloway, in the ninth volume of the Archæologia, p. 49, by Mr Riddell, for an explanation of his title through the Comyns.

LETTER B, p. 150.

Site of the Battle of Harlaw.

In the manuscript geographical description of Scotland, collected by Macfarlane, and preserved in the Advocates' Library, vol. i. p. 7, there is the following minute description of the site of this battle :—
" Through this parish (the chapel of Garioch, called formerly, Capella Beate Mariæ Virginie de Garryoch, Chart. Aberdon, p. 31) runs the king's highway from Aberdeen to Inverness, and from Aberdeen to the high country. A large mile to the east of the church lies the field of an ancient battle, called the battle of Harlaw, from a country town of that name hard by. This town, and the field of battle, which lies along the king's highway upon a moor, extending a short mile from SE. to NW. stands on the north-east side of the water of Urie, and a small distance therefrom. To the west of the field of battle, about half a mile, is a farmer's house, called Legget's Den, hard by in which is a tomb, built in the form of a malt steep, of four large stones, covered with a broad stone above, where, as the country people generally report, Donald of the Isles lies buried, being slain in the battle, and therefore they call it commonly Donald's tomb." So far the MS. It is certain, however, that the Lord of the Isles was not slain. This may probably be the tomb of the chief of Maclean, or of Macintosh, both of whom fell in the battle. In the genealogical collections of the same industrious antiquary, (MS. Advocates' Library, Jac. V. 4, 16, vol. i. p. 180,) we find a manuscript account of the family of Maclean, which informs us that Lauchlan Lubanich had, by M'Donald's daughter, a son, called Eachin Rusidh ni Cath, or Hector Rufus Bellicosus. He commanded as lieutenant-general under the Earl of Ross at the battle of Harlaw in 1411, where he and Irving of Drum, seeking out one another by their armorial bearings on their shields, met and killed each other. He was married to a daughter of the Earl of Douglas.

Sir Walter Ogilvy, on twenty-eighth January, 1426, founded a chaplainry in the parish church of St Mary of Uchterhouse, in which perpetual prayers were to be offered up for the salvation of King James and his Queen Johanna; and for the souls of all who died in the battle of Harlaw.—Diplom. Regior. Indices, vol. i. p. 97.

Letter C, p. 152.

The Retour of Andrew de Tullidiff, mentioned in the text, will be found in the MS. Cartulary of Aberdeen, preserved in the Advocates' Library, folio 121. It is as follows :—

> "Inquisitio super tercia parte
> Ledintusche et Rothmais.

Hæc inquisitio facta fuit apud rane coram Willmo de Cadyhow Ballivo Reverendi in Christo patris, et Dni Gilberti Dei gracia Episcopi Aberdonen : die martis, nono die mensis Maii anno 1413, per probos et fideles homines subscriptos, viz. Robertum de Buthcrgask, Johannem Rous, Johannem Bisete, Robertum Malisei, Hugonem de Kyncavil, Duncanum de Curquhruny, Johannem Morison, Johm Yhung, Adam Johannis, Johannem Thomson, Johannem de Lovask, Johannem Duncanson, Walterum Ranyson, et Johannem Thomson de Petblayne. Qui magno sacramento jurati dicunt, quod quondam Willmus de Tulidef latoris præsencium obiit vestitus et saysitus ut de feodo ad pacem et fidem Dni nostri regis, de tercia parte terrarum de Ledyntusche, et de Rothmais cum pertinenciis jacentium in schyra de Rane infra Vicecom. de Aberden. Et quod dictus Andreas est leggitimus et propinquior heres ejusdem quondam Willmi patris sui de dicta tercia parte dictarum terrarum cum pertinenciis, et licet minoris ætatis existit tamen secundum quoddam statutum consilii generalis ex priviligio concesso hæredibus occisorum in bello de Harelaw, pro defensione patriæ, est hac vice leggittime ætatis, et quod dicta tercia dictarum terrarum cum pertinenciis nunc valet per annum tres libras, et viginti denarios, et valuit tempore pacis quatuor libras," &c. &c. The remainder of the deed is uninteresting.

Letter D, p. 164.

Battles of Baugè and Verneuil.

The exploits of the Scottish forces in France do not properly belong to the History of Scotland, and any reader who wishes for authentic information upon the subject will find it in Fordun a Goodal, vol. ii. pp. 461, 463, and Monstrelet's Chronicle, by Johnes, vols. 5th and 6th. There were three important battles in which the Scots auxiliaries were engaged. First, that of Baugè, in Anjou, fought on twenty-second March, 1421, in which they gained a signal victory over the Duke of Clarence, who was slain, along with the "flower of his chivalry and esquiredom," to use the words of Monstrelet. Secondly, that of Crevant, which was disastrous to the Scots. And lastly, the great battle of Verneuil, fought in 1424, in which John duke of Bedford commanded the English, and completely defeated the united army of the French and Scots.

There is a singular coincidence between the battle of Baugè, and the battle of Stirling, in which Wallace defeated Surrey and Cressingham. The two armies, one commanded by the Duke of Clarence, and the other by the Earl of Buchan, were separated from each other by a rapid river, over which was thrown a narrow bridge. Buchan had despatched a party, under Sir Robert Stewart of Darnley, and the Sieur de Fontaine, to reconnoitre, and they coming suddenly upon the English, were driven back in time to warn the Scottish general of the approach of Clarence. Fortunately, he had a short interval allowed him to draw up his army, whilst Sir Robert Stewart of Railston, and Sir Hugh Kennedy, with a small advanced body, defended the passage of the bridge, over which the Duke of Clarence with his best officers were eagerly forcing their way, having left the bulk of the English army to follow as they best could. The consequences were almost precisely the same as those which took place at Stirling. Clarence, distinguished by his coronet of jewels over his helmet, and splendid armour, was first fiercely attacked by John Carmichael, who shivered his lance on him; then wounded in the face by Sir William de Swynton; and lastly, felled to the earth and slain by the mace of the Earl of Buchan.* His bravest knights and men-at-arms fell along with him; and the rest of the army, enraged at the disaster, and crowding over the bridge to avenge it, being thrown into complete disorder, as they arrived in detail, were slain or taken by the Scots. Monstrelet† affirms, that two or three thousand English were slain. Bower limits the number who fell to sixteen hundred and seventeen, and asserts that the Scots only lost twelve, and the French two men.‡ It is well known that for this service Buchan was rewarded with the baton of Constable of France. After the battle,

* Fordun a Goodal, vol. ii. p. 461. This John, or, as he is called by Douglas, Sir John Carmichael, was ancestor to the noble family of Hyndford, now extinct. The family crest is still a shivered spear.—Douglas, vol. i. p. 752.
† Monstrelet, by Johnes, vol. v. p. 263. ‡ Fordun a Goodal, vol. ii. p. 461.

Sir Robert Stewart of Darnley bought Clarence's jewelled coronet from a Scottish soldier for 1000 angels.*

Having been thus successful at Baugè, the conduct of the Scots at Crevant, considering the circumstances under which the battle was fought, is inexplicable. On consulting Monstrelet,† it will be found that the river Yonne separated the two armies, over which there was a bridge as at Baugè. The Scots occupied a hill near the river, with the town of Crevant, to which they had laid siege, in their rear. Over this bridge they suffered the whole English army to defile, to arrange their squares, and to advance in firm order against them, when they might have pre-occupied the tête-de-pont, and attacked the enemy whilst they were in the act of passing the river. Either the circumstances of the battle have come down to us in a garbled and imperfect state, or it is the fate of the Scots to shut their eyes to the simplest lessons in military tactics, lessons, too, which, it may be added, have often been written against them with sharp pens and bloody ink. The consequences at Crevant were fatal. They were attacked in the front by the Earls of Salisbury and Suffolk, and in the rear by a sortie from the town of Crevant, and completely defeated.‡

The battle of Verneuil was still more disastrous, and so decisive, that it appears to have completely cooled all future desires upon the part of the Scots to send auxiliaries to France. The account given by Bower§ is, at first sight, confused and contradictory; but if the reader will compare it with Monstrelet, vol. vi. pp. 90, 94, it becomes clearer. It seems to have been lost by the Scots, in consequence of the unfortunate dissension between them and their allies the French, which prevented one part of the army from co-operating with the other; whilst, on the side of the English, the steadiness of the archers, each of whom had a sharp double-pointed stake planted before him, defeated the charge of the Lombard cross-bowmen, although they were admirably armed and mounted.||

LETTER E, p. 169.

In this treaty for the relief of James the First, which is to be found in Rymer's Fœdera, vol. x. p. 307, the list which contains the names

* Gough's Sepulchral Monuments, vol. ii. p. 58.
† Vol. vi. p. 48.
‡ Moustrelet, vol. vi. pp. 48, 49.
§ Fordun a Goodal, vol. ii. p. 463.
|| Ibid.

of the hostages is not a little curious, as there is added to the name of each baron a statement of his yearly income, presenting us with an interesting picture of the comparative wealth of the members of the Scottish aristocracy in 1423. The list is as follows :—

Thomas Comes Moraviæ, reddituatus et possessionatus ad M. marc.

Alexander Comes Crauffurdiæ, vel filius ejus et hæredes ad M. marc.

Willielmus Comes Angusiæ, ad vi C marc.

Maletius Comes de Stratherne, ad v C marc.

Georgius Comes Marchiarum, vel filius ejus primogenitus ad viii C marc.

David Filius Primogenitus Comitis Atholiæ, vel filius ejus et hæres ad xii C marc.

Willielmus Constabularius Scotiæ, vel filius et hæres ad viii C marc.

Dominus Robertus de Erskyn, ad M. marc.

Robertus Marescallus Scotiæ, vel filius ejus et hæres ad viii C marc.

Walterus Dominus de Drybtoun (Drylton) vel filius ejus et hæres ad viii C marc.

Johannes Dominus de Cetoun, miles vel filius ejus et hæres ad vi C marc.

Johannis de Montgomery, miles de Ardrossane, vel filius ejus et hæres ad vii C marc.

Alexander Dominus de Gordonne, ad iv C marc.

Malcolmus Dominus de Bygare, ad vi C marc.

Thomas Dominus de Yestyr, ad vi C marc.

Johannis Kennady de Carryk, ad v C marc.

Thomas Boyde de Kylmernok, vel filius ejus et hæres ad v C marc.

Patricius de Dounbarre Dominus de Canmok, vel filius ejus et hæres ad v C marc.

Jacobus Dominus de Dalketh, vel filius ejus primogenitus ad xv C marc.

Duncanus Dominus de Argill, ad xv C marc.*

Johannes Lyon de Glammis, ad vi C marc.

LETTER F, p. 193.

It is not easy to account for the high character of Albany, which is given both by Winton and by Bower. It is certain, because it is proved by his actions, which are established upon authentic evidence,

---

* It may be conjectured, that there is some error both here and in the preceding name.

that he was a crafty and selfish usurper, whose hands were stained with the blood of the heir to the crown—yet he is spoken of by both these writers, not only without severity, but with enthusiastic praise. Indeed, Winton's character of him might serve for the beau ideal of a perfect king :—Vol. ii. p. 418.

Bower, though shorter, is equally complimentary, and throws in some touches which give individuality to the picture. On one occasion, in the midst of the tumult of war, and the havoc of a Border raid, we find the governor recognised by his soldiers as a collector of the relics of earlier ages, (Fordun a Goodal, vol. ii. p. 409,) and at another time a still finer picture is presented of Albany sitting on the ramparts of the castle of Edinburgh, and discoursing to his courtiers, in a clear moonlight night on the system of the universe, and the causes of eclipses. I am sorry I have neglected to mark the page where this occurs, and cannot find it at the moment.

LETTER G, p. 214.

A curious instrument, which throws some light on the state of the Highlands in 1420, and gives an example of the mixture of Celtic and Norman names, is to be found in a MS. in the Adv. Lib., Jac. V. 4. 22, entitled Diplomatum Collectio. It is as follows :—

"John Touch, be the grace of God Bishop of Rosse ; Dame Mary of ye Ile, Lady of the Yles and of Rosse ; Hucheon Fraser, Lord of the Lovat ; John Macloyde, Lerde of Glenelg ; Angus Guthrason of the Ylis ; Schyr William Farquhar, Dean of Rosse ; Walter of Douglas, Scheraff of Elgin ; Walter of Innes, Lord of that ilke ; John Syncler, Lord of Deskford ; John ye Ross, Lord of Kilravache ; John M'Ean of Arnamurchan, with mony othyr,—Til al and syndry to the knawledge of the quhilkis thir present lettres sal to cum, gretyng in God ay listand. Syn it is needeful and meritabil to ber lele witness to suthfastness to your Universitie, we mak knawyn throche thir present lettres, that on Friday the sextent day of the moneth of August, ye yher of our Lord a thousand four hundreth and twenty yher, into the kyrke yharde of the Chanonry of Rossmarkyng, compeirit William the Grahame, the sone and the hayr umquhil of Henry the Grame. In presence of us, befor a nobil Lorde and a mychty, Thomas Earl of Moreff, his ovyr lord of his lands of the Barony of Kerdale, resignande of his awin free will, purly and symply, be fast and baston, intill the hands of the sayde Lorde the Erle," &c. An entail of the lands follows, which is uninteresting.

At page 263 of the same volume, we find a charter granted by

David II., in the 30th year of his reign, entitled, "Carta remissionis Thomæ Man et multis aliis, actionis et sectæ regiæ tum pro homicidiis, combustionibus, furtis, rapinis," &c., in which the preponderance of Celtic names is very striking. The names are as follows :—" Thomas Man, Bridan filii Fergusi, Martino More, Maldoveny Beg Maldowny Macmartican, Cristino filio Duncani, Bridano Breath, Alex^ro Macronlet Adæ Molendinario, Martini M'Coly, Fergusio Clerico Donymore, Michaeli Merlsway, Bridano M'Dor, Maldowny M'Robi, Colano M'Gilbride, Maldowny Macenewerker, et Adæ Fovetour latoribus presencium, &c. Apud Perth, primo die Novemb. regni xxx. quinto.

Letter H, p. 268.

I am indebted for the communication of the following charter to the Rev. Mr Macgregor Stirling, a gentleman intimately acquainted with the recondite sources of Scottish History :—

Apud Edinburgh, Aug. 15, 1451, a. r. 15.

Rex [Jacobus II.] confirmavit Roberto Duncansoun de Strowane, et heredibus suis, terras de Strowane,—terras dimidicatis de Rannach,—terras de Glennerach,—terras de duobus Bohaspikis,—terras de Grannecht, cum lacu et insula lacus ejusdem,—terras de Carric,—terras de Innercadoune,—de Farnay,—de Disert, Faskel, de Kylkeve,—de Balnegarde,—et Balnefarc,—et terras de Glengary, cum foresta ejusdem, in comitatu Atholie, vic. de Perth, quas dictus Robertus, in castrum [sic] Regium de Blar in Atholia personaliter resignavit, et quas rex in unam integram Baroniam de Strowane univit et incorporavit (pro zelo, fauore, amore, quas rex gessit erga dictum Robertum pro captione nequissimi proditoris quondam Roberti de Grahame, et pro ipsius Roberti Duncansoune gratuitis diligenciis et laboribus, circa captionem ejusdem sevissimi proditoris, diligentissime et cordialissime factis.)—(Mag. Sig. iv. 227.)

END OF VOLUME THIRD.

www.ingramcontent.com/pod-product-compliance
Lightning Source LLC
Chambersburg PA
CBHW020325240426
43673CB00039B/924